MW00770934

DAY OF THE WOLF

UNMASKING AND CONFRONTING WOLVES IN THE CHURCH

Coleman Luck

The Sandstar Group

The Sandstar Group
POB 3613
Oakhurst, CA 93644
www.colemanluck.com

Book Layout ©2013 BookDesignTemplates.com
Editing: Coleman Luck, III
Cover design: Carel Gage Luck

Ordering Information:
Quantity sales. Special discounts are available on quantity purchases. For details, contact the "Special Sales Department" at the address above.

Day of the Wolf/ Coleman Luck -- 1st ed.
ISBN 978-0-9888888-6-9

Dedicated to all those who have stood with faith and courage against spiritual wolves for the sake of Jesus and His Kingdom. Your reward is in Heaven.

Though giant rains put out the sun,
Here stand I for a sign,
Though earth be filled with waters dark,
My cup is filled with wine,
Tell to the trembling priests that here,
Under the deluge rod,
One nameless, tattered, broken man,
Stood up and drank to God.

G. K. Chesterton

Table of Contents:

INTRODUCTION

Wolves in the Hospital

Imagine a hospital where the lead surgeon was a carefully disguised serial killer who got pleasure and made money from bringing slow and excruciating death to his victims. Imagine a hospital where evidence about this murderer was beginning to mount. His acts were becoming clear. People were crying out in pain at what he was doing, yet, in spite of all the evidence, almost the entire staff continued to defend him, even blaming his victims for their wounds and throwing them out of the hospital to fend for themselves. Those who were trying to speak the truth were thrown out too. Sound insane? That is what is happening within too many churches and Christian organizations.

Most Christians don't know how to recognize spiritual wolves, nor do they even have the desire to do so. Though wolves may be mauling, Christians turn blind eyes to their attacks, allowing the damage to continue and the cause of Jesus Christ to suffer great loss. In the process, the wounded victims are further victimized by the attitudes of ignorant, cowardly people.

1

A book about spiritual wolves is not easy to write or to read. Nevertheless, considering the wolf crisis in the Christian church today, it is shocking that so few books have been written about the personalities and tactics of spiritual wolves. Most of the writing that has been done is on the Internet and deals with individual experiences and specific situations. Many of these are cries of the wounded and are filled with pain and anger. Others are Biblical examinations of specific false teachings. As important as all of this is, it isn't enough. Almost every week brings the revelation of some new horror.

As I write, a missionary formerly with New Tribes Mission, has just been sentenced to four years in prison for creating and promulgating child pornography. He was a missionary teacher in Brazil and the son of missionaries, who himself had been born in the Amazon. His victims were young girls to whom he was supposed to be ministering. He was caught by U.S. federal authorities after posting his hellish material on the Internet.

The man is very repentant. Only God can judge the heart, however, one can't help but wonder how repentant he would be if he hadn't been caught. How much longer would he have continued his Satanic abuse? There is a debate among some Christians about whether or not his sins should be dealt with publicly within the Body of Christ. The view of some is let the state do its job. The church should just "love". Don't "pile-on" to a fallen Christian brother by publicly confronting his sin. They think this is being true to the Scriptures. They are dangerously wrong.

This book has been written to call us all to account. For spiritual wolves, it is the most serious warning to repent while there is still time. Your soul is at stake. For those who follow and encourage wolves, it is a call to Biblical awareness, repentance and action. For those who have been wounded in wolf attacks, it is a call to forgiveness and healing. For everyone in the Christian Church it is a call to vigilance and, where needed, Biblical, Holy Spirit empowered confrontation, because things are going to get much worse.

To faithful pastors, teachers and leaders, I salute you. Because of the nature of so many cases, what I have written is directed at people who are dealing with wolves in Christian leadership, but many wolves are not found in formal leadership. Thousands of faithful men and women of God have been viciously attacked by wolf packs in their congregations and ministries. Perhaps that includes you. Because of those attacks, you were so wounded that it was necessary to retreat from the battle to experience healing. If so, don't let the retreat for healing become a permanent advance to the rear. You are a warrior and you are needed.

As you enter on this journey with me, you're going to read about some of my experiences. In almost all cases, I do not name individuals and the situations are concealed as much as possible. These experiences are given as illustrations. This book is not intended to confront any specific person or situation. Rather it is meant to be a resource for those who are contending with wolves right now.

Why am I qualified to write this book?

Over the course of decades, I have found myself in many unique and uncomfortable places where wolves have been running free. Hollywood is "wolf central" and for most of my career, I was a writer and executive producer in network television. But how does Hollywood relate to the church?

As far as "wolf observation" goes, the advantage of working in Hollywood is that wolves don't feel the need to hide themselves for very long. But, wherever they are found, they display predictable patterns of behavior. While the external camouflage will change from environment to environment, the essence of spiritual wolves and what they do remains the same, whether in Hollywood, government, the church or anywhere else. This is true over time as well. Going back thousands of years, there is nothing new about the essence of spiritual wolves. However, for very specific reasons, I believe they have always been at their most dangerous and subtle within the Christian church.

There are some people who believe that spiritual wolves are found only in the church. With this I strongly disagree. Wolves are found in every area of human life from the highest levels of society to the streets. And wherever they are found, wolves are spiritual teachers. What do I mean by that?

The two young murderer wolves of Columbine High School taught generations of young murderers who have followed after them. They taught untold thousands of school administrators and parents to be controlled by fear. Example is the strongest form of teaching.

The missionary from hell taught those young girls that he abused in the Amazon. In taking away their innocence, he taught them what "Christian" missionaries were like. He taught them lies from hell about what the message of Jesus means. That teaching will grow in their lives and spread outward for generations.

And so it is with wolves wherever they appear. There has never been a wolf that has not been a spiritual teacher. In the church they wrap themselves in the Bible and a spiritual persona of caring about people. In business, they may wrap themselves in layers of sophisticated management philosophy and a dynamic "can-do" attitude, in government with political philosophy and glad-hand charm, in academia with prestigious degrees and published authority. It doesn't matter. They use their camouflage to teach lies and feast on sheep. They are all of the same species, just hunting among different flocks. We must be absolutely clear. Wolves in the church are no more unique and certainly no more Christian than wolves found anywhere else in the world and are part of the larger genus of spiritual predators.

Sophisticated wolves train protégés who carry on their predatory acts. Both the church and the entertainment industry are full of such "teachers". I had the unpleasant experience of dealing with a number of them in Hollywood. However, far longer than my time there, are the many years that I have spent in the evangelical Christian church in America. Literally, I went to church in my mother's womb. My late father, Dr. G. Coleman Luck, was a Bible scholar and a theologian on the faculty of the Moody Bible Institute in Chicago. Both I and my wife, Carel, attended that school.

As a young adult before going to Hollywood, I worked in several evangelical organizations. These included positions as Supervisor of Production and Talent for WMBI and the Moody Radio Network in Chicago and Advertising Manager for Christianity Today, the leading evangelical magazine of the world. After suc-

5

cess in Hollywood came other contacts with Christian leaders and organizations.

Over the years, I have been a member of local churches, on a number of occasions serving as an elder and Bible teacher. During my career in Hollywood, I helped establish several Christian ministries to those in the entertainment industry. I have lectured in leading Christian colleges and universities. In all of these situations I have met many wonderful people of God. I have also met some wolves and proto-wolves, those in the process of development. Now in retirement and not in any formal leadership position, I am able to step back and analyze what I have experienced from a Biblical perspective.

After reading a draft of this book, one good friend was concerned that perhaps the stories I tell might indicate some residual bitterness on my part and desire to "settle accounts". It's an honest concern and one that I share. All I can say is that, to the best of my understanding, I don't believe that this is the case.

As we walk down the long halls of memory, when we enter certain rooms the emotions of some experiences can sweep back over us. Probably, that will be true for you as you read this book. For me, though many years have passed, recalling certain people and events brings sorrow and the memory of pain and frustration. I remember being angry. This can be depressing as we think about what was lost and our own failures. All of that is natural. Though we may experience such emotions again, they don't have to control us or include bitterness. We don't have to let the Powers of Darkness whiplash us back into emotional slavery.

How can we keep the cancer of bitterness away? As we will discuss later in much detail, healing from all wolf-wounds depends on forgiveness. We're going to study the discipline of forgiveness and how to exercise it. Right now what I would say is that this discipline has been an important part of my life for many years. The heart of it is this: Jesus has forgiven me for so much, how can I not forgive others, even vicious wolves who have attacked and mauled me?

As we journey together, my goal is for us to learn how to recognize and deal with a spiritual wolf quickly, in order to minimize the damage that he or she inflicts. Also I hope that through this study those of us who have been wounded may begin to find healing and bring that healing to people who are suffering all around us. And there are many. Since I began writing this book, horror stories have flooded in. Many in the church are torn and bleeding both emotionally and spiritually, while the wolves continue their predation. This should make all of us angry at Satan and the freedom that he has been given to destroy people in the Body of Christ.

Confrontation with spiritual wolves is spiritual warfare against principalities and powers and demands the wisdom, courage, strength and weapons that can be found only in Jesus Christ. When we are wounded in the battle – *as we will be* – all healing comes from Him.

There is another element to this book that I hope you will find helpful. Since I was a very young man, I have been given the opportunity to hold many different positions of leadership in the military, in business, in the Church and in Hollywood. Rather than simply confronting wolves after they are in leadership, it would be far better to raise up true men and women of God. So I will spend considerable time discussing how I think we might identify Godly Christian leaders. I have come to the opinion that one of the reasons wolves run rampant in the Church is because we no longer understand what a Godly leader should look like. I pray that this study will help us do that. Also seeing Godly leaders should help us identify wolves more quickly.

The book is divided into three sections: Part One: Wolves – Seeing What is Hidden, Part Two: The Fruit of Wolves and the Fruit of Heaven, and Part Three: Wolves – The Confrontation.

But before we begin, I need to issue a very serious warning. I'm so concerned that you understand it that I'm going to re-state it at various points along the way.

Doing a study about spiritual wolves is very much like do-ing a study about demons. I'm sure C. S. Lewis was right when he said that Satan is equally pleased if we see demons everywhere or if we see them nowhere. The same could be said about wolves. While I urge every Christian to know the Scripture and be vigi-lant, it is not my intention that anyone start searching for spiritual wolves in leadership. In Matthew chapter 7 Jesus said that there would be "many" wolves in sheep's clothing, but that doesn't mean that they are in every church, school and Christian organization. It doesn't mean that they are in most.

People have asked me what percentage of pastors and Christian leaders might be wolves? I have no idea. As far as num-bers are concerned, I don't know what Jesus meant when He used the word "many". The only certainty is that by their "fruit" we will know them. Jesus didn't say that by our spiritual "intuition" we will know them. Wolf Hunter isn't among the spiritual gifts given to the Body of Christ.

Because of the emphasis of this study, it may seem as though I think spiritual wolves are everywhere. I don't. But where they do exist, they are well-camouflaged and extremely destructive. When they become known by their fruits, they need to be unmasked and confronted. Those in danger of becoming wolves need to be warned.

But who will do it?

This book is for courageous people. It's time for God's spiritual warriors to rise up and, under the Power of the Holy Spirit, take whatever risks are necessary to cleanse Jesus' Church.

PART ONE

Wolves:
Seeing What is Hidden

Because they are so well camouflaged and come in many varieties, it is surprisingly difficult to establish a clear definition of spiritual wolves. This difficulty is one of their advantages. In a sense this entire book is designed to define what a spiritual wolf is and how he operates. But at the very outset here in Part One I want to present a definition then, through a study of Scripture and applied experience, describe how it works out in detail.

Spiritual Wolves – A Definition

Spiritual wolves are men or women with authority and/or influence within a church, ministry, Christian group or organization who use that authority and/or influence for the primary purpose of advancing their own selfish desires and agendas by exerting destructive control over those under their care, attacking anyone who questions them and doing anything necessary to maintain their profitable and influential positions or advance to greater ones.

Further, spiritual wolves are false prophets/teachers because they justify every selfish act through an appeal to a self-proclaimed, "god-given" authority and/or to Scripture and through the teaching influence of their words and deeds lead weak people away from loving and following Jesus by creating disciples to themselves who will do their will, which means promoting their success and defending their actions.

Through both subtle and overt abuse and disobedience to God's Word, spiritual wolves bring disrepute to the Name of Jesus and to His Body the Church. While advancing themselves, they stand in the way of sinners and emasculate the work of the Church in its task of carrying out the Great Commission. In all of this, they refuse righteous accountability and Godly leadership. When caught and unable to escape the consequences of their actions, spiritual wolves will lie, blame others and even appear to display deep repentance, but all of this is a sham designed to save themselves and re-establish their former positions.

No matter how great their public success and no matter how "godly", powerful and "fruitful" it appears, these men and women are not servants of the Lord. The true, evil fruit of their lives will be visible in the damaged people closest to them and the mauled victims of their predation. Spiritual wolves are either conscious or unconscious servants of Satan and without true repentance, which includes humble restitution and the willingness to follow instead of lead, they are lost forever.

CHAPTER ONE

The Wolf in the Cage

Many years ago, I was writing and producing the CBS/Universal television series, The Equalizer. Our star was an outstanding British actor named Edward Woodward who played Robert McCall, the protagonist of our stories.

In one of my scripts, I gave McCall a strange vision. He saw himself as a wolf out of his natural environment, lost on the streets of New York. To get the sequence on film we needed a real wolf. So our excellent production team in Manhattan set out to find one that we could rent for a couple of days. Sure enough, a wolf was found. (You can find anything in New York if you know who to ask.)

I had written one of the vision sequences to take place in McCall's apartment. Needless to say, the whole thing had to be shot with strict safety protocols. Ostensibly, the wolf we had rented was tame, but even a tame wolf is a wild animal. On our apartment set, the crew constructed a large chain link cage that would not be visible on the film, but would protect the production team. When Edward arrived, he was quick to note one fact. The only person who would be inside the cage with the wolf would be *him*. This was an immediate source of humor for *almost* everyone.

Edward was assured that this wolf was well-trained. The handler was right there (outside the cage) if there were any problems. Though Edward knew the risk, he was such a professional and such a good sport that he agreed to do the scene.

In the sequence, the only thing the wolf had to do was sit on its haunches across the room from McCall and stare at him. Working with animals in a production is always unpredictable and frustrating. For some reason, they just don't think it's always necessary to follow directions and that was the case with this wolf.

I don't know anything about wolves except what is common knowledge. In the wild, they are powerful, implacable predators. They aren't dogs. Our team was as prepared for danger as it was possible to be under the circumstances. But what if the animal leaped across the set and attacked Edward? How much damage could it do before it was restrained? If our star were mauled, it would make headlines, but it wasn't the kind of publicity we needed. Far worse were the potential injuries that might take him out of commission. The whole production would stop and that would cost millions. (Notice that I didn't talk about his pain and suffering, only money and bad PR. That is the way Hollywood thinks.)

As the shoot started, it became apparent that our problem wasn't the danger of attack. Out of its environment, surrounded by the all the lights and people, the only thing this poor wolf wanted to do was crawl under a table. And this it did over and over. We went through multiple "takes" before we could get the animal to sit up long enough for a single usable shot. It may have had the body of a wolf, but in that environment it had the heart of a mouse.

I learned something that day. In the wild, a pack of wolves can be extremely dangerous. Frightening stories about wolves go back many centuries. But isolated and surrounded, under the bright lights, they don't look very terrifying. I'm sure a wild wolf inside that cage might have responded differently than ours. However, even the wildest and most dangerous of them can be controlled. That takes both knowledge and courage. In the case of spiritual wolves, the only One who can bind and tame them is Jesus Christ. But He uses His warriors in the confrontation.

CHAPTER TWO

A First Encounter

As I look back at my life (I am 68 years old), I think my first confrontation with a spiritual wolf in the Body of Christ took place when I was 28 and I was unprepared for it. I have written about that experience more extensively in my book, <u>The Curse of Conservatism</u>, but I'll give a condensed version here.

At the start of 1974, I was recruited to join the leadership staff of a small organization in Buena Park, California called the Christian Freedom Foundation. The organization had existed for several decades as a platform for conservative economic theory, but the founder was very old and had retired. The young president who had taken charge stated that he wanted to bring about significant change in the organization and recruited me and others to help him establish and achieve new goals. I became marketing director.

Several other young men were brought on board to head other divisions. One of them was my old friend, Barrie Doyle, a Canadian who left his position in the news department at Christianity Today to head up our news department.

From the start, my interest was in dealing with critical social issues from a Biblical perspective. Because the president promised a platform for such thought leadership, I moved my family across the United States from Virginia to participate in what I believed would be a new organization speaking with creativity and Christian concern in a chaotic world. For the same reason, Barrie Doyle moved his family the same distance to join the staff. All of us believed in what we were doing.

I'd been there for only a few months when something strange began to happen. The president of the organization started going away for long meetings in other states. None of our leadership team went with him and when he returned he shared nothing about what had transpired. Years later I discovered the truth, which I have written about in my previous book.

The president of the Christian Freedom Foundation had decided to change directions, melding his organization with the goals and money of very powerful people who had a right-wing political agenda. He told none of us anything about this new direction.

Just before Christmas he fired all of his new senior staff. Several of the young men were Southern California natives, so the damage wasn't as great for them. But for Barrie Doyle and me, it was a deep crisis. I was amazed at the cold and callous attitude exhibited by the "Christian" president of this "Christian" organization, who was himself a graduate of a leading evangelical seminary. After bringing us to California where we had worked for only a few months, he thought nothing of cutting us off with no apologies and barely two weeks severance pay. His attitude was, "Well, you're in Southern California. It's a wonderful place to live. Enjoy."

Salaries in Christian organizations are not large. I had no money to move my family anywhere, especially back to my home town of Chicago. We had been renting a house. Suddenly, we had no means of paying our rent. We had to move out, but we had nowhere to go.

God always makes a way where we can't see one. A little church we had been attending let us move our furniture into one of their unused buildings. With the help of Carel's family and God's provision of money from other sources, we were able to make the move.

At the time, the thought never occurred to me that I might have been mauled by a spiritual wolf. I can tell you that for long afterward, I felt the pain of the wounds. As a young man, I was anxious to be successful. The fact that I had been fired after only a few months made me ashamed. Once back home, I didn't want to see any old friends. I didn't want to answer any questions. For an extended period, what had happened to me became a real barrier in my spiritual life. Our success-driven evangelical community doesn't understand wolf attacks. Even though Jesus gave a most serious warning about spiritual wolves, we disregard it.

I am convinced now that the president of that little organization had become a spiritual wolf. You never would have known it to meet and talk with the man. He was an acknowledged "Christian leader" who considered himself a Biblical scholar. He and his family were faithful in their church attendance. He knew how to say all the right things.

The truth of who he was became evident only when the surprise attack occurred. The coldness of it, the total lack of concern for the people under his care and leadership, his willful disobedience of Jesus' command that we should treat others the way we ourselves would want to be treated, his interest only in himself and getting what he wanted, all of these are marks of the spiritual wolf in leadership.

CHAPTER THREE

A Conspiracy of Wolves

The Bible doesn't speak often about wolves, but what it does say is very significant. God gave these words to the prophet Ezekiel:

And the word of the LORD came to me, saying, "Son of man, say to her: 'You are a land that is not cleansed or rained on in the day of indignation.' The conspiracy of her prophets in her midst is like a roaring lion tearing the prey; they have devoured people; they have taken treasure and precious things; they have made many widows in her midst. Her priests have violated My law and profaned My holy things; they have not distinguished between the holy and unholy, nor have they made known the difference between the unclean and the clean; and they have hidden their eyes from My Sabbaths, so that I am profaned among them. Her princes in her midst are like wolves tearing the prey, to shed blood, to destroy people, and to get dishonest gain. (Ezekiel 22:23-27)

There is nothing new about people in leadership who are like ravenous wild animals. They have existed throughout history and they exist now. Someday that's going to change when Jesus, the King, returns to establish His Kingdom on Earth. Until that happens, as far as governmental leadership is concerned, we have to suffer with the rulers we are given. All will answer to God for what they do. But it's clear that the Lord takes special interest in those who are rulers of His people, whether that means the Nation of Israel or the Church. He holds such leaders to a higher standard and a greater account. The Children of Israel in the Old Testament had little choice about who ruled over them. Much more freedom and responsibility regarding the choice of leaders have been given to God's people, the Church.

In the wild, wolves work in packs pursuing their prey until they wear it out. When it is exhausted, the pack circles and attacks. A pride of lions shares in a kill. That's how God describes the leaders of Israel. It wasn't just one wolf destroying His people, it was a pack. It wasn't just one lion, it was a pride. Spiritual carnivores operate the same way today. Wolves congregate and work together, usually around one "alpha wolf" leader. Their purpose is to satisfy their own lusts and desires and protect each other while doing so.

The prophet Zephaniah says this about the judges of Jerusalem, those who were supposed to make righteous decisions for God's people.

"Her judges are evening wolves that leave not a bone till morning." (Zephaniah 3:3)

That is a disturbing image. A pack of evening wolves attacks in the twilight when it is difficult for them to be seen by
their prey. Like gray shadows, they pursue and kill, then gorge all
night. Where were these wolves before evening? They were hidden, waiting for darkness, because they were afraid of the light. In
the light, many people might come against them. But at twilight,
one person might be walking alone. God is calling the judges of
Jerusalem vicious, cowardly beasts who attacked and devoured
people when they were at their most vulnerable. Their motive
was greed.

Such wolves are still at work. And today they have invaded
the heart of the Church.

CHAPTER FOUR

The Ravenous Ones

In the New Testament, Jesus had stinging and revealing words to say about spiritual wolves. What He said points us far toward a definition of spiritual wolves. His prophetic warning is the core of this book. In Matthew 7:15-23 He says this:

"Beware of false prophets, who come to you in sheep's clothing, but inwardly they are ravenous wolves. You will know them by their fruits. Do men gather grapes from thorn bushes or figs from thistles? Even so, every good tree bears good fruit, but a bad tree bears bad fruit. A good tree cannot bear bad fruit, nor can a bad tree bear good fruit. Every tree that does not bear good fruit is cut down and thrown into the fire. Therefore by their fruits you will know them. Not everyone who says to Me, 'Lord, Lord,' shall enter the kingdom of heaven, but he who does the will of My Father in heaven. Many will say to Me in that day, 'Lord, Lord, have we not prophesied in Your name, cast out demons in Your name, and done many wonders in Your name?' And then I will declare to them, 'I never knew you; depart from Me, you who practice lawlessness!'

Jesus is establishing His Church and He gives this warning in a sermon about discipleship. The situation has changed from Old Testament days. Clearly, He isn't speaking about religious and governmental rulers in Israel. There were plenty of wolves ruling in Jesus' day, but the warning isn't about them. It's about future leaders who would rise up in the Body of Christ and how they would subvert the work of carrying out His Great Commission, misleading and destroying the faith of many, even as they claim to be speaking and doing wonderful things in Jesus' Name.

A definition of spiritual wolves starts to become clear:

According to the Bible, a false prophet, a camouflaged wolf, is a person who purports to be speaking messages from God and acting with His authority. He may verify that claimed authority with impressive Bible "preaching" and "teaching" and even miracles. A false prophet isn't necessarily a "foreteller" of the future, although he may pretend to be. Most of all, he is a "forthteller", a person who speaks with claimed authority, telling people lies they want to hear about themselves, about what is right and wrong, about what the Bible says and what God is like. He tells lies about the world and brings the Name of Jesus into disrepute even as he uses that Name to advance himself. His ultimate motives are greed and power. The lies of the false prophet are cunningly woven with just the right amount of truth to draw in and mislead blind sheep. Under the leadership of wolves, the flock is systematically consumed and destroyed.

In John 10:11-16 Jesus speaks of Himself as the Good Shepherd who lays down His life for His sheep. He compares Himself to a hireling, someone who doesn't care about the sheep.

What is a hireling? He is a shepherd, but he's only watching the sheep because he wants money. He has no ownership of the flock. He is a mercenary. Probably whoever paid him to shepherd thinks he will do a good job of protecting and leading. But when danger appears the truth of who he is comes out. All he cares about is his own skin. A false prophet, a spiritual wolf and a mercenary hireling are one and the same.

The modern wolf.

Christianity has become very complex. In our day, a spiritual wolf can rise up to become any kind of teacher or leader in a church or Christian organization. Due to personality, abilities and other apparent qualifications people follow these leaders and depend on them like sheep depend on a shepherd. Very often, they are gifted and popular. But once in control, the truth of who they really are begins to come out and, ultimately, it is devastating.

Because these false leaders are clever, most often the truth about them doesn't appear all at once. Their great skill is in camouflage. This includes building a false sense of their trustworthiness. So when the first attacks begin, people are confused and reject the evidence.

What kind of "sheepskin suits" could a modern wolf wear?

There are many. He or she could appear as a wonderful musician who writes and sings emotional worship songs about the Lord. But built into the songs are subtle lies that put God's people to sleep spiritually turning their hearts away from the real Jesus.

Did you ever think of a musician as a prophet of God? When King David was establishing the service of worship for the

Temple, he set aside a group of musical prophets. 1 Chronicles 25:1 says this:

Moreover David and the captains of the army separated for the service some of the sons of Asaph, of Heman, and of Jeduthun, who should prophesy with harps, stringed instruments, and cymbals.

If there are true musical prophets of God, and there have been many in the history of the Church, certainly there are musical false prophets as well, wolves in sheep's clothing. And what power they have to destroy truth-speaking in musical worship, replacing it with hypnotic wolf-song that focuses everything on me, my needs and how I feel.

The teaching ministry of the musical prophets has been largely destroyed in the western Christian church and wolves are responsible. With all the money and adulation that comes with success in "worship" music, it is coldly predictable that wolves would gather there. The endless lust of church "worship" leaders to be on the "cutting edge" of Christian musical culture makes them complicit in the destruction. Do churches think of worship leaders as musical prophets with a teaching ministry as important as that of the senior pastor? They do not. For many churches, all that matters is crowd-pleasing musical ability. So this aspect of prophetic ministry is left to frustrated rock stars. Enter the pack.

The most disturbing fact of all.

Whatever the position of authority, most disturbing of all is that men and women can become mercenary wolves after years of gifted ministry. Perhaps for decades, people have been blessed, lives have been changed and enriched and all apparently through their work. After such long and fruitful service it seems impossible that they could turn to evil. People who love them refuse to believe it.

Such tragedies unfold with excruciating slowness. Those who see the truth are attacked by those who don't. Those who are wounded by the wolf are accused of being divisive when they report their experiences. One brick at a time, the church or Christian ministry crumbles until a tipping point is reached. Then comes disaster.

Jesus was very clear that wolves can do much apparent good, speaking in His Name with what appears to be great spiritual power even performing "miracles". They *will* bear fruit. But Satan has so perverted the whole concept of "fruit bearing" in the Church, that bad fruit is considered good and good fruit is considered unimportant.

Because we can't tell the difference between bad and good fruit, we do not recognize wolves. Also, we attribute good fruit to wolves though it doesn't belong to them at all. Jesus calls these attractive, fruit-bearing, false leaders ravening or ravenous. The word that is translated ravening is related to a verb that means to snatch or to seize. It speaks of lust and greed and rapaciousness. Wolves seize things and take credit that does not belong to them.

At a certain moment, when people have been lulled, manipulated and perhaps even bullied into weakness and complacency, the wolf will attack leaving his victims spiritually, emotionally (and even physically) robbed and violated. It doesn't just happen to individuals. It starts with a few people, but eventually whole congregations and staffs are destroyed. At the very least, their effectiveness in carrying out Jesus' Great Commission has been deeply compromised.

In particular, Jesus warned that these wolves would be everywhere in the days just before His return. He said these words in Matthew 24:24-25:

For false christs and false prophets will rise and show great signs and wonders to deceive, if possible, even the elect. See, I have told you beforehand.

He was speaking about what would happen in the Days of the End, predicting that there would be a great increase in the number of spiritual wolves and they would be given amazing skill and power to deceive and destroy such as never before in history. There are many reasons to believe that we have entered those days.

CHAPTER FIVE

Wolves in the Early Church

Wolves attacked the new-born Christian church from the very beginning. A classic example is found in Revelation 2:18-29:

"**And to the angel of the church in Thyatira write, 'These things says the Son of God, who has eyes like a flame of fire, and His feet like fine brass: "I know your works, love, service, faith, and your patience; and as for your works, the last are more than the first.**

Nevertheless I have a few things against you, because you allow that woman Jezebel, who calls herself a prophetess, to teach and seduce My servants to commit sexual immorality and eat things sacrificed to idols. And I gave her time to repent of her sexual immorality, and she did not repent. Indeed I will cast her into a sickbed, and those who commit adultery with her into great tribulation, unless they repent of their deeds. I will kill her children with death, and all the churches shall know that I am He who

searches the minds and hearts. And I will give to each one of you according to your works.

"Now to you I say, and to the rest in Thyatira, as many as do not have this doctrine, who have not known the depths of Satan, as they say, I will put on you no other burden. But hold fast what you have till I come. And he who overcomes, and keeps My works until the end, to him I will give power over the nations -- 'He shall rule them with a rod of iron; They shall be dashed to pieces like the potter's vessels' -- as I also have received from My Father; and I will give him the morning star. "He who has an ear, let him hear what the Spirit says to the churches.'"

It is easy to misunderstand what was happening in this church by the strong language that Jesus uses. He calls the wolf/false teacher in question Jezebel. Automatically, this brings up an image of the worst woman in the Bible, a person so clearly evil than anyone should have been able to recognize her. But in Thyatira, it's doubtful that this was the case. Far more likely, the people in the church would have been shocked to learn that one of their respected leaders had been referred to in this way and had been so utterly condemned by the Lord Himself.

This woman was a teacher who called herself a prophetess, which meant that she claimed to be filled with the Holy Spirit and to speak with the authority of the Lord. A significant number of people in the church accepted her authority and her teaching. So what was happening? What was she telling them?

Of all the letters to the seven churches, the one to Thyatira is the longest and the most obscure. But based on what was happening in other cities and what is known about this one, Bible scholars have drawn some logical conclusions.

Thyatira was a wealthy little city, a center of trade along an ancient trade route. It was known for its rich dyes that were used in making expensive textiles. It was a city devoted to doing business and acquiring wealth. Like every city, if you are going to be successful, you need to know and be accepted by the right people. Hollywood is a classic example of such a culture. If you don't know the right people or if the right people don't like you, you might as well pack up and leave. That's the way it was in Thyatira. But how did you get to know the right people?

This little city was a "union town". All business was controlled by trade guilds. To do business in Thyatira at all, much less be successful, you had to be a member of one of those guilds. For a Christian, that was a serious problem because the guilds were inextricably tied to the pagan temple and its worship. They met in the temple and held their feasts there. At those feasts they ate food that had been offered to idols. The guild social and business meetings included worship of the pagan god. To be a member, such worship was obligatory. So what was a Christian to do, give up the idea of success? Or was there another way?

From the letter, it seems likely that this wolf teacher was instructing believers that it was perfectly all right to be involved with guild temple worship and be a faithful Christian at the same time. "Do what you have to do to get along. Follow the forms, they don't mean anything. Tip your hat publicly to the idol, but God knows what's really in your heart."

But there was an even deeper problem. Associated with pagan worship were various forms of temple prostitution. Sexual intercourse was considered a form of worship. Families sent their daughters to "do their time" at the temple and there were male prostitutes as well. Young Christians had grown up in this culture. Just as there are sex addicts today, there were sex addicts then. Apart from making some token sacrifice to the idol, to be a member of the Guild meant putting yourself into a place of tremendous temptation where you had fallen many times before.

Around the cities of the Roman world at that time there Gnostic wolves that were attacking the baby churches by telling the believers that it was perfectly all right to experience anything you desired in the flesh. The body didn't matter. It was evil. It was only the spirit that counted. Do whatever you wanted to do with the body. Your spirit could remain clean while your body was debauched. In fact you should have every experience of the flesh.

For Christians to live this way would take them straight into the deep things of Satan, including demonic influence and possession. Very likely, the woman whom Jesus calls Jezebel was fouling the lives of believers by teaching with the claimed authority of God that it was perfectly all right to live this way. In fact, it would bring you greater power. It was teaching and seducing. In wolf pedagogy, the one always leads to the other. This seduction was a direct attempt to destroy the church by dragging her back and drowning her in the immoral pagan world. Sex was an important part of the strategy.

One of the indicators that wolves are deeply involved in the American evangelical church is the rampant sexual immorality of so many young Christians. In a recent survey, 63 percent of young Christian men and women felt that there was no problem with sex before marriage. We have been drowned by wolf teaching. The Judgment of the Lord cannot be far away.

While there were people in Thyatira who didn't follow the wolf, "Jezebel", they and their leaders had allowed her freedom to teach and destroy when she should have been thrown out. Probably she was charming with a powerful personality. Also, it's possible that she was very influential in one of the Guilds. In Thyatira, women were deeply involved in business. One of the Apostle Paul's converts was a woman named Lydia who was a "seller of purple" from that city. Purple was a color reserved for royalty. Imagine a creative designer visiting wealthy homes around the Roman world. There are some who have claimed that Lydia was the Jezebel of this letter. There is absolutely no evidence that this was the case.

The situation in the church of Thyatira brought the strong rebuke of Jesus. It was not enough to sit back and observe the wolf or even to speak against her. She had to be removed. I'm sure that would have taken courage.

Immediately after the Apostolic period there were traveling prophets going from town to town. Being able to determine who was a wolf and who wasn't came to be very important. About 100 A.D. a book of order was written to help young churches know how to function. It was called the Didache. Included in it was a section on how to determine whether a traveling prophet was true or false.

According to the Didache, a true prophet was to be held in honor. People should listen to what this individual said and take it to heart. Such a person should be given freedom to speak and should not be curtailed. However, "he shall remain one day, and, if necessary, another day also. But if he remains three days he is a false prophet." Such a visitor could ask only for bread and nothing else. If he asked for money, he was a false prophet.

Prophets always claim to speak "in the Spirit," but the Didache presents an acid test. "By their true characters a true and false prophet shall be known...Every prophet that teaches the truth, if he doesn't do what he teaches, is a false prophet." The writers got specific. If, while supposedly speaking "in the Spirit," a prophet ordered a table and food to be set before him, he was a false prophet. "Whosoever shall say in the Spirit, give me money or any other things, you shall not hear him, but if he tell you to give in the matter of others who have need, let no one judge him."

Sometimes such wandering prophets would want to settle down in a Christian community. The Didache gave instructions about that. The prophet needed to have a trade to support himself. If he didn't have one, the church was not to allow him to live in idleness under their care. If he refused to support himself, no matter what came out of his mouth, he was to be considered false. (Didache chapters 11 and 12 as quoted in The Gospel of Matthew, vol. 1, pages 282-283, The Daily Study Bible Series by William Barclay.)

The writers of the Didache understood that a false teacher might begin by teaching the truth. He simply wouldn't be living up to what he was teaching or the full instruction of the Bible. He was a hypocrite. If he stayed for any length of time, eventually he would start making demands to gratify his own desires, create division and lead the people away from the Lord.

The simple test was material. Did the prophet ask to be paid for his prophetic services? It was all right to ask for bread, but claiming to speak for the Lord, did he demand a table and a fancy meal? According to the New Testament, leaders who serve the Lord faithfully should be reasonably supported. The wolf is unfaithful in his or her life and teaching, yet expects to be well-supported at the expense of the sheep.

No matter where they are found, all wolves love to feast on money and power. When we think of money and power, it's easy to get the most extreme images in our heads, huge cathedrals and mega-churches, yachts, fancy cars and trophy wives. Yes, there are spiritual wolves who bask in that evil glut and claim it is all a gift from God for their faithfulness, offering themselves as examples of spiritual maturity and success.

But to follow the lead of the early church, we should be cautious about looking only at extremes, because very few wolves have such freedom. When we are looking for extremes it's easy to miss the real wolf that is close to us because he is much more conservative and careful. Most wolves don't have the opportunity to feast on the wealth of millions. A wolf can get pleasure from the power of abusing employees in a small Christian organization. Wolves are hungry no matter the size of the enclosure or the flock.

We like to think that we live in a very sophisticated age compared to that of the early church. However, all this means is that modern wolves have far more resources available to expand their predation, while the sheep are just as weak and gullible as in the first century.

The Didache was concerned about accountability. It urged constant watchfulness. How difficult such accountability is today! Wolves in the leadership of Christian organizations often answer to boards that have almost no contact with the victims who work in those organizations. Some denominations establish rules that make it almost impossible to get rid of a "pastor" wolf. People follow "tele-wolves", giving their faith and money to someone they never see in person and who is unaccountable to anyone they know.

Making accountability even more difficult is the fact that the modern spiritual "alpha wolf" always surrounds himself with protection. This was true in the days of the early church. The wolf came in and through his teaching created division, surrounding himself with followers. And so it is in the 21st century. Protecting every alpha wolf will be lesser wolves, fearful, enslaved sheep and other leaders whom the wolf has flattered and cultivated as friends. When he feels threatened by an individual, he will destroy that person, casting him out of fellowship or the organization, bloodied and mauled. Then, he will spiritually justify everything he did and his cabal will add their agreement.

CHAPTER SIX

Wolf Words

Shortly before he died a martyr's death in Rome, the Apostle Peter wrote these words:

But there were also false prophets among the people, even as there will be false teachers among you, who will secretly bring in destructive heresies, even denying the Lord who bought them, and bring on themselves swift destruction. And many will follow their destructive ways, because of whom the way of truth will be blasphemed. By covetousness they will exploit you with deceptive words; for a long time their judgment has not been idle, and their destruction does not slumber. (2 Peter 2:1-3)

Deceptive words! What kind of words are those? The Greek word that is translated "deceptive" is plastos. From it we get our word "plastic". Peter uses it to describe how false teachers will use words. They will mold them into images that appear to be real, but are not. That is the heart of all idolatry.

In the Old Testament, God warned His people that they were not to worship images made by the hands of man. But where did those physical images come from? They came from thoughts and words. Ancient religious leaders, claiming to speak for the gods, instructed craftsmen with words, describing how to make an idol that would depict a god. Words were molded long before an image was formed.

Today spiritual wolves carefully mold words into attractive, authoritative shapes in order to deceive and mislead. Their subtle heresies are nothing more than new forms of ancient idolatry.

A physical idol is a blatant image of a different god than the One of the Bible. With great cunning and deceptive words, spiritual wolves present a different "Jesus" than the one of Scripture. Theirs is not the Jesus of the Cross or the Great Commission. It is not the Jesus of repentance from sin or of servanthood or of the Narrow Way. It is not the Jesus of love, mercy and forgiveness based on the atoning Blood Sacrifice that took place at Calvary. It is not the Jesus who is seated at the Right Hand of God who will judge the living and the dead, sending some to Heaven and others to hell. The subtle teaching of the wolf replaces the real Jesus with a powerless idol molded out of words.

A wolf may shift the focus away from Jesus and loving obedience to Him, by introducing endless, distracting minutiae that can appear to be sound Bible teaching. This may include obsessive emphasis on God's blessings of prosperity, or politics, or imagined details about the End Times, or spiritual gifts, or tithing, or Biblical rules and law, or fascination with the meaning of Greek words, or the positive, "seeker-sensitive" messages of the Bible and on and on. But all of it brings about one result. With subtle, almost hypnotic power, the gifted wolf incrementally reshapes love for Jesus into praise, love and worship of himself. In the process,

Jesus is never forgotten. He's just molded into a lovely, lifeless statue.

The gifted wolf may teach the Bible and theology in great detail without ever bringing hearers to an understanding of the need for repentance from sin, the receiving and giving of forgiveness, or the absolute surrender of the life to Jesus' Lordship. He or she may teach much about discipleship, but create no disciples to the Lord. He or she may teach much about the "power" and "gifts" of the Holy Spirit, but never teach the true evidence of His Presence, which is an ever-deepening love for Jesus that leads to a holy life set apart for Him and His Kingdom.

As Peter tells us, in all that they do spiritual wolves cause the "way" of Truth to be blasphemed. What is the "way" of Truth? It is the Narrow Road to Eternal Life and the means for entering into the Kingdom of Heaven by the atoning sacrifice of Jesus Christ. It is the manner in which Jesus empowers His true followers to bear fruit in this world for that Kingdom.

While the wolf's followers are hypnotized by his gifts, non-believers see the results of his brutish, selfish actions. They see mauled people crawling out from under his stifling "ministry". They see foolish Christians who follow blindly no matter how they are abused. They see lawsuits and bankruptcies. They see people who claimed to be Christians turning away from the faith. And when they see all of this, they mock and blaspheme the only way into Heaven, which is through Jesus Christ.

The Apostle John wrote in 1 John 4:1: **Beloved, do not believe every spirit, but test the spirits, whether they are of God; because many false prophets have gone out into the world.**

41

Throughout history, the Church has suffered from wolves dressed like sheep. From every denomination and branch of Christianity come personal stories about wolf attacks.

"The priest was just the most wonderful man, so caring and loving. We trusted him. How could he have done what he did to those little boys?"

"He taught our Sunday School class for years. He was such a man of God. So when he offered us the opportunity to invest in his business, promising that we would double our money, we believed him. We prayed about it together. Of course, from our new wealth we would tithe for God's work. He stole it all. How could God have allowed this to happen? We feel like such fools. Now we don't trust anyone."

"It happened so naturally. He was my pastor and we were in ministry together. He was such a godly man and God blessed our work. We prayed together every day. I loved and respected him so much that I wanted to do anything to help him. It was clear that his wife didn't love or deserve him. She didn't care about his ministry at all. When we started sleeping together it didn't feel wrong. It seemed like a natural expression of the love God had given to us. He told me that he would leave his wife. It had never been a true marriage before God anyway. Well, it didn't happen and now I know he was lying. He was just using me. Finally, he tossed me aside for another woman. I feel filthy, like I've been raped. And what makes it so much worse is that I helped him do it. But where was God in all of this? Why didn't He show me what this man was really like before it went so far?"

Cases such as these are only the most blatant examples of spiritual wolf predation. There are untold thousands of others

42

where the wolf isn't so easy to observe, where the attacks and damage are far more subtle, where years of comfortable false teaching is sending people to hell or where years of spiritualized abuse have destroyed all faith in a loving God.

Wolf words seduce people into spiritual darkness.

In Matthew 7:15-23 Jesus could not have been clearer. At the very beginning, He uses a word that is translated *beware.* In the original language it means *Pay Attention Because There Is Danger! Be Cautious! Keep This Always In Your Mind*! Why does He use this word? Because we do not have to be ravaged by spiritual wolves.

In 1968 I was a young infantry First Lieutenant in Vietnam. During that time, I led a rifle platoon. When we were out on patrol we would set up for the night in a specific way. We would establish a system of guards. During the night, at least one soldier had to be awake scanning all around us with a night seeing device called a starlight scope. We were a little group alone and vulnerable, so every minute of the night a guard needed to be watching for the enemy. We did it in shifts.

Several times I awoke to check on our status only to find that the soldier who was supposed to be on guard had fallen asleep. I was not pleased. Our lives depended on constant vigilance. Constant vigilance is tiring. We want to stop, close our eyes and rest. But to do so is death.

Until we get to Heaven, we are in enemy territory. It is dark and dangerous here. Guarding a flock that belongs to Jesus traveling through such territory cannot be left to one person or even an entire elder or deacon board. Every mature believer should be spiritually awake and listening, carefully weighing all that is said and done in the church against the eternal Truth of the Bible. Every mature believer should know how to recognize spiritual wolves and how to deal with them. This can be done only through the wisdom and power of the Holy Spirit.

CHAPTER SEVEN

Does God Speak Through Wolves?

This is a very controversial question. Many Christians believe that the answer is, no. God only speaks through his sanctified, chosen vessels. In this they make a terrible, potentially lethal, mistake. This error allows wolves much greater freedom and much more time to wreak destruction.

Jesus said that it is the "fruit" of a leader's life that must be scrutinized to determine "wolfhood" and we're going to examine what He meant by "fruit" in a coming chapter. In the meantime, we need to be clear that a true spiritual wolf is either a conscious or unconscious representative of Satan. No matter how wonderfully he or she may have ministered in the past, or how spiritually "gifted" he or she may appear to be, no matter what Christian schools the individual attended or ministerial degrees that he or she may hold, no matter that a thousand Bible verses may be known and quoted, no matter that thousands of people may have been blessed/taught/saved/healed/delivered under that person's "ministry", he or she is **not** a member of Jesus' Kingdom or a child of God.

Just writing those words is so difficult. And I know how difficult they will be to accept, but I see no other way to understand and apply Jesus' warning in Matthew chapter 7.

You may say, "But my problem leader knows the Bible and preaches it so well." Knowing the Bible and having wonderful preaching ability is not proof that a man or woman is a true member of Jesus' family. The Pharisees of Jesus' day knew the Bible better than anyone. There were gifted teachers among them, yet they were condemned. You may say, "But people have come to know the Lord and have grown in their faith through this person's ministry. Are you telling me that God speaks His Truth through Bible teachers and preachers who really don't know Him at all?"

That is exactly what I am saying.

Charles Templeton was a well-known Canadian pastor and evangelist. Many people came to know Jesus through his gifted ministry. In the 1940's, he along with several other pastors and evangelists including Billy Graham, founded Youth for Christ, International, an organization that exists today and has had a wonderful ministry for many years. It was very influential in my life when I was a teenager.

Templeton and the first president of Youth for Christ, Torrey Johnson, toured Europe together on an evangelistic crusade, often staying in the same room. They prayed together. On that trip and others, many people came to know Jesus. There was much "fruit". But in the years that followed, Charles Templeton lost his faith and became a well-known agnostic, arguing in the media against what he had preached. Had he ever believed at all? Only God knows.

So what happened to those who met Jesus through his ministry? Did his lack of belief mean that theirs was invalid? Of course not. God's Word is powerful far beyond the person who speaks it. It is the Holy Spirit using God's Word that transforms lives. I've known people who came to trust in Jesus through a Hollywood movie done by those who didn't know Him at all.

Was Charles Templeton a spiritual wolf? No. As sad as it is, he was honest about his loss of belief. He didn't try to fool anyone. Many others are not so honest. There are numerous reports about men in the ministry who have become atheists, yet continue in their positions, never telling their parishioners about their true beliefs. Instead, they write about them anonymously on the Internet. What is the reason for their dishonesty? They don't want to lose the money and the prestige. They are wolves.

Does God speak through wolves? Indeed He does. And He does it to show His omnipotent Glory. In the Old Testament, the prophet Balaam is a wonderful example of a man who was not a child of God and instead was evil, yet God spoke through him. King Balak tried to get Balaam to curse the Children of Israel, but God wouldn't let him do it. Instead, through that evil man the world was given one of the most beautiful predictions of the coming Messiah, Jesus. Did the gift of that message do Balaam any good? He died like a dog as an enemy of God.

There is another reason why God's blessing and fruit can seem to come from the ministry of wolves. Often, working beneath wolves in humble positions, are many sincere believers who suffer under wolf leadership. These good people struggle to do the true work of the Lord. I believe that God blesses them in spite of

47

their false leaders. Needless to say, wolves are happy to take credit for all such blessing.

CHAPTER EIGHT

Sheep in Wolf Suits

At this point in our journey, it's time for another serious word of caution. Let's be honest, in the Body of Christ there are many foolish people, immature people, insensitive people, sinful people, stubborn people, insulting people, ignorant people, proud people, selfish people and more. Such people get into leadership. While, in their sinfulness and ignorance, they may damage others, this doesn't automatically mean that they are spiritual wolves.

You can be an ineffective, foolish leader and not be a spiritual wolf. You've just been promoted to your level of incompetence and should be removed from that position until you mature and discover where your real gifts lie. You can be a teacher making mistakes in your teaching, even passionately, though unconsciously, teaching things that are wrong. That doesn't make you a spiritual wolf. It makes you an ignorant teacher who shouldn't be teaching others until you have more knowledge. You can be a leader who falls into temptation and sin. That doesn't mean you are a spiritual wolf. It means that you need to be removed from leadership, repent and learn to serve others with chastity, compassion and humility, making restitution where possible and accepting a more humble position in the Body of Christ.

A great danger and sin in the Church is to accuse someone of being a wolf (false prophet, false teacher) when it isn't true. Because a teacher/leader disagrees with you about baptism, or the End Times, or tithing, or freewill/election/predestination, or the sign gifts, or the role of women in the church, or how a Christian is to act and minister in the world, or how a church is to be organized and led, etc., does not automatically make that individual a wolf. He may be wrong, but all of us are wrong in many particulars. Part of maturing in Christ is recognizing how little we know and looking at others with compassion and humility, hoping that we will be viewed in the same way. If we constantly "cry wolf" no one is going to believe us when a real wolf appears.

There is an old saying that "the devil rules by fashion". This isn't just true in the world, it's true in the church. A person may have a style of communicating that you find grating, irritating, out-of-date, immature, boring (add your own adjectives). Your dislike of that style may color your thinking about everything that person says or does to such a degree that you undermine his or her leadership.

Often old Christians stand in rigid judgment over stumbling and bumbling young Christian leaders and teachers, deciding that they are of little value. Young Christians refuse to listen to old Christian teachers and leaders viewing them as out of touch, irrelevant and judgmental.

When this happens, and it's happening in so many churches, be clear about one thing. It is paving the way for a wolf to take leadership. The wolf always appeals to the desires of the dominant crowd. He or she knows exactly what is fashionable with that crowd and how to use it. So while you undermine godly leaders, the wolf is at the door.

At this period of history (2014) so-called "social media" have made it possible to malign people, especially Christian leaders, beyond anything imaginable in the past. Too often I read someone's diatribe against a Christian leader calling that person a false teacher. These are passed from person to person in an endless slandering chain.

In one recent case an accusation made by a spewing "Christian" was disproved with evidence in that very "thread". No matter, the spewer just went right on and his pack followed though it was clear that none of them knew what they were talking about.

Jesus said that we would account for every idle word. That includes the words that we post on-line. If you are too lazy to do your own research about a particular leader to determine the truth or falsehood regarding accusations against him, the least you can do is remain silent. If you believe every rumor and out-of-context statement attributed to a particular leader, adding your own ignorant accusations and spewing all of it into the world, there is a very great possibility that *you* are a wolf.

Remember, all wolves are not in leadership. There are thousands of mangy curs wandering around in churches and in cyber-space, doing what they can to maul with many varieties of false teaching, including false teaching *about* false teaching. So examine yourself. Are you following wolves? It doesn't take a master hunter to hear the howling of a pack and know what animals are making that noise. Be vigilant about your own heart.

CHAPTER NINE

The Spiritual Food Chain
of Death

As I have done specific research for this book, I have become more and more disturbed. I asked myself what kinds of wolves are there in the church and where do they come from? I've come to the conclusion that they fall into two categories. The first we might call Process Wolves. These are people who did not start out to be wolves, but through the selfish choices of their lives and the power that has been given to them, that is what they have become. The longer it continues without humble repentance and restitution, the more wolf-like and destructive they are.

It is easier for me to understand these people. I believe that all strong leaders are tempted in these directions. Truly there, but for the Grace of God go many of us, including me. I believe that almost all of the "wolf stories" that I tell in this book are about Process Wolves. My discussion regarding growth into wolfhood relates to this group.

But there is a second category. These I call Born Wolves. I hope and pray that they are in the minority as far as wolves in the church are concerned. However, even if this is so, their numbers will vastly increase in the days ahead. For Born Wolves, it is not a matter of developing into a wolf. They are wolves from their earliest years. The only question is how far they will descend into evil.

It is not pleasant to think of ourselves as food at the bottom of a spiritual chain of predation, yet that is how Satan and his dark lords view us. His human wolves share in the hungers of their master.

All spiritual wolves are consumed with selfishness and greed. They are hungry for two kinds of food – money which brings prestige and creature comforts and power which means control over others. The wolf wants constant praise without criticism. This he will view as nothing more than his due. What he gives in return is charm. For a limited period of time, charm can pass for respect, love, friendship, kindness and even spirituality. It is none of these. Charm is wonderful, but in itself it is not a measure of anything. I'll speak more about charm very soon.

To maintain control over the lesser wolves and foolish sheep that he needs as an inner circle of protection, a wolf will give tangible rewards for unquestioning obedience and loyalty. These can include money, titles, power and other perquisites. To receive them will mean that you agree to accept his abuse, which can be either subtly manipulative or blatant and brutal. Loyalty means silent obedience.

Recently, some wolves in Christian business and ministry have been demanding that those who work for them sign non-disclosure and non-compete agreements. Such demands are a sure indicator that something is wrong. There are all sorts of rationales presented for these requirements, but the real reasons won't become apparent until you are in the belly of the beast. They have to do with a fear of openness and a viciously competitive spirit, neither of which have a place in the Body of Christ.

To be in a wolf's inner circle there are rigid requirements. For the rest of the flock, the wolf's abuse may be subtle, such as instilling false guilt at not accepting without question all of his instruction and leadership or creating fear that if his guidance is not followed disaster will result. (Maybe even eternally in hell.) His abuse may be slathered in charm to the point that it almost feels good when his teeth go in. Only afterward will there be suffering when the teeth tear and the wound begins to bleed.

Because Satan is a legalist, his spiritual wolves are always legalists. A wolf establishes his own rules and expects everyone to live up to them. Of course, those rules do not apply to him and may change at his discretion. He changes the meaning of words, especially words in the Bible, to give authority to his legalistic code. The legalism of a wolf may require lawlessness among his followers. He may tell them, with the apparent authority of God, that they are free from certain Biblical principles of ethical and moral behavior.

However they are presented, the rules of the wolf do not promote true freedom and maturity in Christ. They do not lead the sheep into green pastures. They keep the sheep spiritually penned and starving while the wolf enjoys the pasture along with periodic feasts of lamb. The greater the power that is given to him, the greater will be the lies and manipulations that he uses to maintain his position and continue feasting on the flock.

As we said, the church is supposed to be a spiritual hospital where damaged people come for healing in Jesus and loving support from His people. There are some who come with so many wounds from the past that they are more than just weakened. Their awful experiences have conditioned them to think that they are worthy only to be abused. Though they are miserable, abuse is what they expect and all they know. It represents home.

Such damaged sheep are a particular delicacy for wolves. They have a sixth sense that draws them into relationships that become feasts of servitude and dependency as the "need" for abuse is spiritualized. Cults and cult-like churches are built on such hellish relationships that lead ever deeper into evil. It is a form of seduction that is both spiritual and, all too often, physical.

CHAPTER TEN

The Black, the White and the Gray

Within the Church, a wolf may express himself in a variety of ways. We might call the extremes black wolves and white wolves.

The black wolf feeds on those damaged sheep that are desperate for the acceptance of a powerful father or mother figure whose favor it is difficult to gain. These poor sheep find security in having someone tell them what to do and brief moments of pleasure when they receive a shred of favor. They don't like to make difficult choices. They want someone to do it for them. They feel at home only in narrow pens constructed of rules and guilt over breaking those rules. They are fearful of wide, green, open pastures. They resent sheep who refuse to stay in their pens with them.

After a period of time these pitiful sheep internalize the attitudes and desires of the black wolf to such a degree that they are dependent on him. They think with his thoughts and perform his desires without considering any other alternatives. These people see God as distant or perhaps as a hard father and cruel taskmaster who punishes disobedience. His love must be earned and that takes a lot of effort. The wolf is ready to guide them.

The white wolf appeals to those who want someone to tell them how to be happy and successful. They have no real interest in being true disciples of Jesus if it means the acceptance of any kind of loss or suffering, so the white wolf assures them that this isn't necessary. He tells them that suffering and loss are of the devil. All God wants for His sheep is prosperity. To get it, they must follow simple rules and proclaim simple statements that the wolf has twisted out of context from the Bible.

Obedience to the white wolf means trying to live with a legalistic, unwavering, iron-like faith, not in God, but in the wolf's Christianized mantras, which he or she blends with just enough truth to make the lies difficult to discern by the ignorant, the narcissistic and the lazy.

Both kinds of sheep that follow these wolves want the same thing. They want happiness as they have come to define it from their damaged experiences and sinful, selfish desires. Both kinds of wolf are masters and mistresses at weaving webs of legalism that appear to give their sheep what they want. However, both kinds of legalism lead to disillusionment, guilt, anger, fear, self-pity, enslavement and death. In the process, no matter their color, the wolves are well fed.

Among spiritual wolves, probably there are more gray wolves than any other variety. In the light of day, the gray wolf remains hidden between the extremes, trying to appeal to the widest possible prey. With great care, the gray wolf assures that his teaching is "Biblical". His subtle deletions and accretions are not easy to spot, yet they emasculate the Word of God, destroying its power to transform lives. And in the evening, the gray wolf attacks. By morning, the one he has attacked is gone from the church or the organization. Half asleep, the other sheep either ignore the loss or excuse it and keep grazing.

You may work for a gray wolf in a small Christian ministry, mission, school or church. You are working as hard as you can, but he keeps you on edge with stated or implied threats all couched in "spiritual" jargon. The gray wolf knows the Bible and quotes Bible verses. He says he's encouraging you, trying to build you up, even trying to "disciple" you, but the effect is the opposite. The more contact you have with him, the more discouraged you get and the further away from the Lord you feel. As the frustration and discouragement deepen, your patience grows short. You may respond in a manner that isn't "Christian". The wolf uses that to prove you are weak and immature, perhaps caught in sin.

The gray wolf may flatter you one day and rage at you the next, creating constant insecurity. He may say wonderful things about you in public and vilify you in private or vice versa. Or he may *never* build you up, causing you to endlessly doubt yourself.

All varieties of wolves want to dominate. If you show the slightest sign of courage or leadership by disagreeing with them, even if it is ever so respectfully, you become a threat and a target. You may need your job. Or all of your friends are in his church. The wolf knows your need and takes advantage of it. And the pack around him is watching, reporting to their leader.

Many wolves in churches are not pastors. You may be a pastor with a gray wolf on your elder board. This isn't just a stubborn person or someone who doesn't share your vision. It isn't someone whose personality doesn't jibe with yours and who irritates you. Often God puts people like this in our lives to speak truth to us.

A gray wolf elder begins by moving behind your back, manipulating others, speaking lies and causing nothing but dissension. In other words, such a person is an "evening wolf" who will wait to strike. When the open attack comes it will be when you are most vulnerable and after he has established his authority with a pack of lesser wolves and weak, foolish sheep. Do not be amazed at how easily his slander and outrageous lies are accepted. He has groomed his followers to do that. And every vicious, self-serving act will be perpetrated in the Name of Jesus and for His ministry.

Eventually, all varieties of spiritual wolves will attack individuals. Whether the attacks are open or carefully camouflaged, they leave angry, broken victims. The mauling by a spiritual wolf tempts weak and immature Christians to blame God and the Church, which is what Satan intended from the start. In their pain, wolf-wounded people often become blind and deaf to legitimate Christian teachers and leaders who speak with the authority and Love of the Lord. As part of the spiritual food chain of hell, angry, bitter, wolf-wounded people often take many others with them.

CHAPTER ELEVEN

The Good-Old-Boy Wolf

Let me tell you about a pastor in a small town in the western United States. When he first arrived in the town, he seemed like a great guy, personable, down-to-earth, jovial. He was middle-aged and previous to his position as a senior pastor had been an associate pastor for years. Upon his arrival, several people tried to establish a friendship with this man and his wife, but it just didn't work. Something wasn't there. They discounted it as a quirk of personality. Some people "click" and others don't.

As the months passed and the man began his ministry, disconcerting things began to happen. A woman who had led the Christian school that was associated with the church, began to come under sniping fire from the pastor. Week after week, he picked apart her work, denigrating her in front of others. When finally she left, the pastor's wife took over her paid position.

Next came the popular worship leader of the church, a young man who was studying for the ministry. His worship leading was done for free. On the paid staff, he was the part-time janitor. The pastor decided that he didn't like his worship leading style. Suddenly, nothing the young man did as a janitor was adequate. The pastor and his wife picked it apart. He was blamed for things that weren't his responsibility. He and his family left the church and entered another denomination where he ministers as a senior pastor today.

After that came the youth pastor, a young man who had grown up in the church and also was very popular. He had an excellent ministry with the junior high and high school young people, spending a lot of personal time in discipleship. The congregation enjoyed his preaching. He had a strong love for God and an enthusiasm for ministry. Like so many youth pastors, he hoped one day to be senior pastor in a church of his own.

Over and over this young man shared ideas for expanded ministry with the senior pastor. Over and over, his ideas were rejected. After a period of time, it became clear that the senior pastor didn't have a real vision for the church and would not allow this young man to pursue his vision. The relationship between them grew tense.

Though he had grown up in this church, with great sadness, the youth minister began searching for another church. When the offer came for him to become senior pastor of a small church across the state, he went to his pastor and pleaded with him, telling him that he didn't want to leave, that he was sure they could work out their differences. He was turned down cold.

The young man took the new position. Since that time, his former pastor has done all he could within the denomination to hurt his career.

Needing a worship leader, the pastor found a young man within the congregation who had great musical talent, but who had almost no church experience of any kind. Because of home circumstances while growing up, he had rarely attended church and knew little about how things were supposed to work within a congregation. He was just learning the Bible.

With no concern for his lack of experience, the pastor elevated him into worship leader. Thankfully, the young man was very dedicated and struggled hard to learn, though he received no help or guidance from his pastor.

The new worship leader was paid a small amount per Sunday for his work even though he was asked to do other things, which included practices during the week. After two years, he requested two paid Sundays off per year for a vacation. His family did not have much money and they depended on his part-time ministry salary to survive. Inexplicably, the pastor refused, accusing him of being greedy and not being dedicated to the ministry. In sadness and frustration, the young man and his family left the church.

In all these situations, the pastor's vindictiveness did not end when an individual left the congregation. He continued to do all he could to destroy each person's reputation. He is known for continuing to say terrible things for years.

The cold selfishness, his utter lack of interest in discipling the people on his staff, in particular, the young men in spiritual leadership beneath him, his lack of vision for the church and his unwillingness for anyone else to have a vision, undergirded by the unsurprising shallowness of his preaching, qualify him to be categorized as a wolf. Yet to this day, he is still the jovial, good-old-boy pastor of that church, though many, many people, including senior men and women of God, have left the congregation because they know what kind of man he is. Those who remain also know what kind of man he is, but blindly overlook it.

After watching his terrible actions for years, one individual joined his board just so he could restrain him from hurting more people. It's clear that restraining is not what is needed. Yet, through misunderstanding of Scripture, difficulty caused by denominational rules, fear of consequences and pure apathy, the man is allowed to continue. Filled with shallow charm, he still slaps people on the back and newcomers think he is a great guy. But always, he is very concerned when people do not respect him. He doesn't like it when anyone uses his first name without referring to him as "pastor".

Of all the traits that define a spiritual wolf utter lack of Christ-like love is the most important. Jesus said in John 13:34-35

"A new commandment I give to you, that you love one another; as I have loved you, that you also love one another. By this all will know that you are My disciples, if you have love for one another."

Perhaps the clearest proof that the Good Old Boy "pastor" is a wolf comes from his frigid lack of compassion. He dislikes helping anyone in financial need. There is a story that he loves to tell and has told it over and over.

One day in a former church, a young couple met with him. They were in great financial difficulty and wondered if their church might help them. He told them the church would help them *to the level that they had tithed*. Well, they were poor and had not been able to tithe much. He checked the records and gave them back exactly the amount that they had given. The man is very proud of this act. He uses the story to encourage tithing.

One cannot look at what he did without thinking of Jesus' parable of the talents and the unfaithful servant who hid his money in the ground and gave back to his master exactly what he had been given. If Jesus is in each of those who love Him, then that spiritual wolf was the steward of the money Jesus had given through that young couple. The same thing that the master said to the unfaithful servant might be said to him, "At least you could have given back the money with interest."

It is frightening to think of what this man will say when he stands before the King. It is also frightening to think of what Jesus will say to the church that has allowed him to remain "pastor" in spite of all the evidence about who he really is.

CHAPTER TWELVE

Why Does the Sheepskin Suit Look So Good?

In Matthew 7 Jesus warned that spiritual wolves won't appear snarling and roaring. They will come in wearing perfect sheepskin suits. What did He mean by that? Quite simply, you won't be able to tell that they are wolves just by looking at them. More than that, you will swear that they are outstanding sheep, the best specimens of the whole flock. Not a strand of wolf fur will peek out. Appearing to be the best specimens, they will rise to leadership.

There are skilled prosthetics creators in Hollywood who make full head masks so real and amazing that even close up you can't tell that they are masks at all. As real as those masks are, the sheep costumes worn by spiritual wolves are far more realistic, because they aren't worn just on the outside. But let's look at the outside first.

A wolf in a church, Christian school or organization will dress and act like a sheep of that particular flock. Whatever the external conventions of that community might be, he will express them with skill. Are specific clothes or clothing styles necessary to fit in? He will wear them. Do Christians of that community demand obedience to certain rules of behavior in relation to the secular culture? The wolf will be passionate about obeying those rules and requiring others to do so.

Is there a litmus test for full acceptance in a Christian community such as belief in a pre, mid or post-tribulational Rapture or freewill, or predestination? The wolf will defend the required position to the point of driving people away who express the slightest variance. Is it necessary to speak in tongues? The wolf will croak, stutter and blather with impressive glossolalia. Is a seminary degree needed for leadership success within a group? He will graduate, perhaps with honors, from an acceptable school.

Most of all, a wolf will be charming to the people who matter. But let's look deeper. To be effective, the sheepskin suit must hide the "wolf spirit" *EVEN TO THE WEARER*. What do I mean by that?

If I were thirty years old and wanted to convince you for a full day that I was an old man of 70, I would have to do a lot more than put on a mask. I would have to speak like an old man and move like an old man. I would have to try to think like an old man. In other words, to convince you for any significant period that I *was* an old man, I would have to be a consummate actor.

As a writer and producer in Hollywood, I have had the great privilege of working with many highly skilled professional actors. A professional actor prepares for a major role by doing research into the kind of character that he is going to portray. He will attempt to understand not just *how* that character would act in any given situation, but *why* he would act that way.

He will want to know about his background and the details of his life. He may talk to people who are like that character. He will spend time imagining that he is that person. Ultimately, the actor will reach deep inside himself to find those elements in his own personality and experience that relate to that character. When the moment of performance arrives, he puts on that persona. For a brief period, he believes that he *is* that imaginary individual.

There are a few actors who are so passionate about "becoming" the character they are portraying that they refuse to get "out of character" during the entire period of the performance, both on and off the set, even at home. Sometimes for months, they choose to, not only believe a dramatic "lie", but, to as great an extent as possible within the law, *live it*.

Here's an interesting question, if you decide to tell a lie, but in the process of preparing to tell it, convince yourself that it's the truth, is it really a lie when the words leave your mouth? Perhaps you have convinced yourself so completely of its truthfulness that you could pass a lie detector test. You have reconstructed your memories so that they fit the "reality" that you want to believe. If you believe completely what you are saying, are you a liar? In our relativistic age where there are no absolutes, that is a serious question.

The wolves that Jesus is warning about are consummate actors. Until they reveal themselves to their victims, they look like true followers of His. Why are they so successful in carrying off the subterfuge? Like the most committed method actors, they have convinced themselves that they really are sheep. And not just any old sheep, the very best and finest of the flock. Even while they maul and pillage, they refuse to think of themselves as wolves.

A professional actor understands the difference between what's real and what isn't. At the end of the day, he knows that he isn't the character that he is portraying. I am convinced that the vast majority of the group that we have called Process Wolves, do not understand who they are. They have lied for so long even to themselves, that without a merciful act of God, they will believe those lies all the way to hell. How can someone be so self-deluded?

First steps into a wolfhood.

Have you ever told a lie and were so committed to it that you came to believe it to the point where your memories were reconstructed to match the lie? Have you ever treated someone badly, then justified the way you acted so completely that you convinced yourself that what you did wasn't wrong at all? After doing something wrong, have you ever wiped it from your memory by consciously focusing elsewhere, especially on all the good things you do? In getting something that you wanted, have you ever justified doing something that you knew was wrong? Are there areas of sin in your life where you have refused to repent, instead continuing to sin until it didn't bother you anymore? Have you learned how to use people to get what you want without even thinking about it? All of these and more are steps toward becoming a spiritual wolf.

In Jesus' warning in Matthew 7, it is strongly implied that when most spiritual wolves stand before Him someday they will be shocked to discover that they have never been part of His flock. They will argue with Him, trying to prove their sheephood by their success in ministry. It will be eternally devastating for them to discover that, though they had convinced themselves they were sheep, in reality they were wolves. His words will strip them of the sheepskin suits that had camouflaged them to the depths of their souls.

Many will say to Me in that day, 'Lord, Lord, have we not prophesied in Your name, cast out demons in Your name, and done many wonders in Your name?' And then I will declare to them, 'I never knew you; depart from Me, you who practice lawlessness!' (Matthew 7:22-23)

When Jesus uses the word "many," that's got to mean a very large number. And the words "practice lawlessness" are powerful. In the original language they imply working at a career of evil lawbreaking as though it were a craft or a trade. If you're going to become good at something you have to believe in it and work hard at it for a long time. That's what Process Wolves do. And as with any craft, they get better at it over time. But how can you live that way? What would you need to believe about yourself?

If you are a writer in Hollywood, there is a basic rule you must follow if you want to create realistic antagonists or villains in your scripts. Here's the rule: The villain always believes that he is the real hero of the story and when you are dealing with his character, you have to write him that way.

The greatest antagonist in the universe is Satan, the monstrous fallen angel once called Lucifer, the Light Bearer. I am convinced that, in his monumental pride and commitment to lies, he considers himself the real hero of cosmic history. In his mind, he has a justification for every horrific, brutal act of rebellion that he has ever perpetrated. The fact that Christians don't consider him the hero fills him with rage and a cosmic case of self-pity. I'm sure he believes that he has been terribly misunderstood. He had to do what he did, there was no other choice. Whatever he has become, he was forced into it. None of it is his fault, it's God's fault. And on and on.

It is interesting that, more and more, both in occult literature and popular culture, Satan/Lucifer and those who live lives of evil following him, are being presented as heroes. More and more, absolute evil is being fed to us as the only logical alternative for these twisted protagonists without the slightest intrusion of love, grace, repentance and mercy. All of this is in preparation for the End of Days, when the ultimate Satanic Wolf Hero will be presented as the savior of the human race.

Jesus called Satan a liar and the father of lies. We trivialize the whole concept of lying. Too often, we think of lying the way a child lies. That kind of lying is on the surface. The child wants something and lies to get it. He lies out of laziness to escape work, to get something he wants, or he lies to evade the consequences of a misdeed. Satanic lying and the lying of his wolves, is on a much more sophisticated level.

The most heinous lie and the heart of all monstrous lying is to convince yourself that, even though you are a selfish liar, you really are a truth-telling hero, simply misunderstood as you sacrifice your life for the good of others. This leads directly into justifying every awful thing that you might do. The voice of darkness inside whispers that, painful as it was, you had no choice.

I am convinced that it's possible to be so adept at lying to yourself that you actually pray yourself into sinful, destructive beliefs and decisions, thinking that God has spoken to you and approves. Yes, you prayed all right, but the one you have been hearing from wasn't the God of the Bible. Wolf prayers can feel just like real ones.

All of this may help explain the successful performances of so many spiritual wolves, why they can fool so many thousands. Process Wolves grow into their predatory roles over time through an increase of power and more and more spiritualized selfish choices.

But there is another variety of wolf.

CHAPTER THIRTEEN

Serpent Wolves

Decades ago, the late psychiatrist, M. Scott Peck, discovered a disturbing group of people among his clients. Even with all of his training, he found no way to categorize them. The things they did were utterly cruel. Worst of all they had no conscience, not a shred of remorse about any horrible act that they perpetrated. For example, a mother and father had a son who committed suicide. The following Christmas, as a gift, they gave their other son the gun that his brother had used to kill himself. And they thought nothing of it. It was how they had always dealt with their children.

As Peck discovered more and more such people, he had to create a new category for them because they didn't fit into anything in his training. The category he created was "Evil". Dr. Peck documented his experiences in an important book entitled, The People of the Lie.

The late Roman Catholic priest, Father Malachi Martin, who served at high levels in the Vatican, discovered the same kind of people. But he called them demon possessed and created a new category of possession for them. Some of his experiences are documented in his book, Hostage to the Devil.

When we think of demonic possession, automatically into our minds come images from The Exorcist, and other books and movies. They present a set of symptoms that many Christians equate with evil spirit possession. These symptoms appear because, to varying degrees, the victims are fighting against the demon that is overwhelming them. However, Father Martin discovered people who were not fighting at all. The demon was an integral part of them. They were comfortable with its presence and didn't want to change. He called these the Perfectly Possessed. While their actions and attitudes were extremely disturbing and destructive, they didn't manifest the traditionally understood symptoms of possession.

Let's try to imagine a man who is in this state of willing enslavement. (It could be a woman.) Either knowingly or unknowingly, this individual is a servant of Darkness walking through the world with the specific assignment to harm as many people as possible. With him he brings chaos. Does he know that he is possessed by an evil spirit? Whether he does or not, isn't important. He is totally comfortable with who he is and sees no need for change. This makes him the ultimate spiritual wolf.

According to the Bible, Satan can appear as an angel of light and so can his servants, so let's imagine a man who could wreak the most havoc. Wouldn't he present himself to the world in the best possible way? If he were good-looking it would make him that much more dangerous. Certainly, he would be very charming. People would be attracted to him. There would be something exciting about him. He would be creative and forceful, unafraid to take risks. His view of things would be different than the average person. Average people are filled with insecurity, but this man wouldn't be insecure at all. He would always be certain of what he wanted to do and how he wanted to do it. Consequently, many would view him as a natural-born leader.

Gifted as he was by Satan who has known humans for eons, this perfectly possessed man would know exactly what to say and how to say it in order to build friendship, trust and even romantic love. He would be very bright and could talk on many subjects with what appeared to be authority. Understanding the need for humor in building relationships, he would be funny. This would include self-deprecating humor.

He would be a great storyteller. Though his stories might be a little disjointed and a bit odd, the way he told them would be compelling. Probably, they would be stories about the wild things he had done and his many accomplishments. They would be fanciful and would always present him in the best light, but this would be mitigated by how fascinating they were and so filled with humor. It would be refreshing to see such a gifted person who had done so many things, yet was humble and didn't take himself too seriously.

This unique individual would be a student of culture and human psychology. He would understand the nuances necessary to establish good relationships. With what appeared to be amazing speed and sensitivity, he would learn your likes and dislikes and would do thoughtful things for you. If you were part of a tight-knit group, he would join in with an intuitive understanding of what was expected of members. In short, to those around him, he would appear to be an ideal friend...for awhile.

But the more some people got to know him, the more disturbed they would become, especially if they were mature Christians. Something was not quite right. If you were the specific target of his attentions, it's likely that you wouldn't notice it. If you had very little contact with him, you wouldn't notice it either. Only those who were around him, but not one of his targets, might see it.

But let's imagine that you are the focus of his attention. For you, his special friendship would be mesmerizing. He would appear to understand and appreciate you on a level that few ever had. You might even believe that you had found your "soul-mate" or at least the closest, most understanding friend that had ever entered your life. Just the way he looked at you with such amazing intensity and concentration would take your mind off his words. If friends didn't like him and expressed concern, you wouldn't understand what they were talking about. You would brush off their warnings, thinking they were jealous.

Not that there wouldn't be frustrations in your relationship with this charming, perfectly possessed individual. There would be. In all human relations, whether love affairs or friendships, there is a desire to get to know the other person on a deeper level. But in the case of your special friend, in spite of all his talk (and he would talk a lot), in spite of his knowledge, humor and apparent interest in you, in spite of the fact that you spent significant time with him, slowly there might come the realization that you didn't know him at all. Whenever you attempted to learn something about his family and background, almost anything really personal, the inquiries might be deflected. He might tell you some piece of information, but the next day it would change. You could never pin him down.

Or he could take the exact opposite approach, building an entire detailed picture of his past, including much very personal information that would gain your sympathy and trust. You would relate to it emotionally because it was so similar to your own past. Only later would you learn that none of it was true.

Some of your friends would say that all of his wonderful talk was glib and superficial. They might tell you that everything he did and said, everything he desired, was self-centered. When he appeared to be doing something for others it was really for himself and under his charming façade was a gigantic ego.

You would become defensive. You would tell them that everybody has flaws. You are a Christian and you are certain that he is as well. He has shared with you his deep struggles and profound faith. Perhaps he has shared that he had serious problems when he was growing up. You have compassion for him. You know what he needs. You have decided that you will be very open, honest and vulnerable so that he can heal and learn how to trust others through your loving example.

But over time, something would become clear even to you, the target. No matter what you did to help him, your close friend doesn't ever change. He may talk about positive change and how much he wants it, but it never happens. He *is* totally self-centered. Most frustrating of all, he never takes responsibility for anything he does wrong. In his mind, he is never wrong. When he does something that is clearly wrong or hurtful, either it isn't important to him and he glosses it over or he blames someone else. Often, he blames you. When confronted, it's amazing how quickly he can change the subject without any attempt at a logical connection. Or he may get really angry.

If you become intimate with him, you would grow increasingly disturbed because he has no interest in rules or laws of any kind, whether the unwritten rules of personal relationships or an established legal code. He knows the Bible and can quote verses, but it seems to be all in his head, not in his heart or actions. While he has many rules that he wants you to follow, he considers any kind of moral code a minor impediment, rules for others and not him. He claims to be a free, creative spirit who is sharing God's love. His electrical impulsiveness, which had been charming at the start, would begin to bother you. When he sees something that he wants, he takes it, no matter what it is and thinks nothing of hurting people in the process.

If what he does to get what he wants is very destructive and hurtful, there is not the slightest sense of guilt, certainly no remorse or sorrow. At first, you wouldn't understand this because he apologizes even in tears, promising that it will never happen again, telling you that the Lord has forgiven him so you should too. But shortly thereafter he would do exactly the same thing and grow angry when you called him on it.

Soon you would realize that he didn't understand the very idea of guilt, remorse and sorrow. It was like a foreign language that he didn't know. Even if what he had done was something truly awful and cruel, he would feel no guilt whatsoever. When he seemed to show remorse, sorrow and repentance, it was just play acting. The only reason he did it would be to get out of the current predicament by doing what was expected of a Christian. And he would be a very good actor. Most disturbing of all would be the creeping realization that he had no sense of moral proportion. He would view the most heinous, even vicious, acts as no more important than minor traffic violations. It would take time to accept the reality of all this because it is so unlike how you view the world. As a Christian, you struggle to believe the best about other people. But the longer you were with him, the more your life would turn to chaos.

If you could enter the mind of this perfectly possessed individual who is so charming and has become such an intimate friend, if you could see the world and other people the way he does, you would be shocked and terrified. Within his consciousness, there would not be the slightest drop of love, compassion, empathy or sympathy for any living creature. His only concern would be for himself, what he wanted and how to get it. He would do anything, use anyone in any way necessary to satisfy any desire or urge that came upon him. Whatever apparent good he did would only be to achieve his dark goals. The alien coldness of his mind would freeze your heart.

Like his father Satan, he would be a masterful liar, willing to use deceit and total manipulation whenever it served him. His only hunger would be for status, pleasure, money and power. His goal in any relationship would be absolute control. Within his mind there would be no fear or insecurity. The only emotions that would mean anything to him would be rage, frustration and lust. In fact, even these would be experienced only on a minimal level. Controlled as he was by an evil spirit, his entire emotional life and personality would be extremely shallow.

Eventually, after you had been used and abused, drained of any value that he had seen in you, you would be abandoned. Without any apology or goodbye, he would be gone. Too late, you would realize that there was no way to humanly reach him, no appeal to human sympathy or empathy that would have meant anything. You might as well appeal to a computer voice on the telephone. Here is the strangest part. Even though you are aware and ashamed that you have been duped, when he was gone you would miss the tremendous "connection" and "intimacy" that you had experienced, which would break your heart even more.

Normal people couldn't begin to understand a perfectly possessed man or woman. Normal people would consider it impossible that anyone could live as a cold, calculating predator one hundred percent of the time. This would make normal people very susceptible to such a person's charm, lies and manipulations. His victims wouldn't understand how completely they were being "gamed" until he had vanished from their lives, leaving emotional, financial and even physical devastation. This could include children that he had fathered, but didn't care about. His victims would be shocked to see that, from the moment he had met them, he had targeted them because he considered them vulnerable. With great care he had assessed what he could take from them, then overwhelmed their resistance with his charm and false friendship.

As an astute observer of people, he would have carefully probed to determine specific areas that were vulnerable to assault. He would have learned a target's secret hopes and fears, then created a strategy designed to appeal to their specific needs and weaknesses. He would have created a façade of history and personality designed to mirror his target's history and personality. To like and love him would be like liking and loving yourself. Finally, when the moment was right, the wolf would strike, exploiting the target, leaving them devastated, lonely and ashamed at their gullibility.

Now let's expand our imaginary scenario. Imagine that instead of targeting just one person, such a perfectly possessed serpent wolf spent his life targeting churches, Christian schools and ministries. Being a fabulous actor and having done his research, he would say all the right words with the right emotion, he would fabricate suitable credentials and background, so that he would be accepted easily by any Christian group. Because of his skill and extreme likability, which would include his knowledge of the Bible and Christian culture, in a short time he could worm his way into positions of trust. Then, whether his goal was money, sexual pleasure or pure control over others, the flock would be open to his depredations. With subtle charm, lies and backstabbing, he would destroy anyone who stood in his way. Those above him he would charm into being his loyal patrons. Those below who could be of use, he would turn into willing pawns.

Could someone like this actually exist? What I have called perfectly possessed people, psychologists call psychopaths.

CHAPTER FOURTEEN

Ice in Their Moral Veins

Because of popular media, most of us believe that psychopaths are serial killers like Ted Bundy or Richard Ramirez, the Night Stalker. But such monsters are only the tiniest portion of the psychopath population. One expert, Kent A. Kiehl, Ph.D., estimates that one in every 150 people in the United States is a psychopath. This would mean that, at any given time, there are several million such people literally hunting for prey in America. The vast majority are men, but there are women psychopaths as well.

Could psychopaths have been in the human community since the very beginning? Recall the story of Cain and Abel. As revealed in Genesis 4, the personality of Cain is disturbing. Something was wrong with him. When he and Abel brought offerings of worship to the Lord, his was not accepted. It wasn't the offering itself that was the problem, God does not condemn that. It was the heart of Cain that made the offering unacceptable. When confronted, his response was not contrition and repentance, but jealousy and anger that finally erupted in out-of-control rage and violence to the point of murder.

And after the crime, what do we see? Utter coldness and amorality. First, Cain lies to cover up his murder. Even though it is the first murder that has ever been committed and he should be shocked, he doesn't care at all. Clearly, it has no more importance for him than the death of an animal. He doesn't care about his parents and their horror and sorrow. When God makes him face what he has done, Cain admits no wrong and displays not the slightest guilt or remorse. When he is condemned, his only concern is for himself. All of this is classical psychopath behavior. So, based on the evidence of Genesis, we have to say that it seems very likely the first child born to the human race after the Fall was a psychopath. How fitting a result of sin and how predictive of the future!

Psychopaths have been in the human community ever since, bringing enslavement, misery, death and hell with them. Some have risen to become vicious, bloodthirsty leaders. The personal histories of many despots reveal that they were psychopaths. But recently, something new has been happening. Their numbers are increasing. Psychologist, Robert D. Hare, Ph.D., who is considered by everyone in the field to be the modern-day father of psychopath research, believes that we began to see a significant increase starting in the 1960's and 70's.

Within American society, where do you find these charming, ruthless, unfeeling, dangerous people? Psychopaths who are less sophisticated and not "well-bred" commit every sort of crime and wind up spending multiple terms in prison. Their offenses run the gamut from cons called affinity scams (the targeting of groups with members who trust each other, such as churches) to child molestation and murder. But many more psychopaths have learned to walk on the edge of the law, never quite breaking it enough to run afoul of the authorities.

While they don't break the law, these serpent wolves wreak devastation on everyone close to them, including multiple marriages with brokenhearted wives and husbands, fatherless and motherless children, emptied bank accounts, angry, abused fellow workers and a host of people who feel ashamed at having been duped and promise themselves that they will never trust anyone again.

Many less sophisticated psychopaths lead marginal lives on the edge of society, but many others excel. Because of family connections, their gifts and skills, or simply their ability as imposters and con artists, they have learned how to thrive. The most skillful rise to top levels in business, the arts, law (including law enforcement), the military and politics. Their energetic drive, which conceals shallow creativity, coupled with ruthless, domineering amorality, is rewarded as leadership by those above them, while their co-workers and those beneath, including their families, suffer immeasurably.

I'm convinced that there are many psychopaths at high levels in Hollywood. I know of a writer/producer/director who has been extremely successful in both film and television who fits the pattern. For decades, he has consciously chosen to make life hell for the people under him. While I have never worked for him, close friends of mine have.

For many years, child actors have made allegations about the existence of an organized community of child molester psychopaths who are extremely powerful within the entertainment business. Those making the allegations have been afraid to name names. Their fear isn't just for their careers. These wolves are so powerful and ruthless that their victims fear for their lives. Hollywood isn't the only place where powerful psychopaths wreak every kind of havoc.

Because they are wolf predators, psychopaths gravitate toward any area where vulnerable people may be found in significant numbers. Consequently they choose to be doctors, nurses, psychiatrists, teachers, professors and counselors, etc. Could there be a greater opportunity than a vulnerable person in long-term psychotherapy? Psychopaths who are sexual predators, have set up group homes for abused teenagers. It should be no surprise that they are drawn to the church in large numbers.

If ever there was a vulnerable group waiting to be exploited and abused it is the Christian community. We believe in and teach the need for vulnerability in the Body of Christ. Many of us think that being nice and charming and saying the right words indicate spiritual trustworthiness. We want to be friends with our brothers and sisters in the Lord. When someone has a broken past, we want to help them rebuild after they accept Jesus as their Savior. If someone tells us something about their past, we believe them. We are unprepared for charming, ruthless, amoral liars.

Within the Body of Christ, rarely are the details of a life resume ever checked. Though the Internet offers great opportunity to examine a person's history, few Christians use it. Many states require background checks on all those who work with children. But more than a few psychopath child molesters have been clever enough to evade the system. Some move frequently, creating multiple identities with sophisticated supporting materials and letters of recommendation.

Making matters much worse, Christians want strong, good-looking, charming, creative leaders. If such people know the right words and speak to our emotions that's all that is needed for them to be accepted. We make our decisions about trustworthiness and spiritual maturity based almost entirely on emotion. Also making matters much worse, psychopaths recognize each other and work together to accomplish their goals of predation. If one is in a church or ministry, there may be several more. The wolf pack.

Some serpent wolves' goals are short-term, such as stealing money. The psychopath enters, assesses, targets and mauls within a few months or at the most a couple of years. Then he vanishes. As bad as it is, in some ways a financial affinity scam is the least damaging of a wolf's potential destruction. But his involvement with a group doesn't have to be short-lived.

Such an individual might have targeted Christians and Christian ministry long ago as a vulnerable category, then gone to all the right schools and churches establishing legitimate credentials, which would allow him to enter and potentially become a top leader of a Christian church, denomination or ministry and remain as a spiritual wolf feasting on the flock for a lifetime. Is it almost impossible for you to imagine someone who could be so consciously malevolent and appear to be a great Christian? The serpent wolf depends on your inability to imagine it. He depends on our blindness, gullibility and fantasy thinking.

But let's understand something: We do not need to be victimized by these predators.

Jesus told us to be wise as serpents and gentle as doves. What does it mean to be wise as a serpent? At the very least, we should be able to recognize a serpent when it starts crawling through our house. By the fruit of a person's life we can know who that individual really is. But because we don't understand what the New Testament means by fruit, we misread evidence or don't look for it at all.

Why do I call psychopath predators "born wolves"? This is the most troubling part of the entire discussion. Where do psychopaths come from? In dealing with all psychological aberrations we search for causes so we can fix them. Psychopaths defy our efforts. On a legal level, they are not insane. While they don't care about right and wrong, they know the difference and are culpable for their actions. Every study indicates that true psychopaths have been this way since early childhood.

While some may come from neglectful or abusive homes, many do not. Many of their families are normal and loving. Yet, from their early years, psychopaths wreak chaos in those families. From the time they can make decisions, their selfish impulsiveness, viciousness and amorality, their total lack concern for others, guide their choices. In many cases, as they grow older they bankrupt their parents and siblings who are locked in a pattern of bailing them out of their self-inflicted crises. In adulthood the pattern continues with husbands and wives who love them no matter what they do and want to "save" them from themselves. The pattern continues with people in their community who like and trust them. It continues in the church.

What causes psychopathy? Medical researchers in the field do not know. It is clear from fMRI tests that patterns in certain areas of the brain are different with psychopaths than with the general population. What causes those differences is not known. Damage to certain parts of the brain can trigger psychopathic tendencies and activities in people who have not experienced them before.

Is the deep evil that psychopaths perpetrate nothing more than the result of brain abnormalities? If so, why should this be so? Why shouldn't such a brain abnormality cause a person to be overwhelmingly righteous, empathetic, loving and good to everyone far beyond the norm? Why should brain abnormalities take people into every sort of destruction and perversion? Can the psychopathic abnormality be corrected? Studies and trial programs are continuing, however, professionals who deal with psychopaths state that, to date, no therapy has proven to have any positive, life-changing, long-term effects. Some psychopaths have actually used therapy to help them become more efficient predators. Psychopaths convicted of crimes have by far the highest rate of recidivism.

So, is it all just physical? If you are a materialist, that would be your position. But a materialist viewpoint doesn't account for a psychopath's consistent and conscious choices that can only be described as unrestrained evil. Could there be another answer? Could the physical deformity of the brain be caused by an unrestrained deformity of the spirit?

The spiritual deformity of absolute evil is in all of us. Only by the Grace of God are we not all psychopaths without the slightest concern for anyone but ourselves. Is it possible that psychopathy is the "normal" moral state of fallen humanity under the power of Satan and only the work of the Holy Spirit restraining evil in the world keeps the human race from becoming entirely psychopathic?

Are psychopaths the living image of what the whole human race will become in the Final Days when the restraining of the Holy Spirit will be removed? Certainly, the morality of psychopaths is the same morality as that of demons and fallen angels and for a period of time in the Days of the End Satan and his hosts will control the world – very likely, a world where the vast majority have no conscience or sense of guilt or remorse. According to Revelation, even when terrible judgments are inflicted on them, the people of that day refuse to repent.

But right now, is it possible that certain people are chosen by the Powers of Darkness to have that unrestrained evil released in and through them? As troubling and as controversial as the idea is, could it be possible that there are people who are chosen from birth and even physically molded by Satan to be special servants designed to embody who he is and what he desires for the human race? Could such people offer the opportunity for a unique kind of perfect possession?

From the earliest years of childhood, true psychopaths display no conscience, remorse, love or empathy and bring chaos and destruction to those around them. Parents see it very early and become distraught because no form of discipline has any effect. And it grows much worse as the years pass.

Satan is territorial and views certain families as belonging to him down through their generations. The late evangelical scholar and occult expert, Dr. Kurt Koch, wrote about this in a number of books including Christian Counseling and Occultism: A Complete Guidebook to Occult Oppression and Deliverance and Occult Bondage and Deliverance: Counseling the Occultly Oppressed. Also in dealing with occult influences, I recommend,

Demon Possession and the Christian: A New Perspective, by my old friend and former professor at the Moody Bible Institute, Dr. C. Fred Dickason.

I believe in the Power of Jesus to save and sanctify the vilest sinner. I believe that there is no sin beyond His ability to redeem or His Blood to cleanse. But as we consider psychopaths, we face a cold reality. Salvation requires belief that Jesus can save and a desire to be saved. It requires true repentance for sin.

The Lord is not slack concerning His promise, as some count slackness, but is longsuffering toward us, not willing that any should perish but that all should come to repentance. 2 Peter 3:9

To repent means that you understand that you have sinned, you have a sense of guilt for that sin and you desire to turn away from it and be forgiven. In a true psychopath, there is no agreement that sin has been committed. There is no sense of guilt, no remorse and no sorrow. No matter how heinous the crime and how awful the suffering he caused, the true psychopath simply does not care. Over and over, by their direct statements during psychological interviews and by their subsequent actions, any apparent remorse, sorrow or desire for forgiveness has proven to be a sham act. The Apostle Paul writes about consciences that have been seared as with a hot iron. That doesn't seem to be the situation for psychopaths. From all indications, they have never had a conscience that could be seared.

It is a miracle when any sinner is saved, but it would take a spiritual and psychological miracle of healing, deliverance and transformation for a true psychopath to repent. To be permanently delivered from the Powers of Darkness, an individual must put their trust in Christ so that He can come and live within them. If they are delivered from an evil spirit and the Holy Spirit does not enter in, it is like the house that Jesus warned might be cleansed, but then re-infested by far worse spirits than the ones that had been ejected.

Psychopaths present a unique challenge to the church. The most gifted of them are extremely difficult to recognize. Even trained professionals who are fully aware that they are dealing with known psychopaths have been duped by their charming lies and manipulations. Especially this is true if you are the target of their "charm initiatives". Those who are not the targets may have an easier time discerning the truth about an individual. If an entire church or organization is the target, it may take outside observers to have the necessary objectivity.

Adding to the complexity of the problem, there are people who may display several psychopathic traits, but are not psychopaths. Even in churches and Christian organizations certain psychopathic traits are rewarded as creative, energetic leadership.

Because of their gifts and charm, when a psychopath becomes a pastor, elder, Sunday School teacher, financial administrator, camp director, youth worker or other Christian leader, many in the church or organization will support that individual, making excuses for his or her destructive actions until great harm has been done. In fact, the only person a psychopath can never fool is Jesus Christ. Therefore, it is extremely important that the Holy Spirit give great wisdom and strength in identifying and confronting these serpent wolves.

There is much more to be learned about psychopaths. I recommend three books: Without Conscience: The Disturbing World of Psychopaths Among Us by Robert D. Hare, Ph.D. and Snakes In Suits: When Psychopaths Go To Work by Paul Babiak, Ph.D. and Robert D. Hare, Ph.D., also The Psychopath Whisperer: The Science of Those Without Conscience, by Kurt A. Kiehl, Ph.D.

Dr. Hare has created a checklist of key symptoms of psychopathy that is used by professionals. I will give you those symptoms with the same warning that he gives. You can't run down the list applying the symptoms to an individual in order to make any final determination that he or she is a psychopath. The checklist is to guide professionals trained to use an extensive scale that goes with it. It takes hours of professional interviews to reach a final assessment. There are many people who show a number of the symptoms, but who are not psychopaths. I give the list here as a general guide. If a particular individual shows many of the symptoms, it may indicate a serious problem.

Key Symptoms of Psychopathy

Emotional/Interpersonal:

1. Glib and superficial (often witty and articulate, but consistently shallow in interpersonal communication)

2. Egocentric and grandiose as though the world revolves around him or her.

3. Lack of remorse or guilt. Absolutely no concern about the effects his or her actions have on others. No conscience and no sorrow.

4. Lack of empathy. Emotionless, almost like androids in their inability to feel real compassion for someone else no matter what they do to that individual. If they appear to show empathy it is an act. They are only displaying what they believe is expected. Some of them carefully study to know what is expected.

5. Shallow emotions. A kind of emotional poverty that limits the range and depth of their feelings. Typically, when asked what he understands about love, a psychopath will describe sexual experiences that brought pleasure.

Social Deviance:

1. Impulsive. They do what feels good without thinking. Psychopaths are poor planners, which is one reason why the less sophisticated of them are often caught.

2. Poor behavior controls. Aggressive over-reaction to any perceived insult or slight, including explosive and often vicious rage.

3. Need for excitement. A hunger to "live on the edge". Most often this means breaking rules and laws.

4. Lack of responsibility. Commitments and obligations don't mean anything. Promises of all kinds are made and broken with ease.

5. Early behavior problems. In childhood extensive, serious and persistent destructive behavior that can include lying, theft, substance abuse, vandalism, violence, animal abuse, running away, early and promiscuous sexual activity, etc.

6. Adult anti-social behavior. Breaking laws and being convicted of crimes doesn't bother them. Often they are proud of criminal behavior.

In particular, total lack of remorse or sense of guilt and total lack of empathy are key indicators of a psychopath personality. For more extensive descriptions, please read the three books that I have recommended.

Both Process Wolves and Born Wolves in sheep's clothing look so good in large part because they are empowered by the greatest illusionist in all of history, Satan himself. The beautiful illusion that makes a sheepskin suit fit with perfection is charm.

CHAPTER FIFTEEN

The Charm Initiative

What is charm? One dictionary defines charm as "the power of pleasing or attracting as through personality or beauty. A trait or feature imparting this power." The key word is power. A person gifted with great charm has real power to deeply and emotionally influence the attitudes and actions of others. There is nothing wrong with this gift. It is from God.

I have a friend who has been in Christian ministry for many years who is one of the most charming people I know. She loves God and communicates that love to those around her. Her gift of charm is empowered by His love. Because of her charm, she can get people to do things that they wouldn't do for anyone else. She uses her gift selflessly for the Lord.

The power of charm can take the toughest, most cynical person off guard. If you possess charm, it can make people fall in love with you. Sometimes it is coupled with physical beauty, but not always. When it is coupled with great creative, intellectual or financial ability it can take a person to the pinnacle of power. When charm is used by the Powers of Darkness, it brings temptation, destruction and hell into people's lives. It is one of the greatest weapons of the elite of Hollywood.

The Myth and the Man

I first met him at dinner in one of the finer restaurants in Los Angeles. No question about it, I was in awe. As an actor, he was a legend. We were having dinner because both of us were represented by the same leading Hollywood literary and talent agency. The series I had helped write and produce for almost four years, The Equalizer, had ended. During those years I had written for one of the greatest actors of his generation, Edward Woodward.

As a writer, my relationship with Edward couldn't have been better. I can say with absolute confidence, that he had loved everything I wrote for him. But due to a war between CBS and Universal, that experience had come to an end.

It was a new day and I was going to create a series of my own. The agency had "packaged" me together with this famous actor and a "hot" television director. An agency makes much more money on a project if they sell a "package" of talent rather than individual elements. Our package was being sold through a major studio to a major network. So the dinner was a chance to meet and get to know each other. Hopefully, we would establish a long and fruitful creative partnership. He was an older man. When he smiled and laughed there was such joy in it. The sun seemed to shine a little brighter. He was very charming.

I came away thinking what an opportunity this was, to write for yet another great actor. It was the kind of work that a writer/producer would kill for in Hollywood. This was in my mind as I wrote the one hour pilot script.

We were thrilled when the network chose to have it produced. Dozens of pilot scripts are written and paid for each year that are never produced. I had set the story in a major Midwestern city, so all of us went there to shoot what I had written. It was an expensive production that took three weeks to complete.

While we were on location, several times I tried to make some personal connection with our star. As an executive producer, you don't expect to become close friends with your lead actors, but you do look for creative camaraderie, a shared vision. Though we spent several evenings together, I just couldn't find a personal connection with this man. He was always charming, but there was something intangible that seemed to stand between us. In all the years of The Equalizer, Edward Woodward and I had been able to spend almost no personal time together, yet there had been deep creative agreement. We shared a vision about the character he was portraying and the stories we would tell.

The first sense that the charm was a facade in our lead actor came in an unexpected way. My wife, Carel, had arrived in the city and one day she visited the location where we were shooting. It happened that when she was ready to go back to the hotel that our star had finished his work for the day and was going back to the same hotel. One of our cars would take them both.

We had been shooting in a downtown building. Carel and this man came out to the street to find a group of little boys on the sidewalk with their parents. They had heard that this famous actor was in town and hoped to get an autograph. (He had played a notorious villain in a series of feature films.) One of the little boys had a picture book with a photograph of the villain in it and he hoped to get an autograph on the page.

As the man was getting in the car, the child approached with the open book and asked if he would sign it. The star took the book and pen and proceeded to scribble all over the photo. Then he got in the car and shut the door. It wasn't an autograph. The little boy didn't know what to say. He just stood there. My wife was shocked along with everyone else who had witnessed what had happened. It was the first piece of tangible evidence that this man was not what he appeared.

We were the only new dramatic series picked up by the network that year for their fall schedule. We went into production in Los Angeles with our sets built on the Warner Bros lot. As a writer, my goal was to continue doing the same kind of stories that I had done with great success for almost four years on The Equalizer.

But as I began to write scripts, very soon it became clear that I had a significant problem. The star disliked what I wrote. The charm began to slip away. He would complain about specific dialog, telling me that he didn't know how to perform it. If I had been an inexperienced or insecure writer, his criticisms could have been devastating. Thankfully, I was neither. I had just come off a long period of writing for a very great British actor who never had a single problem with the scripts I gave him.

During all my time on The Equalizer I had written stories about redemption. This had been done in various ways. When it was appropriate, I had not been afraid to talk about God. My intention was to continue telling those same kinds of stories.

Soon my problem came into focus. The star hated any mention of God. He would call from the set complaining about a scene and want me to remove it, claiming that he didn't know how to say the words. I would reply to his complaints that I would rewrite a scene as many times as necessary for him to be comfortable with the dialog, but I wouldn't remove it. Always such scenes had to do with faith and God. Never were these scenes "preachy" or heavy handed. I consider myself a commercial Hollywood writer/producer.

We were polite with each other, but our positions were clear. It wasn't long before the wolf attack began. True to the manner of wolves, first our star gathered a small pack around him which included some people who were working for me. After only five episodes, they pressured the studio and the network until I was fired. With me out of the way, the man became much more aggressive in his attacks. Though I was gone, the writing staff that I had hired was still in place. I got disturbing reports. Dealing with the star was a nightmare. He hadn't had the courage to deni-grate me or my work to my face, but he felt no such constraint with the other writers. Though he had the most charming façade, what lay beneath was not charming at all.

As word got out that I had been fired, I began to hear sto-ries from people who had had other negative experiences with this man. They were shared very quietly. Because of his fame, power and appeal, people were afraid to level any public criticism against him. And that continues to this day.

The series went downhill rapidly. It was picked up for on-ly half of a second season. The first season had floundered so bad-ly that they tried to resurrect it by restructuring and renaming it. It didn't work and was canceled. However, the star received an Emmy for the role that I had created for him. Two other actors received Emmys for their work on our destroyed series. I didn't see the presentation, but I was told that when he won, the star thanked everyone who had been involved except me.

By that time, I had moved on to a different company. The day after the Emmys a vice president at my former studio called to thank me for all the work I had done on the series. He told me it was shameful that the star had not even mentioned my name. It didn't matter. I hadn't been watching. But that isn't quite the end of the story.

The experience on that series had been very painful. I had put so much into it that when it was over I went through a period of grief and loss. On a larger level, great damage had been done to my career. But all things are in God's Hands and my faith has always been in Him. He is the One who has determined my path, so in the middle of all that had happened, I experienced sorrow, but also I had peace. There has been no bitterness.

When the illusion of charm is stripped away and you are attacked by a wolf, your first reaction is pain and shock. Very quickly, this is followed by confusion. You may question your own senses. "Did this happen the way I think it did? How could it have happened? *Why* did it happen? Did I do something to make it happen? Have I not performed as I should? What have I done wrong?"

You second-guess every decision that you made leading up to the attack. You may become fearful. Faith in your own abilities may be shaken. Often this confusion continues for a long time. As you look back at the experience it can seem incredible. Maybe you are misremembering? You may even start blaming yourself for what occurred. (The wolf will blame you as well.)

All of this is part of a destructive cycle designed to tear you down, destroy your effectiveness and control you. The more obvious and vicious the attack, the more shame and self-doubt you may experience.

As the years passed, I asked myself many questions about what had happened on that television series. As a Christian, I prayed about the whole thing, "Lord, what did I do wrong there? Did I misrepresent You? Certainly, I could have done my job better. What should I learn from this?"

My prayer for wisdom was answered in an unusual way. Eight or nine years after the series had gone off the air, the star was performing in a TV movie. It happened that a consultant on that production was a personal friend of mine and a strong Christian. One day on the set, she walked up to the man and said, "I just want to tell you how much I've loved your work, especially what you did on (and she named our series)." She referred to a specific scene that I had written for the pilot and that he had performed so well.

The star got a strange look on his face and replied, "Yes, well, the man who created that had a *spiritual agenda* and *we* can't have that in television." Always a quick thinker, my friend just smiled and said, "Doesn't everyone have a spiritual agenda?" Then she walked away.

How very odd! All he needed to say was, thank you. And my friend was right. Everyone in television does have a spiritual agenda. They might not describe it in those terms, but that's what it is. And who is the "we" that he was referring to? How sad that every time he looks at his Emmy, he is forced to remember my "spiritual agenda". (Okay, I'm not all that sad, but I do pray for him.)

When my friend told me what had happened, it was both a clarification and a confirmation that what I had experienced was not of my doing, but was instead a powerful wolf attack. I had been a small casualty in a great war. Into that war, the enemy sends his armies. Many of them are charming wolves.

Hollywood is the perfect place to observe the power of charm and its destructive uses. The leaders of Hollywood are some of the most charming people in the world. This is true of everyone from studio executives, producers and agents to stars. When they want to, they know how to "turn it on". Always this involves what appears to be deep interest in you and your work.

Charm can pass for respect, love, friendship, kindness and even spirituality. A charming person can appear to be your "new best friend". When this kind of attention is showered on you from a powerful or beautiful person, it can be overwhelming. When charm is coupled with real love and caring it can build up people. When it is used to manipulate and control, the result will be devastating.

Just as easily as wolves can turn on charm, eventually they *will* turn it off. When the wolf has gotten all he can from you and decides to discard you, or when he decides to control you more fully through fear, it can be an emotional whiplash. The attack can seem to come out of nowhere and be about almost nothing. The shock of a vicious wolf attack by someone you may have trusted and even loved makes the pain far worse.

When you thought you knew a person, but realized that you didn't, you feel foolish and betrayed. It strikes our pride.

That's one of the reasons the wounds of a wolf are so deep. Because you mistook charm for true friendship and caring, you had made yourself vulnerable. Knowing that you were used is scalding.

The terrible loss of a perceived friendship that you valued is made far more painful by the clear evidence that the friendship was never real at all. Too easily, what comes out of that is rage, bitterness and cynicism. You swear to yourself that you won't ever be hurt like that again. Even worse, if you feel trapped and unable to leave the wolf's control, the attacks may become increasingly vicious, beating you down into a form of slavery. Unless you are freed from the wolf's power and the wounds are healed, not only can they last a lifetime, you can pass the spiritual infection on to others.

In Hollywood, you develop "wolf radar". You watch for manipulation, distrusting appearances. You create your own "armor of charm". It is not an easy way to live. You can lose your ability to trust anyone and that is depressing. In response, many people become wolves themselves.

But I want to be quick to say that even in Hollywood, everyone is not a wolf. I have worked for some powerful leaders at the studios and networks who treated me with great respect and fairness. Without their help, I never could have achieved what I did. Though they do not share my religious beliefs, I consider those people to be gifts from God and I pray for God's blessing to be upon them.

So it is important to understand that, even in Hollywood with all the wolves that are there, and even after you have experienced vicious attacks, you cannot allow yourself to become so cynical that you think everyone you meet is a wolf. That poisons potentially good relationships. When we allow that to happen, the wolves have won.

Hollywood should be very different from the Church. But is it? When you enter Hollywood you are vulnerable, the terrain is new and you don't know the unwritten rules. You want to trust everyone who seems to be interested in you, but you learn that such naivete is dangerous. You stop being vulnerable or you will be eaten alive. But that doesn't mean you aren't angry. Hollywood is one of the angriest places on earth. Creative people remain only because they are paid so well to be savaged.

People enter the Church to *be* vulnerable. Life is difficult and we need a safe place where we can share our sorrows and find strength to keep going. The last thing we need is to be constantly on guard watching for wolves. And so we don't watch, which makes the Christian Church the greatest hunting ground for wolf packs in the world.

Where are the shepherds and sheepdogs who should be guarding the flock? Many times they are attacked by the very people they are trying to protect. When they are silenced and shoved out, the wolves grow even stronger. What is the wolf's most powerful camouflage in the Church? It is not just charm, but spiritualized charm, the mantle of the pseudo-holy spirit.

CHAPTER SIXTEEN

Meet the Pseudo-Holy Spirit

He was the most charming man. We met in a Sunday school class at the First Presbyterian Church of Hollywood. He had a warm smile and the love of God just seemed to flow from him. When that man prayed, it was real praying – such passion, such power.

Over a few months, we got to know him and what a story he had to tell. He was a Bulgarian pastor who had left his country after great persecution by the Communists. For years, he had done what he could for the poor Christians he had been forced to leave behind, broadcasting the truth of Jesus to them over the radio, encouraging them and smuggling in what resources he could. He had his own little mission that he and his family operated out of their home.

Not long before we met him, the Communist regime in Bulgaria had fallen. There was a new administration in Sofia and a new Bulgarian ambassador in Washington. After decades of horrible oppression, the country was free. But with freedom came great need. Our Bulgarian pastor friend had contacts in the country. They had told him that the hospitals were out of insulin for children and other pharmaceutical supplies.

One evening, a few of us sat in my living room and decided that we had to do something to help the people of Bulgaria. Why couldn't we take some medical supplies to them ourselves? None of us had ever done anything like that, but why not give it a try? We pulled out our date books and found a week when all of us were free. It was a go.

The Bulgarian pastor would coordinate the many details of the trip once we got in country, but the major preparations in the United States were up to Carel and me. Though she had never done anything like this before, Carel went to work pulling together as many medical supplies as we could take with us. None of us would carry personal luggage beyond a small suitcase. She got drug companies to donate insulin. She got the airline to allow extra weight in our checked luggage. Carel was assisted in this by a good friend, Ken Whitten, who runs a mission out of New Hampshire that ministers to people's spiritual and physical needs around the world. Ken traveled with us on this adventure.

From my office in Hollywood, I called the Bulgarian ambassador in Washington and got through to him. He was a gracious man who gave us a letter telling all the authorities in Bulgaria to let us go anywhere and do anything we wanted. (We used it throughout our trip.) Also, he scheduled a meeting for us with the new President of his country.

The trip really was an adventure. To be in a formerly communist nation only a couple of years into freedom was exciting. It was also tragic. We saw the tremendous need of the people. We spoke to Christian groups both large and small and met people who humbled us. In spite of lifetimes of oppression, they had been faithful to Jesus. Though they were so poor, they gave what little they had to make us feel welcome. I will never forget it.

Everything went well. When we arrived in Sofia our Bulgarian pastor friend was our guide. His adult daughter was our translator. During that trip, I didn't see anything amiss. There were no red flags.

After we got home, the Bulgarian pastor asked me to join the board of his little mission, which I was happy to do. We continued to work with Ken Whitten and his team in New Hampshire to send shipments to Bulgaria. But it wasn't long before I started to get reports that were disturbing. Something was wrong. Ken had a system in place to make sure that anything they sent to any country was distributed in a fair and ethical manner so that no one could take personal profit from it. The Bulgarian pastor was abrogating that system. When Ken confronted him about it, the charm slipped away and he got very unpleasant. It appeared that the man was trying to take advantage of our shipments for his own gain.

When I got the report, I went to the man's home in Los Angeles to discuss the situation. The response from him was ugly. The mask of the pseudo-holy spirit came off. He would stand for no one questioning any of his actions. He would be responsible to no one but himself. Of course, I resigned from his board and had nothing more to do with him.

It was over twenty years before I heard anything further about this man. One day Carel and I were visiting a church in Los Angeles, when his daughter came up to us. She told us that, long before, her father had left her mother, his wife of many years, and had run off with his secretary.

Another member of our old Bulgaria team had become friends with a gentlemen in the Bulgarian Christian community of Los Angeles. From him we learned that the man who had claimed to be a persecuted Bulgarian pastor was mostly a fraud. Yes, he was from Bulgaria, but his stories of persecution were lies and he had milked American Christians for decades with most of the money going into his own pocket.

I don't regret having gone to Bulgaria and doing what we could to help the good people there. I do regret that, with our presence, we lent credibility and authority to that man, even taking him with us to meet the president of the country. I consider my wolf radar to be pretty well calibrated and with the first evidence of dishonesty, I confronted him. But it took quite awhile. Before the evidence appeared, I was certain that this was a truly humble and godly man. After all, he was so charming and he could preach and pray with such power. Satan is an expert illusionist and many of his wolves are gifted to make them look like servants of God. To complete the camouflage, he fills them with a pseudo-holy spirit.

We do not attempt to understand or take seriously enough the words of the Apostle Paul in 2 Corinthians 11:12-15:

For such are false apostles, deceitful workers, transforming themselves into apostles of Christ. And no wonder! For Satan himself transforms himself into an angel of light. Therefore it is no great thing if his ministers also transform themselves into ministers of righteousness, whose end will be according to their works.

CHAPTER SEVENTEEN

Nice vs. Good on the Elder Board

A primary reason why wolves are so successful in the church is because Christians have lost all understanding about what is "good". We think "nice" is the same thing as "good", but that is not always true. "Nice" is charming and makes us feel good. "Good" doesn't always make us feel good. Sometimes it hurts. Sometimes it comes in rough and abrasive forms. Sometimes it doesn't smile. But "nice" is always smiling.

Many years ago I was an elder in a small congregation. The board was made up of only the pastor and three or four men. It was a relatively new congregation, so ours was the first elder board that had been formed. I didn't know some of the other men well, but they all seemed very nice. Because of our backgrounds, each of us brought certain strengths to the group.

But as we began to meet month after month, something strange started happening. We just couldn't get anything done. We prayed and shared and tried to do the work of the church with vision, but it felt as though we were swimming in a pool of warm, murky soup. The frustration grew. What was wrong here? There were no arguments. Everyone got along. We just couldn't get anything accomplished. I had never experienced anything like it. After a year and a half of this, I left the board and ultimately began attending a different church.

A couple of years later I received some very illuminating information. It had come out that one of the men on that board had been leading a double life. Though married to a lovely Christian woman, when he went away on frequent business trips out of the country, he was involved in sexual promiscuity with men. When the truth came out, though it destroyed his marriage, he was unrepentant.

Month in and month out, this man had sat with us, praying, talking, presenting the image of a mature Christian. He was very nice. I liked him. Never was he argumentative and often he contributed good ideas. He was such a friendly, smiling, inoffensive wolf. There were no vicious attacks. As a representative of darkness, his presence simply choked the work of the Lord. With even greater power and influence in the church, how much more damage might he have done? As always, eventually the façade covering this wolf was ripped away and people close to him were mauled.

CHAPTER EIGHTEEN

Welcome to the Weed Patch

Where do so many spiritual wolves come from? What is their natural habitat in the Body of Christ? Jesus told a parable in Matthew 13:24-30:

Another parable He put forth to them, saying: "The kingdom of heaven is like a man who sowed good seed in his field; but while men slept, his enemy came and sowed tares among the wheat and went his way. But when the grain had sprouted and produced a crop, then the tares also appeared. So the servants of the owner came and said to him, 'Sir, did you not sow good seed in your field? How then does it have tares?' He said to them, 'An enemy has done this.' The servants said to him, 'Do you want us then to go and gather them up?' But he said, 'No, lest while you gather up the tares you also uproot the wheat with them. Let both grow together until the harvest, and at the time of harvest I will say to the reapers, "First gather together the tares and

bind them in bundles to burn them, but gather the wheat into my barn.""""

The explanation of the parable follows a few verses later in Matt 13:36-43:

Then Jesus sent the multitude away and went into the house. And His disciples came to Him, saying, "Explain to us the parable of the tares of the field." He answered and said to them: "He who sows the good seed is the Son of Man. The field is the world, the good seeds are the sons of the kingdom, but the tares are the sons of the wicked one. The enemy who sowed them is the devil, the harvest is the end of the age, and the reapers are the angels. Therefore as the tares are gathered and burned in the fire, so it will be at the end of this age. The Son of Man will send out His angels, and they will gather out of His kingdom all things that offend, and those who practice lawlessness, and will cast them into the furnace of fire. There will be wailing and gnashing of teeth. Then the righteous will shine forth as the sun in the kingdom of their Father. He who has ears to hear, let him hear!

So what is a tare? It isn't just any old weed. There is a vicious weed that has grown in the Mideast for eons called bearded darnel. It's a species of rye grass that looks very much like wheat until it is mature. But if you harvest both together, then grind and eat the mixture, the result can be deadly. Darnel can cause drowsiness, apathy, trance, convulsions, drunkenness, trembling, slurred speech, vomiting and even death. It kills sheep and cattle. When it is mature, it's easy to tell this seed from real wheat because darnel is much smaller. But before that time, it's almost impossible.

Jesus is saying that in the world there are many, many people who do not belong to Him at all. In a sense, they have been "planted" by Satan and they serve him. The fruit of their lives is poisonous and destructive.

So could it be possible that the "people of the tares" might be well represented in the church? Could there be many who appear to be wonderful Christians, but in reality are sons and daughters of the Evil One? Would Satan plant his weeds in abundance everywhere but in the church? Could their deep involvement in the church be a primary tactic of the enemy to bring scandal, disrepute and disgrace to the Body of Christ? Doesn't that sound like something that Satan would love to do? But there is a serious warning in Jesus' parable.

So often we think we know who the poisonous, destructive people are who belong to Satan. Isn't it clear? All around us in the world are those who do sinful things. What they do isn't hidden at all. It's right out in the open for everyone to see. Over and over they may reject the message of salvation in Jesus. They may jeer at Christians. They may even persecute us. In our hurt and anger, we give up on them, viewing them as lost forever.

In this cabal of darkness are prostitutes, pimps, druggies, drunks, thugs, thieves, slanderers and the murderers who kill Christians. In it is the business person who cheated you and the guy who cut you off on the road, flipping the finger. There are atheists who rant against God and all those who believe in Him.

117

There are people who just don't seem to care, who never lift a hand to help anyone. Among them is the nasty person in the next cubicle and the boss who makes your life miserable. Among them are promiscuous, Hollywood stars and sleek studio executives.

But in this evil group spread around the world, we do not know who will come to repentance. We do not know which of these awful people will be our brother or sister forever in the Kingdom of God. Many that we consider lost may very well surprise us by their appearance in Heaven. At the last possible moment of life they may repent, proving that they were the chosen of God all along. So we take the message of God's Love to everyone because He is not willing that any should perish, but that all should come to repentance. Remember, God loves them all, whether they are tares or wheat, for He loves the whole world.

Jesus isn't warning us about obviously sinful people. In Matthew 13 He is warning us that there are many, many people who will look the opposite. In the church, they will appear to be good Christians. We will trust them. We will allow them into our homes and lives. But when we get to Heaven we will be shocked to discover that they are not there.

These "nice" people sing worship songs and raise their hands, they take up the offering, teach Sunday School and hand out bulletins. They serve on church committees and make tasty potluck dishes. Yet not a single one of them belongs to Jesus and never will. Though they may not even know it themselves, they have been planted by the Enemy to impede and poison the work of the Kingdom of God.

I know this is shocking to consider, but I don't believe that there is any other way to understand Jesus' warning. I'm sure that

Satan wants to plant his tares wherever the real work of the Gospel might take place. Wherever discipleship could happen, that's where the evil seed will be sown.

According to Jesus, the Enemy is always generous with his scattering. Consequently, it's likely that there are so many of what might be called "darnel people" in every area of Church life that to try and weed them out would be dangerous. Dangerous to whom? Immature believers, because immature wheat and immature darnel look almost alike. Jesus and His angels will take care of the weeding when the harvest is ripe. In the meantime, the Body of Christ suffers from the presence of these people. But even this is in the will of God.

The Apostle Paul wrote these words in 1 Corinthians 2:13-3:3:

These things we also speak, not in words which man's wisdom teaches but which the Holy Spirit teaches, comparing spiritual things with spiritual. But the natural man does not receive the things of the Spirit of God, for they are foolishness to him; nor can he know them, because they are spiritually discerned. But he who is spiritual judges all things, yet he himself is rightly judged by no one. For "who has known the mind of the LORD that he may instruct Him?" But we have the mind of Christ.

And I, brethren, could not speak to you as to spiritual people but as to carnal, as to babes in Christ. I fed you with milk and not with solid food; for until now you were

not able to receive it, and even now you are still not able; for you are still carnal. For where there are envy, strife, and divisions among you, are you not carnal and behaving like mere men?

According to this passage, there are three kinds of people in the world. First, there are those who are spiritually mature in Christ, empowered by the Holy Spirit, who know His Word and are trying to live it. Second, there are those who are "carnal" or babies in Christ who are immature and live like it. Then there is a third group that Paul calls "natural". They do not know God. The things of the Spirit of God seem unimportant or even ridiculous to them.

We should remember that, at one time, all of us were part of this third group. Only by the grace and mercy of God expressed in the atoning sacrifice of Jesus were we moved from the category of "natural" lost people into the Body of the Messiah.

To varying degrees, people in the group that the Apostle Paul calls "natural" are enslaved to Satan. Their eyes are blinded and their minds darkened. But this group can be divided into two groups, those who have been chosen before the foundation of the world to someday place their trust in Jesus and accept His atoning sacrifice for their sins and those who are not part of the Family of God and never will be. It is from this last group that Satan plants his tares in the Church.

The task that Jesus gave to His Church is to go into the world, preaching the Good News about Him, baptizing and making disciples. Satan plants his sons and daughters to keep that from happening. Though most are unconscious of it, he works through them to wreak havoc and destruction. Jesus told us how they would do that.

CHAPTER NINETEEN

The Scandal of the Tares

Does it seem to you that the Church is wracked with one awful scandal after another? Every other week we read about something horrible that some Christian or Christian group has done or said. Does this enrage and frustrate you? Do you find yourself ranting about ignorant, selfish, sinful Christians? Do you target whole groups with your disdain? Have people in your church done and said things that were vicious, disgusting and ignorant? Have you gotten so disillusioned that you left a church and perhaps even gave up on church altogether? Have you allowed yourself to become bitter about the Body of Christ? I know how you feel. I've been there.

I have a suggestion for us. Let's stop being dupes of Satan. Let's step back and think strategically. As we do so, let's be guided by Jesus. We need to take a hard look at the people of the tares and how they operate. There are several good reasons for doing so. One is that it's from within the tares that many wolves may appear.

According to what Jesus said in Matthew 13, darnel people operate in at least two main ways: First, they *offend*. The word that He used that is translated "offend" is the Greek word scandalon. From it we get our word scandal, which means a disgraceful action which brings damage to a reputation. It includes defamatory talk or malicious gossip. Probably, the Greek word is derived from a word that means a trap or a snare.

Remember that tares remain hidden. Wolves may try to remain hidden, but because they have a congenital need for money, praise and power their fruits reveal who they are. Tares are different. Whatever awful things happen, they don't want the onus to fall on them. Wolves don't worry about falling onuses. They charm and beat their way through them. Consciously or unconsciously, tares are agents provocateurs, spreading scandal, disrepute and disgrace through facilitating temptation and sin, while keeping their own hands apparently clean. This can happen in many ways.

A darnel person may discover something sinful that is taking place in a church. Instead of dealing with it in a Biblical manner, he or she may promote scandal with malicious talk often couched as "prayer requests", trapping others into sin with them. Or perhaps nothing sinful is going on at all, but this self-righteous individual stands in judgment, painting innocent activities as sinful and attacking others through innuendoes and gossiping slander. (We're going to discuss gossip in a later chapter.)

A darnel person may appear to be very righteous on Sunday, but watch him all week long. While proclaiming himself to be a dedicated Christian with a Bible on his desk, he may treat people horribly, bringing disrepute to all who bear the name of Jesus. Not wanting to be associated with such a person, other Christians are silenced in their witness. Instead of carrying the Love of God into the world, because of darnel people and their actions, true Christians are defensive and spend their time disparaging each other and the church.

Satan must be well pleased. How many scandalous words and actions instigated and promoted by tares are spewing around Christian churches all over the world, bringing division, mockery and even physical attacks? In America, I'm sure many tares are at the heart of the movement to mix conservative politics with the Christian faith. That guarantees that half the population will reject Jesus as just another political issue. (See my book, The Curse of Conservatism.)

Second, in His warning, Jesus tells us that the "people of the tares" act lawlessly. What does that mean? It means that they act as a law unto themselves. They are their own little gods. Their greatest concern is fulfilling their own desires. This can manifest in an unwillingness to follow true godly leadership in the Body of Christ. And more than just not follow, they impede through laziness, stubbornness, subversion and even willful, direct disobedience.

Lawless people are selfish people. All they care about is what they want and are willing to do whatever is necessary to get it. Selfish people always place unreasonable expectations on others, especially Christian leaders. When those expectations are not met (and they never can be), tares become enraged and attempt to retaliate. They are experts at bringing false accusations and creating false guilt. Because they appear to be such "excellent Christians", their selfish accusations are taken seriously. Many effective leaders and ministries have been deeply harmed by traps set among the weeds.

The work of the church is to disciple. *Tares cannot be discipled.* You cannot disciple a corpse. Tares are spiritually dead people. It may appear that they are listening and learning, but it isn't true. Probably this is the source of much discouragement among God's faithful leaders. As the burden of pastoral care grows year by year, they forget that tares exist. Satan will use his tares to burn you out.

Being Masters of Lethargy, a large percentage of tares will show little interest or enthusiasm beyond minimal participation, leaving only a few dedicated people to do the work. They use people and resources without giving back. As burnout and discouragement spread, important ministries grind to a halt. Other tares are Masters of Frenetic Activity and will be the first to volunteer for everything, bringing discord with them. Tares love to support wolves that may rise up from their midst.

How should we respond to the knowledge that spiritual darnel is around us? First, if you are a pastor or leader, preach and teach the Cross. Preach and teach about God's love that led Jesus to die in our place. Preach and teach about the Blood that was shed to free us from sin, about Jesus' death and resurrection. Preach and teach about His Power as He sits at the Right Hand of the Throne of God. Preach and teach about the Narrow Road of discipleship and the broad road that leads to destruction. Warn them about the reality of hell and the Judgment of the Great White Throne. Preach and teach about His soon return. If there is one way to get rid of some tares without searching and weeding, I think it will be this kind of preaching and teaching. If they are awake enough to hear you, I doubt that they will like it.

Second, as Jesus commanded, do not try to determine who the darnel people are. Instead, love everyone and do the work of the Kingdom. Never forget that we are called to love the lost with the Love of Christ, whether they are tares or not. Remember that immature Christians can act a lot like tares. The moment you start thinking that someone is a tare and will never be transformed, that's when God will show you a miracle. Never stop trying to disciple all who seem willing. With the patience that comes from Jesus do not give up and do not be discouraged.

Third, stop counting the heads of the plants to determine success in ministry. Our whole approach in determining success in ministry is one of the reasons that wolves and tares thrive among us. When you start head-counting remind yourself that an unknown, but significant percentage, will be tares.

Think of it this way, the more tares that are planted in your ministry, the more it proves that Satan is afraid of the work God is doing in and through you. In his fear, he is trying to destroy you in every way possible. Don't help him by giving in to anger, discouragement, disobedience or laziness. Do you want the weeds to win? Live your life for Jesus so that you are worthy to be attacked. And then don't be surprised when you are. God will carry you through.

CHAPTER TWENTY

The Wolf and the Vacation

While Jesus said that we aren't supposed to search for tares in the Church, it is our duty to be on the lookout for wolves. All wolves are not in formal leadership. There are plenty of small vicious ones creeping around in miserable little packs, hunting for prey. They search for weakness. When they find it, they attack.

In 1979 I was teaching a Bible study in a private home in Beverly Hills. The people who owned the home were new believers in Jesus. A mutual friend, now with the Lord, had introduced us. They wanted someone to lead a Bible study so he recommended me. It was a large, beautiful home with two Academy Awards on the piano won by the host for his outstanding work as a theme song writer in feature films.

It was an "open" Bible study. Anyone who wished could attend and we had a sizeable group each week. Since it was LA, I'm afraid many of the people were drawn more by the Academy Awards than anything else, but we were glad for anyone who came. While teaching that study, there were a number of strange experiences that I could never have imagined happening. One of them was a confrontation with a small, but dangerous wolf.

One night, a woman came into the study. Almost immediately, she began trying to establish her authority with the group. After my teaching time was over, she attempted to exercise her "spiritual gifts". Deep in my spirit I sensed that something was very wrong with this individual and wouldn't allow her to "perform", because that's what it felt like she wanted to do. Opposing her meant that I was attacked by her friends who accused me of not believing in the power of the Holy Spirit.

1979 was a very difficult year for my family. I had left the job that had brought me to California and had paid for graduate school. I was struggling to break in to the entertainment business, writing scripts, having meetings, doing all the things that a novice writer is supposed to do. The one thing I wasn't doing was making any money. God took care of us that year, but it was not an easy time.

For awhile, one of the things that we couldn't afford was a telephone, so every morning at 10 o'clock I would go down to the laundromat a few blocks away and call my agent. Gracious woman that she was (who later trusted in Jesus and became a dear friend), she always took my call because she knew it was the only time I would be reachable other than by carrier pigeon.

The teacher of a Bible study bears spiritual responsibility for the people who attend. For several years my friend who owned the home in Beverly Hills had been struggling with agoraphobia. During that period, we, along with a number of other Christians, were standing with him and his wife as they battled this monster of fear that had so much control of their lives.

In particular, it kept him from flying on planes. This was difficult because often his work called for him to travel to other cities. A number of times, flight reservations would be made for an important trip. A little team of us would go to his home and spend several hours praying with him. Then we would go to the airport and pray with him there.

Vividly, I remember my friend getting on a plane with his wife while all of us continued to pray at the gate. (This was in that ancient day when an un-ticketed person could go to the gate.) The time of departure would arrive and we would be joyful. He was onboard. Then, at the last possible moment, he would rush off the plane with his unhappy wife behind him. The battle to conquer agoraphobia was difficult and frustrating, but he didn't quit. Ultimately, through the power of the Lord, he overcame it.

For me, there was one important moment. After months of battling his fear, my friend got to the place where he thought he could take a vacation. His wife was thrilled. She made the reservations for a trip to Mexico. But a few days before they were to leave, I was contacted by our mutual friend. (I wasn't reachable by phone.) He told me that the woman who had been so concerned to make sure everyone's legs were the right length had been at work while I was out of contact. With all of her "spiritual authority," she had informed the couple that they must not get on that plane to Mexico because it was going to crash.

I was furious. I reached them and gave them this message, "Do not be afraid to get on that plane. It's not going to crash. You are safe. Jesus will be flying with you. Either that woman is right or I am right. If she is wrong, she is a false prophet and no one should listen to her."

When they got on the plane the first flight attendant they met was an Hispanic man named "Jesus". Not exactly what I meant, but a good reminder. My friends had a wonderful vacation and reported that the flights in both directions were the smoothest that they had ever experienced. The wolf vanished from their lives.

But what would have happened if they had listened to her and not taken their trip? She would have burrowed deep into their home taking more and more control. Very often, that is how a spiritual wolf works. He or she doesn't just instill fear. The purpose for the fear is to create dependence. With dependence comes more authority, control and predation.

CHAPTER TWENTY-ONE

How to Bring a Wolf to Your Church

I live in the mountains of central California. This is a ranching area. Many of the people who live here know a lot about livestock. Our pastor, Marc Phillips, is one of those people. Recently, he said this, "Horses and cattle know how to take care of themselves in the wild. You can release cattle in the high mountain ranges and let them roam all summer. Horses can take care of themselves too. We look after them because we want to, not because they actually need it. But sheep are different. They need constant care because sheep search for ways to kill themselves."

Jesus called all of humanity sheep and he was right. Like sheep, we search for ways to kill ourselves. We need a shepherd and Jesus offers to be our shepherd. Under His leadership as Chief Shepherd, he makes available faithful under-shepherds to guide us away from self-destruction. But in our stubborn blindness and stupidity, we don't recognize or follow them. Why? Because we have our own foolish sheep criteria for what a shepherd should look like. He should look like a beautiful, talented sheep.

We get this idea from the world. In America, specifically Hollywood and the sports industry. Because we're addicted to following attractive and gifted sheep, the wolves run free. Beautiful, sheepskin suits fit them perfectly.

Many years ago, I was an elder in a small church in North Hollywood, California. At a certain point our pastor moved on and we had to start the process of finding his replacement. As we began our search, the district supervisor of our denomination met with us and confided to me an important principle in the choice of a new pastor. At first I thought he was joking, but he wasn't. In his opinion, after many years of guiding evangelical churches in southern California, he had determined that there was an important qualification to assure a man's success in the pastorate. All things being equal, it would be good if he were a jock.

What?

That's right, a *jock*. Being a jock (okay, a former jock was acceptable) would give him the ability to relate more effectively to his church members and the more prestigious a jock he had been…well, you get the picture.

Now the district supervisor was a good and godly man. There was nothing cynical about him. He was honestly giving me the wisdom of many years during which he had dealt with scores of churches and hundreds of pastors and had been a pastor himself. He knew his target audience. Granted, southern California is unique. Some of the world's most ignorant sheep congregate here. But in almost every area of culture we have proven to be a bellwether for the whole nation (to say nothing of the world).

Over three decades after my experience in North Hollywood, we might add another element to the guidance given by the district supervisor. Today, besides being a jock, it would be helpful if a prospective pastor had some significant experience as a successful rock musician. This is because, since the 1960's, in most of our churches, music has become more important than preaching. Many evangelicals/charismatics choose their church depending in large part on the quality of the musical "worship" experience.

In many of our congregations "worship" can go on for 45 minutes or even longer on a Sunday Morning. But God help the pastor who preaches more than half an hour. If sermons consistently drag out beyond the thirty-minute barrier the perpetrating pastor had better be one of the greatest storytellers in the world. And no matter how good he is he should never talk past noon. Why? Because it will encroach on two other vastly important Sunday activities – getting to restaurants for lunch and home for the games on TV. (Do you see the nexus between the jock pastor and preaching?)

Our little church in North Hollywood had another problem. Not a lot of people attended because we were within five miles of several "mega-churches" with "superstar" pastors who drew large crowds and generous offerings. Their churches could afford all the amenities. Why waste your time in a little church with a non-superstar pastor when you could attend a Grand Event that would truly "meet your needs"?

While we were searching for a pastor, I ran into an ugly reality of evangelical church growth. With a few striking exceptions, I discovered that most of the mega-churches had not grown from reaching the non-believers of their communities. Like spiritual Wal-Marts, they had sucked up the market and destroyed the weaker competition. These churches have grown at the expense of hundreds of small churches.

Was there some pseudo-spiritual capitalistic conspiracy behind this? No. It just happened because great numbers of evangelical Christians are anxious to sit under the ministry of a "superstar". And being children of the Internet/TV/movie/sports event age, they feel very comfortable in large crowds where there is little personal contact. They like the emotion that can be generated in a huge audience and think that equates to the Presence of God. (I'm afraid that if we took away the thunderous sound systems, His "Presence" would go with it.)

What is a Superstar pastor or teacher? First, he or she is a Great Communicator. The Superstar is skilled in melding his or her personal gifts with technology so that large numbers can be deeply swayed through the Power of Emotion. More than most other preachers and teachers, the Superstar seems to have an ability to open his heart, to communicate with amazing honesty and vulnerability in front of thousands. He preaches with passion, appearing to relate on a personal level with each individual in the arena-size room. Now many of these people are quite legitimate. They are what they appear to be – honest, caring, gifted individuals struggling to perform a difficult job. But more than a few are *wolves*.

We know that God prepares people to serve Him. From the womb and through all the experiences of their lives, He is at work building men and women to have the joy of doing His Will. In Hollywood I came to understand that Satan prepares his representatives as well. He wreaks havoc in the lives of creatively gifted men and women, bringing damage that they will spread to millions when they are in positions of power.

I believe that the star I wrote about in a previous chapter and who created such difficulty for me, is such a "prepared" man. When he was a child, his parents abandoned him. He grew up in the home of his grandparents who did two things that warped his whole life. They beat him unmercifully and took him to church. Satan doesn't just prepare men and women for leadership in Hollywood, he prepares them for leadership among the people of God.

Too often, charming, attractive and gifted wolves are projected into positions of authority in the Body of Christ based on one terrible error. Christians automatically assume that numbers and spectacle equate to God's Presence and blessing. Consequently, we make a very dangerous and unbiblical leap. We assume that if there's great visible "success", the pastor's moral and spiritual life must be exemplary. He must be a true "Man of God". We ask ourselves, would God fill a dirty vessel? Over and over these assumptions have trapped us. Either He fills dirty vessels or we don't have a clue what the "filling" of His Spirit is all about.

Do you want a wolf to lead your church? All you have to do is use the spiritualized standards of worldly attractiveness and success as the basis for your choice. Satan has gifted people waiting who will fit that job description.

CHAPTER TWENTY-TWO

Christians Love Their Fantasies

During all the years that I wrote and produced network episodic television I learned something very important. When you are creating an episodic series you must do your very best to cast actors that people will want to invite into their homes each week. This kind of casting is an art in itself. Also you must tell stories that draw the viewer deeper and deeper into the imaginary lives of the characters that those actors portray.

When you are successful in casting and storytelling, a strange thing happens. Viewers in their homes will relate to those actors and their fantasy characters as though they were real. The manufactured emotions on the screen will be miniaturized and experienced by the viewer. As Hollywood writers write their scripts, they are consciously creating scenes that they hope will addict their audiences, making them want more. At a very deep level, people come to care about these imaginary characters.

When a series is successful, people may start thinking that in real life the actors are like the characters they portray. On our series, The Equalizer, Edward Woodward portrayed a brilliant former espionage professional who was trying to make amends for all the terrible things he had done in the past by helping people in need. If you were in trouble with nowhere to turn and the "odds were against you", you could call The Equalizer.

Edward portrayed the character of Robert McCall so well and the audience related to him so deeply, that people would walk up to him on the street and ask for his help. It happened so often that he took to carrying phone numbers of public agencies where real help might be received.

But it goes even deeper than that. Several years ago a woman wrote to me from Australia. She said that when she was a little girl, she would watch The Equalizer each week. Her home life was so bad that our series was the only thing that gave her hope. It helped her believe that out there somewhere was a father who really cared. How tragic and heart-rending.

There have been many other stories like this that have come to me about a scene or an episode that spoke to a person on a deep level of need. So much good could come from the amazing storytelling power of Hollywood. Instead there is so much evil. The people who are responsible for such a misuse of their gifts will answer to God someday.

As sheep, we desperately desire shepherds. In our culture we have chosen evil shepherds. They are the celebrities, the actors, the rock stars, the sports figures, the politicians and, yes, many religious leaders who spill onto our screens and into our lives. These are some of the people that Jesus calls wolves.

As a race, we have a desperate weakness. We create our little celebrity gods in our own image. By "our own image," I mean in the way that we want to see them. Once we have created a fantasy image about someone, we don't want to give it up. We cling to it with desperation. Disbelieving evidence that is right in front of us, we refuse to accept that we are following wolves until we are mauled.

We are the "Me" generations. Everything revolves around meeting our "needs". How does a "Me" generation member know that God is speaking through a Christian leader? The same way we relate to an actor on the screen – charm, attractiveness, and the powerful emotion of a story that draws us in. If we like what we see and our hearts are moved, then the message must be from Heaven. Let's be honest. It's likely that far too much of what we consider to be "God's Power" in our pulpits is nothing but the Grand Illusions of story, celebrity charm, the performing arts, technology and their hypnotic influence on crowds.

Am I saying that there should be no drama or emotion in preaching, teaching or music? No. Our emotions are God-given. Our love of "story" is from Him. I want to hear passionate preaching. I want music to stir my soul. I'm a professional storyteller and I want to be touched by stories. But when attractive personalities and emotion are the measure of truth instead of the Bible, we are vulnerable to every trap and disaster that can befall us. We beg for the wolf.

One of the great lies of Hollywood storytelling is that when you are "in love" somehow a deeper "wisdom" enters your life. You can understand truth that no one else sees. When you "follow your heart" everything will be all right no matter how foolish a particular decision may be. Almost everyone who has lived beyond 35 years old knows from painful experience how idiotic that philosophy is. But we Christians display our own version of such romantic foolishness when we fall in love with and idolize our superstar pastors, musicians and Christian media celebrities. It is a form of idolatry.

But let's go deeper toward the core of the disease that makes us susceptible to wolves. The most dangerous addiction is one that we Christians *reward* in our leaders. The more they are controlled by it, the more we revere them. What is this addiction?

The Hunger for the Glory of Spiritualized Power.

The attitude of a spiritual wolf (or a person in transition to full wolfhood) might be verbalized in this way: "God has blessed me. I am gifted. Many people hang on my every word. Obviously, I am doing God's Work. Look at how many lives are being changed, healed, delivered. Look at the financial resources that have opened to accomplish my vision. The Mantle of the Apostles is upon me. I live in the bubble of my own special dispensation. The people around me are to be used to fulfill the Great Work that God has given me to do. Because My Vision is God's Vision, what I set out to accomplish justifies the means that I choose and anyone who stands in my way must be removed."

While this is a crude statement of the philosophy, it is operationally accurate and is the credo of wolves. Throughout my adult life, I have seen it play out with the most damaging results in a variety of churches and evangelical organizations. The more successful and powerful many spiritual wolves become, the more we idolize and reward them. No matter how charismatic they are, beyond all else, these people are concerned about themselves and achieving their own goals. They are their own little gods and we reward them for their idolatry.

If we want Godly leaders we need an entirely different system of values and measurement.

CHAPTER TWENTY-THREE

Two Wolves

Meet the National TV Reverend.

This man is an ordained minister who exudes charm and caring while on camera. Off camera he is well known for his short temper and lack of concern for the employees in his own large organization. He is infamous for saying foolish, insensitive, unchristian things on the air, yet promotes himself as a wise and godly expert on a plethora of subjects. Many people are left stupefied by his cavalier ignorance. He is known for being involved in morally questionable businesses on other continents.

Like all spiritual wolves, the National TV Reverend blends truth with his falsehoods. Working under him in his "ministry" are a host of fine, humble people. I'm convinced that it is their presence and not his leadership that is responsible for any good that has been done by his organization.

My own experience with the National TV Reverend took place over a four-day period a number of years ago. I was part of a small group that stayed with him in a private villa that he had rented in England for our meeting. He was on his way back from Russia where he had bought some expensive horses and we had to meet in England because he wanted to attend Wimbledon. The purpose for our meeting was to work on a project that he was funding. He is a very wealthy man.

Having no personal experience with the National TV Reverend, I came to the meeting with an open mind and a lot of enthusiasm for the task in front of us. However, it wasn't long before our group crashed into the reality behind the mask. The arrogance and elitism of this "Christian" celebrity were breathtaking. It was clear that he considered himself to be regal and expected everyone around him to have the same attitude.

For four days we were with him from breakfast in the morning through an excellent gourmet dinner each night. During that time he made it clear that he had no personal interest in anyone but himself. In our little group there was at least one non-Christian. Though the National TV Reverend trumpets his commitment to world evangelism, he showed utter disdain for this person.

Among the unpleasant realities to be observed in this larger-than-life "minister" was his clear lack of Bible knowledge. Though we were working on a story from the Bible, he had little interest in the source material. He was concerned only with his own opinions. If the Bible disagreed with those, he got irritated.

Let me be quick to say that I had no personal conflict with this man. When the project was finished, he was very complimentary about our work. But I left our four-day meeting deeply disturbed about the millions who follow his spiritual leadership and contribute millions to his causes.

Meet the Christian TV Mogul

This is a man who has been well known within powerful circles in the entertainment industry. Because of his prominent position, often he has been pursued to act as sponsor of various evangelical events. The Christian Media Mogul is brash and arrogant. Like all wolves he can be very charming. Within Hollywood his reputation is for making one right decision years ago that brought him great wealth, followed by a long string of foolish decisions. Also, he is well known for deceit.

Several years ago he boasted to me about 20 different individuals and organizations that were suing him because of the way he had consciously created contracts so he could breach them with impunity. To him, it was just good business and he was proud of his cleverness.

As bad as Hollywood can be, within the industry your word is your bond. Long before contracts are written, deals are entered into based on a handshake. For the "Christian" Media Mogul, even written contracts meant nothing. For wolves, the end justifies the means.

Foolish Christians fawn over men such as these two and many more like them. Instead of being petted and feted, they should be placed under church discipline for the good of their souls to see if repentance is possible. Of course they would never stand for such a thing. And who would consider attempting it? In the evangelical world, there is no church with authority that they would recognize. But what about a Christian peer group? Aren't there other mature, evangelical leaders on their level who could take them to task?

From what I can determine, the opposite is true. Instead of a peer group that would hold each member accountable, there exists across the United States (and even out into the rest of the world) an elitist "evangelical Christian" clique of very powerful men. These individuals are leaders in media, politics, business, the mega churches and the Christian academic community. I have had friends who have touched the periphery of this clique. The members protect each other, fund each other, and promote each other. Unless someone in the group does something particularly egregious that embarrasses everyone (such as the antics of the Reverend Ted Haggard) normal, everyday arrogance, narcissism, and deceit on a grand scale remain acceptable and hidden.

Because they are wealthy and powerful, these men receive special "spiritual" treatment. I don't know whether it still exists, but a few years ago there was a regular telephone "Bible study" taking place among them. Every week or two, a group of these wealthy men would gather in a conference call and a leading evangelical minister would give them a short "devotional" message over the phone.

What do these people need? Not fawning, special treatment, but a tough, godly group of "powerless" men who care nothing about their fame and fortune and will tell them the truth for the good of their eternal souls.

Are all wealthy Christian leaders wolves? Certainly not, but too often wealth and power blind those who aren't to those who are. Too easily, they accept and promote wolves as brothers and sisters in Christ because they are in the same economic stratum and claim to be Christians. Thereby they give tacit approval to a wolf's actions.

In Luke 6:43-45 Jesus gives important guidance about why a spiritual wolf acts in the way that he does.

"For a good tree does not bear bad fruit, nor does a bad tree bear good fruit. For every tree is known by its own fruit. For men do not gather figs from thorns, nor do they gather grapes from a bramble bush. A good man out of the good treasure of his heart brings forth good; and an evil man out of the evil treasure of his heart brings forth evil. For out of the abundance of the heart his mouth speaks."

In the Middle Ages the Roman Catholic Church was governed by a cabal of sleek, charming and vicious wolves. To an ever-increasing degree, the evangelical church in the United States has resurrected that awful system. One of the reasons that we accept this situation is because we do not understand what the New Testament means when it speaks about "fruit" and "fruit bearing". It's time we learned.

PART TWO

The Fruit of Wolves and the Fruit of Heaven

CHAPTER TWENTY-FOUR

How Not to Eat Radioactive Fruit

For those of us who are city folk, when we think of "fruit" the image we get is of a fruit stand or the produce department at a grocery store. To us, fruit is limited to the end result. But the word has a broader meaning in the Bible than simply what appears at the end of a branch or vine.

The literal meaning of the Greek word that is translated "fruit" includes the concept of fertile ground, the plant and its nurture, in fact, the entire growing process, not just what appears at the end. So if you want to recognize good fruit, you start by looking at the ground from which it is growing. Would you plant a vegetable garden where radioactive waste had been spilled? Would you eat the vegetables that grew there just because they looked and tasted so good? On a spiritual level, Christians do this all the time.

The fantasy stories that we believe about leaders, their gifts and charm and the succulent "fruit" that they seem to present distract us from considering their spiritual soil. This is a major reason why wolves have such freedom in the Church. To distinguish between wolf fruit and the real fruit of Heaven, we need to understand the difference between wolf soil and heavenly soil.

First and basic to everything else, the fertile soil
of Heaven is humble ground.

When Jesus came He revolutionized the whole concept of humility. Before He came, the majority of Greek philosophers equated humility with groveling, with being mean-spirited, slavish, servile and even stingy. A few philosophers such as Plato and Aristotle took a higher view that foreshadowed the New Testament. For them humility equated to having prudence, wisdom and moral integrity. Such a person they classified as a "Great Soul" who, though realizing its greatness, would not boast about it. That's where the philosophers failed. If you think you are a "Great Soul" you will boast about it, but your boasting will be with such subtlety that it will enhance the appearance of humility.

We could call it humble bragging.

It's generally accepted even in Hollywood that unvarnished pride is ugly. So both in the church and in Hollywood, pride is carefully varnished. Proud leaders learn how to boast in a way that makes it appear that they are humble, while in reality they are guiding people to worship at their altars.

It works like this: A leader receives compliments. A few of them might even be deserved. Most, however, are given by people who simply want the leader to notice and appreciate them and this is the only way they know how to get his attention. The more these people appear to be "appreciated" by the leader, the more flattery they pour on. So he continues "appreciating" them. Whatever truth was in the original compliment is lost in a mountain of fantasy.

Though the leader would never admit it, no matter how fantastical the compliment, in his soul he believes it is well-deserved and preens himself with it. While he appears to display humility, perhaps even gently brushing aside the compliment, secretly he hopes that others hear it and the news of his greatness spreads. A bit of false humility in the form of self-deprecating humor can encourage the expansion of this bloated propaganda. The truth is that self-deprecating humor can camouflage monstrous pride.

What does true humility look like? It's the mantle of Heavenly power and Jesus Christ wore it perfectly. He elevated humility from the dirt where Satan had buried it to the highest virtue. He showed Godly humility for what it really is...a sword into the heart of Darkness. "Fruit unto Heaven" only grows on humble ground.

Do we want the humility of Jesus in ourselves and our leaders? Leaders are an accurate expression of the people they lead. If we want humble leaders, we'd better start learning to be humble ourselves.

CHAPTER TWENTY-FIVE

I Hate Being Lowly

I really do. I like being noticed. I like for people to think I'm important. When I was a young man, my father was so well known in the evangelical Christian community around Chicago that when I visited some churches I would be recognized from the pulpit as his son. That felt good. It stroked my pride. But in Romans 12:14-16, the Apostle Paul stands against all of that. He shares the secret of how to have a life of Heavenly humility because that is the only spiritual "ground" that can bear much fruit. Here is what he says:

Bless those who persecute you; bless and do not curse. Rejoice with those who rejoice, and weep with those who weep. Be of the same mind toward one another. Do not set your mind on high things, but associate with the humble. Do not be wise in your own opinion.

In the Greek, two concepts are presented here. One is collective, the other individual. They work together and stand as a barrier against wolves and their fruit.

Collectively, Christians are to assure that no "spiritual aristocracy" is allowed to rise up in the Body of Christ because we are all of the same mind. What mind is that? The Mind of Christ. I Corinthians 2:16 says that we have the Mind of Christ. If we really have His Mind, we're not lofty in our self-image and desires.

In Hollywood, there are powerful people who insist on being treated in certain ways by those they consider beneath them. They insist that very specific items be waiting in their hotel rooms. If they aren't in place when they arrive, they throw a fit. One star demands that no one make eye contact with him when he walks on a film set. These are extreme examples, but the disease of an inflated ego is everywhere.

Paul says that a person in leadership in the church is no better and is of no more value than the lowliest disciple of Jesus. He tells us that this will be displayed in very practical ways. There should be such unity between those in leadership and the lowliest believers that they can rejoice and weep together through all the experiences of their lives. That's how Jesus relates to each of us. He rejoices and weeps with us. Only when we get to Heaven will we understand the depth of our Oneness with Him.

When our King walked this earth, He set the perfect example of humility.

John 13:12-17 records: **So when He had washed their feet, taken His garments, and sat down again, He said to them, "Do you know what I have done to you? You call Me Teacher and Lord, and you say well, for so I am. If I then, your Lord and Teacher, have washed your feet, you also ought to wash one another's feet. For I have given you an example, that you should do as I have done to you. Most as-**

suredly, I say to you, a servant is not greater than his master; nor is he who is sent greater than he who sent him. If you know these things, blessed are you if you do them.**

Jesus' disciples were like Christians today. They had a never-ending problem with humility and the servanthood that naturally comes from it.

Luke 22:24-27: **Now there was also a dispute among them, as to which of them should be considered the greatest. And He said to them, "The kings of the Gentiles exercise lordship over them, and those who exercise authority over them are called 'benefactors.' But not so among you; on the contrary, he who is greatest among you, let him be as the younger, and he who governs as he who serves. For who is greater, he who sits at the table, or he who serves? Is it not he who sits at the table? Yet I am among you as the One who serves.**

Jesus wasn't humble just because it's nice for people to be that way. With His humble coming, life and humiliating death, He overthrew the entire system of Satanic rule. He did it by destroying its foundation which is based on pride expressed in an elitist hierarchy.

The temptation to elitism has been in the Church from the beginning. It is the glory of spiritual wolves. Elitism, "the consciousness of or pride in belonging to a select or favored group" is the heart of the Satanic world system.

The belief that you are part of a select or favored group because you are better than others, the lust to be part of such a group, or the resentment that you are not in that kind of group, is the underlying force of oppression, racism, war, class hatred, religious bigotry and even occultism. It is the soul of everything from Gnosticism to the Communist Party and the annual conference of the Bilderberg Group. It is the heart of the Hindu caste system and every religious system that offers higher levels of spiritual attainment through initiation and personal effort. It is the seed of failure in democracy.

Elitism is the core of the original temptation dangled in front of Adam and Eve in the Garden of Eden. Satan whispered to Eve that there was a much higher level that she might attain. Far above her was an elite group called the "gods". She could be as one of them knowing good and evil. All she had to do was disobey God and establish her own authority to be part of that rarified society. The lie inflated her pride, inflamed an evil desire and blinded her to destruction.

When Satan took Jesus to a mountaintop and showed him all the kingdoms of the world and their glory, when he offered those kingdoms to Him if only He would bow down and worship, he was trying to institutionalize pride forever. He was trying to establish forever the evil, elitist system that he uses to rule the pitiful creatures that follow him, for Satan exerts his control through an ancient, iron-clad hierarchy of principalities and powers. To him the lowest slaves of all are humans who bear the Image of God.

Pride, lack of humility, is death in the church. Jesus will not be present where pride is in control. Elitism is the institutionalization of Satanic pride. The goal of the Powers of Darkness is to establish a spiritual aristocracy within a church, for that is the seedbed where pride can grow and choke out the fruit of Heaven. Satan accomplishes this through his wolves and tares. Elitism is the fruit of their lives. A spiritual hierarchy of evil is their natural home and foolish sheep are willing and anxious to help them establish and maintain it. Too often, how we choose our leaders in churches and Christian organizations simply spiritualizes that Satanic system, opening the door to wolves.

But Jesus has shown us another way. He established humility as the mark of Kingdom leadership. *Consequently, if you want to choose a leader who will bear much real fruit for eternity, humility is the first measure to determine whether his "life ground" is fertile or not.* Without humility, a leader cannot bear Heavenly fruit, no matter how impressive his or her ministry may be.

My little sister, Virginia, suffered from Down Syndrome. Her mind never progressed much beyond that of a four-year-old. She was one of the "least of these" that Jesus spoke about. There were loving people in her church who dedicated themselves to ministering to my sister and others like her. They spent time with the most humble of Jesus' followers. Their love was palpable.

It is people such as these who should be raised up to leadership in the church because their humble lives are fertile ground that bears good fruit. But very often, these are the people who won't volunteer for leadership because they don't think they are worthy or gifted enough. You won't find wolves spending much time with the poor and the mentally disabled. Oh, they may show up for a "photo op", but after that they are gone.

161

How do we stand against the Satanic system of pride and elitism? Through the Power of the Holy Spirit, collectively and individually, we must cultivate humility and help each other toward that goal. All of us, including our leaders, should seek out the lowliest of believers, not just to minister to them, but so that they can minister to us. A literal translation of our Romans passage could read that we should let such lowly people "lead us by the hand". Lead us where? Into the Presence of Jesus by reminding us of what Jesus did.

Philippians 2:5-8 says, **Let this mind be in you which was also in Christ Jesus, who, being in the form of God, did not consider it robbery to be equal with God, but made Himself of no reputation, taking the form of a bondservant, and coming in the likeness of men. And being found in appearance as a man, He humbled Himself and became obedient to the point of death, even the death of the cross.**

Personally, I hate being of "no reputation". I don't want to be considered just one of the servants laboring in the scullery. Certainly, I don't want to be considered a criminal. Yet that is what Jesus chose and far worse. Are we willing for Him to teach us how to be humble? It means being humiliated.

While we were in England with the National TV Reverend, one night an invitation to dinner came from a wealthy member of the British aristocracy. There were eight of us in our group. The National TV Reverend divided us into two parties. The most important people went with him to the dinner at a mansion, while the rest stayed behind.

It was clear what he was doing. The unbeliever in our party was not invited to the dinner. My wife and I weren't either. It was humiliating. While it stung at the time, it was good that we remained behind. We were able to get to know our unbelieving friend and speak with him in a way that was impossible with that wolf, the National TV Reverend, present. Where would Jesus have been that night? Of course, He is everywhere, but in a special way I think He was with us...giving me a little lesson in humility.

CHAPTER TWENTY-SIX

Four Kinds of Rotten

If we don't want wolves in leadership, we can't allow their natural habitats to exist in the Body of Christ. One of Satan's most successful strategies is to create division through proud leaders and the establishment of elite groups. His wolves and darnel people are well equipped to carry out this ministry from hell. What kinds of aristocracies does Satan like to form? Let me suggest a few:

The Spiritual Aristocracy

This is one of Satan's oldest and most successful subgroups. It was a spiritual aristocracy that stood against Jesus and nailed Him to a cross. Today in the church, Satan convinces his aristocrats that they have more of the Holy Spirit and are more spiritually mature than other Christians. He encourages them to prove their spiritual superiority by expressing their potent spiritual "gifts" or deeper spiritual "life" in ostentatious ways.

Depending on the church, those in the Spiritual Aristocracy may display their membership in the group by "sharing" their rigid dedication to daily devotions and prayer, endless "godly" DVD watching, End Times book reading, bloviating public prayers, "words of wisdom" and/or raucous speaking in tongues. They will be the first to give "guidance" to anyone and everyone. Satan encourages them to insert themselves into positions of leadership where their superior spirituality can best be seen and will have the most influence, intimidating and frustrating many.

In some churches the Spiritual Elite prove their status by slavishly following a set of structured rules and letting everyone know of their obedience. The Spiritual Elite use a rich vocabulary of jargon which must be mastered if a person ever hopes to be accepted in their group. But acceptance isn't going to be easy. You will need to spend a lot of time listening to them and doing as they instruct. A spiritual aristocracy is the natural home of wolves.

In too many churches, spiritual elitism is institutionalized by organizational structure. Years ago, I was a member of a large church. The pastor, a good man who loved the Lord, had a large board of elders. I became one of them. I discovered that he liked to maintain tight control over everything. He informed all new elders that he didn't want any surprises in an elder meeting. If we had anything of importance to share we should clear it with him beforehand. He governed through an executive committee. All major decisions were made by that small group and presented to the full board for approval. Basically, we were a rubber stamp.

There was no insidious intent behind this system. After too many years and too many meetings, this pastor just wanted to expedite business. However in the process, he established an elite group. Those who were not in the group resented it. Division was created. Such discontent is an open door for wolf leadership to arise.

Wolves love to surround themselves with a Spiritual Aristocracy, boards of directors and elders who are proud of their positions and will do the wolf's bidding. For a wolf, a Spiritual Aristocracy creates many layers of additional camouflage, a kind of human fortress that is difficult to penetrate.

The Financial Aristocracy

Satan is very wealthy. He has made sure that in Western civilization financial success is worshiped like ancient pagans worshipped their idols. A man or woman with significant money is idolized as much in the church as anywhere else in society. How many churches and other Christian organizations bend over backwards to put a wealthy man on their board? His spiritual life may be in the toilet, but who wants to take a serious look at that? God has blessed him, so he should be in leadership.

Forget the warning in the Book of James against giving preference to wealthy people. Forget Jesus' warning about how difficult it is for a wealthy person to enter the Kingdom of Heaven. Bring the rich guy in and elevate him. Isn't it practical? The church can use his financial knowledge, to say nothing of his cash. On the basis of worldly success alone, men and women are elevated to leadership and the result is disastrous.

Satan loves to breed wealthy wolves. In leadership, they speak with loud voices and can control all the ministries of a church including the selection of pastors. They can change the entire direction of a Christian organization.

The love of money corrupts in many subtle ways. Whether you love it or not is expressed in how you waste it and what you waste it on. (Truthfully, I've wasted plenty of it in my life and for that I must repent.) At the time of this writing, it has been discovered that a very successful Christian author who has made millions and who is chairman of the board of trustees at a Christian school has been involved for years in high stakes gambling. It is not surprising that after over a century, the code of conduct at that school has suddenly been watered down to reflect his values.

Now this man is an acquaintance and I do not believe that he is a wolf. He has done many good things in service to the Lord. However, his foolish immaturity in this situation makes it clear that he should be removed from leadership. But that hasn't happened and I doubt that it will. When we glorify money and those who have it, overlooking sin and immaturity to place them in leadership, we are being disobedient fools. We are inviting Satan to assist us in ministry.

The ability to acquire wealth can be a gift from God. Whether wealth is of God or Satan will be determined by the humility of the heart that possesses it.

The Creative Aristocracy

I know a lot about this group. These are the musicians, the writers, the actors, the artists. We creative people are capable of the most horrible elitism and Satan loves to encourage it. He loves to plant artistic tares and wolves among us.

Most creative people are elitists by nature. Those who aren't creative we don't find very interesting. We resent those who don't appreciate our gifts. Satan whispers that we are the ones with "vision". God has given us special abilities to *see* and *understand* and *express*. Whatever gifts God may have given, Satan loves to twist them into bloated fantastical lies. And we creative people suck them right up.

Humility and creativity don't often go hand in hand. I'm afraid that's true especially in me. Under the gentle guidance of Satan, both in the church and the world, creative people can be miserable narcissists making life hell for those cursed to be close to them. I've seen it in Hollywood and in the Church, especially among our Christian "celebrities".

Creative people whine about how other Christians don't understand or appreciate "the artist and art". When we aren't fawned over, we sulk. Personally, I love to gripe about the total lack of esthetic sensibilities in most evangelical churches. Never mind that beautiful churches can be dead as stone coffins. At least they are lovely bone boxes. You just have to get used to the odor.

In American evangelical Christianity a person may have one great creative gift which he or she displays with tremendous power. In everything else, that person may be a selfish dolt. No matter, in the church we reward them with adulation. We make sure they know that they're *very special.* In the process, we help destroy any hope that these creative souls might become mature, humble people of God, which is the only way their gifts will mean anything. This idolizing of creatively talented people is straight out of the world system and is Satanic idolatry.

As this book is being written, a number of large churches are discovering that they have put talented musicians in position as "worship" leaders who may not know Jesus at all. They have the attitude and bloated self-image of rock stars and act that way. Frustrated because they haven't made it in the rock world, they are in church to perform and make good money doing it. The congregation is there to appreciate their talent. The worship that they lead is self-worship and all self-worship is Satanic. Real worship can't take place until these false leaders are removed. It's time to clean out the musical wolves. It may sound like worship to you, but it's just howling to God. It's time to stop idolizing creatively talented people.

During his so-called "Christian period", my wife and I spent a number of evenings with the singer/songwriter Bob Dylan. He was in our home for dinner and for hours we discussed the Bible. He had done some serious study. Dylan told me that he couldn't go to church like a normal person. He had to slip in the back after the service started and leave before it let out or he would be mobbed.

Celebrity worship is a curse in the Western Church. Not only does it establish an elite group, Satan uses it to fabricate life-crushing false goals for so many young people. Where does this spirit of elitist celebrity worship come from? Hollywood and the entertainment business, which includes professional sports.

Hollywood operates with an elitist caste system that is almost as rigid as that of the ancient Hindus. Like the silversmiths who made idols to the goddess Diana in Ephesus, Hollywood knows that celebrity worship sells product. The many huckster wolves in the evangelical church know this too, so the church has been trained to ape the world.

When creative people are lifted up with no concern for their spiritual maturity and with no accountability, you can be sure that wolves are waiting to exploit them. When we look only at a person's apparent "gifts", we help destroy him. Often we help to turn him into a wolf.

Young creative people should be guided into being disciples of Jesus. The root of the word disciple means discipline. A creative person must be *willing* to learn from those who aren't very creative at all. Creative elitists need to be told the truth about their spiritual condition, not isolated and idolized in their imaginary grandeur.

The Intellectual Aristocracy

I do believe that Satan holds a thousand doctorates and endows multitudes of university chairs. The Intellectual Aristocracy in the Church is made up of people with advanced degrees from seminaries and other institutions of higher learning. They may hold positions in the Christian academic community. In my opinion, it is within this group that Satan has made some of his most important gains that have been so destructive to the Body of Christ.

I have experienced intellectual elitism in Christian organizations. Christian colleges and universities are rife with it. When degrees are viewed as the primary proof of wisdom and knowledge, when the status of a degree is necessary for a leader to be respected or even employed, fools are in control and wolves will be among them.

I know of a Christian college that wanted to hire a man to be president. He was a gifted leader who met all of their qualifications except he didn't have a doctorate. The school found a way to get one for him. The fact that they believed this was vital, says worlds about the influence that intellectual elitism is having on that institution. And they are not alone.

The destruction of Christian higher education has been caused by capitulation to a world system that requires not just advanced degrees, but for maximum status, advanced degrees from particular institutions. Men and women who have those degrees are chosen for employment though in many cases, from the standpoint of spiritual knowledge, wisdom, discernment and discipleship, a janitor is more qualified.

At the very least, this guarantees that true discipleship to Jesus is not instilled in students within the academic disciplines of a Christian college or university. At worst, it assures that spiritual wolves will find their way into those schools. These men and women will subtly inculcate the values of the world into the lives of young people during a time when they are vulnerable. As in a war, beachheads for spiritual wolves are established within specific departments. From there the dark influence spreads outward all the way back into homes and churches.

Young people are leaving the Christian faith in frightening numbers. For too many, this can be directly attributed to attending Christian colleges and universities and what they have been taught there. The teaching of so-called "theistic" evolution has undermined faith in the authority of the Bible. During the past several decades it has become fashionable among some "evangelical" scholars to denigrate the very concept of evangelical scholarship and intellectual life. These scholars place the highest value on acceptance by the intellectual elites of the world.

Intellectual elitism is a virulent disease. Many years ago, I observed the editors of a major Christian magazine, men and women who were considered "thought leaders" in the evangelical world, try to fire a man who worked on the business side of their publication. The quality of his work was not in question. Their only problem was that he didn't have a college degree. Their elitist values and bloated image were all that mattered. The editorial staff

172

had little to do with people on the "business" side. By their actions, they communicated that those people existed to further their "thought leadership".

Is it wrong to work for an advanced degree? Of course not. God has given the church brilliant men and women who should be respected and whose gifts should be utilized. As servants of the Lord, they are vital to the life and health of the Body of Christ. Thankfully, in my life I have known many brilliant Christian intellectuals who were not elitists.

My own father was an intellectual with several advanced degrees including an earned doctorate. He was a humble man of God who delighted in having fellowship with everyone. I grew up knowing many professors at the Moody Bible Institute, where my father taught. These men and women were intellectually brilliant, yet humble servants of Jesus. Their lives still speak to me though most are with the Lord in Heaven.

Over the years, I have enjoyed teaching the Bible to various groups. That might never have happened except for one man. When I was in my early twenties, a very brilliant Christian intellectual named Dr. Charles Horne was teaching a Sunday School class at our church in Wheaton, Illinois.

Dr. Horne (now with the Lord) was a professor of theology at Wheaton College and had been a professor at the Moody Bible Institute. In his Sunday school class were other college professors and many educated people. One Sunday when he had to be away, he asked me to substitute teach for him. Me! Certainly I was no scholar and, at the time, didn't even have an undergraduate degree. When I told him that I didn't think I was qualified, he just laughed.

I was scared to death, but I did it. Dr. Horne's trust was a great gift to me. It opened the door to the possibility that I might be able to teach the Bible someday, something that I felt unqualified to do.

Thank God for the many Christian intellectuals who refuse to be part of an intellectual aristocracy. They infuse their students with the blessing and Presence of Jesus as He is manifested through their lives. Some of them are in the forefront of the war, standing for the Lord against a secularist onslaught within their disciplines. We need them. But they need the humblest members of Christ's Body to "take them by the hand" and lead them to Him.

When we allow and encourage elitism or any kind of spiritual aristocracy in the church, we guarantee the presence and leadership of wolves. In our ignorance and disobedience, we open the door to Satanic destruction.

CHAPTER TWENTY-SEVEN

Antidotes to Wolf Rot

As we think about the fertile ground of humility where true "fruit unto God" can grow, let's look at that passage in Romans again:

Bless those who persecute you; bless and do not curse. Rejoice with those who rejoice, and weep with those who weep. Be of the same mind toward one another. Do not set your mind on high things, but associate with the humble. Do not be wise in your own opinion. (Romans 12:14-16)

We said that in the Greek, two concepts are presented to guard us from spiritual pride and elitism and guide us to humility. One is collective, the other is individual and they work together. We've looked at the collective emphasis, now let's look at the individual.

Along with the admonition against the establishment of a spiritual aristocracy, we are given a strong personal admonition about having a humble view of ourselves. When Paul says not to set our minds on "high things," he means don't focus on our own lofty dignity. Don't consider how intelligent, creative, gifted and elevated we are above others.

My career in Hollywood was never stellar. But I experienced enough success to know that it changes you in disturbing ways. At the heart of that change is a kind of mystical exhilaration about winning, a subtle sweetness in knowing that you have succeeded where the vast, vast majority of gifted people have failed. When your name appears on national television or major theater screens, it is a thrilling moment. Your friends cheer. Vague acquaintances talk about knowing you. There, for all of the world to see, is proof of your amazing ability. Without the slightest effort you start basking in the Wonder of You.

With major success come lofty perks. The perks of Hollywood are like helium for the soul. You suck it in whether you want to or not because it's the only thing available to breathe. After awhile there's so much of it in you that it just feels like you are rising off the ground above everyone else.

During my years of success in Hollywood, there was a single airline that came to personify this whole gaseous reality. Yes, an airline and its name was MGM Grand Air. This delightful collection of jets flew between New York and Los Angeles and every inch of them was First Class. None of this pretense to grandeur called "business". And certainly no hordes of smelly bodies crammed into constriction seats in a cattle car called coach.

To fly MGM Grand Air, a limousine picked you up at home and transported you to a private terminal. No need to wander around through the unwashed masses. From the private terminal you were ushered onto the aircraft. On board you were seated in a huge, soft, lounger style chair with plenty of legroom. Fine wine and caviar were served followed by a delightful selection of gourmet meals. An hour or so before landing, the staff would bake chocolate chip cookies. (I am not lying about any of this.) I came to look forward to a hot chocolate chip cookie that would sweeten my arrival on either coast.

The rear of the plane was divided into cubicles with four big lounge chairs facing each other two by two. One night flying back to LA, I was alone in a cubicle. Just for me the staff collapsed the loungers into a queen-sized bed. (Isn't this sickening?) As I lay there looking out the window I knew without a doubt that God loved me more than anyone else.

But the ultimate subtle joy in flying MGM Grand Air was the other passengers. Not on one of those planes would you be crammed in with the riffraff and illiterati that slosh down the aisles of Southwest Airlines. You weren't even subjected to the lesser mortals who flew first class on American. (Some of them might have been upgraded. You just couldn't tell.) Every time you boarded the plane there was the quiet assurance that MGM Grand Air catered only to stars and moguls, truly important people just like you.

I won't mention any of my seatmates on those flights. Being from Hollywood, I hate to drop names. Suffice it to say that just to walk on board and sit down made you feel as though you had pierced the inner circle. Flying MGM Grand Air at studio expense became a delicious form of gaseous flattery. I loved it.

Too bad they went bankrupt.

Jesus knows how susceptible we are to flatter-gas, how much the mental methane makes us think foul lofty thoughts about ourselves. Very, very few leaders can take a steady flow of flatter-gas and not choke to death spiritually. I couldn't. The

177

Apostle Paul was dealing with inflated egos when he wrote these words to the church in Corinth.

Now these things, brethren, I have figuratively transferred to myself and Apollos for your sakes, that you may learn in us not to think beyond what is written, that none of you may be puffed up on behalf of one against the other. For who makes you differ from another? And what do you have that you did not receive? Now if you did indeed receive it, why do you boast as if you had not received it? (1 Corinthians 4:6-7)

Paul knew how prone we are to self-inflation, so he gave us an antidote. It is the individual admonition found in Romans 12:14-16 and it's a vital key to humility.

Bless those who persecute you; bless and do not curse.

In Hollywood, people are paid well to be persecuted. When you reach the very top, you may not be persecuted, but you've experienced so much of it on the way up that the rage stays with you. The most successful people in Hollywood are some of the angriest. With their inflated egos, they hold serious grudges that go on for years. Many take joy in doing to others what people have done to them...only worse.

The Greek word that's translated "bless" is eulogeo. It is a compound of two Greek words. To give them a literal definition we would say that these words mean "speaking good things about someone out loud". From eulogeo we get our word eulogy. At funerals people eulogize the dead person. Usually, this means that someone stands up and says only nice things about him, leaving out most of the truth. It is a conscious attempt to speak only good and celebrate their memory with praise.

So when I am told to bless a person who is persecuting me, that means I am to speak well about him to others. It means asking God to give that individual all the things I want for myself, to prosper him and make him happy, to bestow good on him, *all while he is doing the opposite to me and won't stop.*

The mark of a man or woman of God whose life is fertile ground where much fruit unto God will grow is the humility with which they deal with those who cause them grief or with whom they strongly disagree. *A spiritual wolf will bestow many gifts upon his friends, but he will never bless his enemies with kindness. He is no more capable of doing so than his father, Satan.* Any kindness that he appears to show will have chains, not just strings, attached.

In choosing a leader for the Body of Christ, watch how that person handles those who "persecute" him. If he makes enemies and keeps them, if he excoriates those who challenge his leadership, if he is vindictive and retaliatory, no matter what his gifts and other qualifications may be, *he should not be in leadership.* There is every possibility that he is a wolf.

CHAPTER TWENTY-EIGHT

Humble People

Have you known any humble people who have taken you by the hand and brought you to Jesus? I have.

When I was growing up, my family spent every summer in a small town in northern Oklahoma called Tonkawa. As I write this chapter, in my mind are the good, down-to-earth people who were in the little church we attended. In particular, I remember a pastor named Charles Holgate. He was a middle-aged seminary graduate ministering in a church of less than 50 people. Even as child, I could see how he loved them. Whatever they were going through he was beside them in it. He and his wife couldn't have children so they showed amazing love to all the children. In his shop he took the time to make wooden swords for my brother and me. Of all the gifts of childhood, that is one of only a few that I remember.

My grandfather, William Heldenbrand, was an honest, hardworking farmer, a truly moral man with an impeccable repu-tation in Tonkawa. But it was very difficult to have a conversation with him because he just never talked. I mean to anybody. Until his death when I was ten years old, I don't remember him saying more than five words to anyone in my presence. His silence was intimidating. I don't remember him ever saying anything to me.

My grandfather was so silent about everything that after he died, my grandmother was terribly worried about his soul. They had been married well over 50 years and loved each other deeply, but he had never talked to her about Jesus. She didn't know whether he knew the Lord or not. But Charles Holgate knew. My grandfather trusted him and that trust had broken through the silence. They had talked about Jesus and how to know Him. Reverend Holgate gave my grandmother great peace. There was no question about whether Bill Heldenbrand was in Heaven. They had prayed together. Charles Holgate, humble pastor in a humble church, cared about the eternal life of a very old man. That pastor lives in my memory as an example of the loving humility of Jesus

When I think about humble people, I remember Art Lundahl. Art was a businessman who commuted to Chicago every day. But once a week he gave an evening to be a leader of a boys club at our church. Art didn't have any sons, so one evening a week he became a father to a whole bunch of rowdy urchins. I was in the group.

Art was a storyteller. I was ten years old and by that point I had read and heard hundreds of stories. But Art's were different. He made up the stories that he told and I had never heard anyone do that. And they were *good stories.* He created a character called Sheriff Pete. About once a month Art would tell us a new story about Pete and his adventures dealing with bad guys and helping people. I don't remember any of the details. What I do remember is that when he came in with a "Pete Story" every boy sat in rapt attention. And when he was finished, we always wanted more.

I'm a professional storyteller. I've written screenplays and novels. I've created network TV series. I know now how much it takes to create a story. Art Lundahl, who was a busy man with a job and a family of his own, spent a lot of time on those stories. I don't think he ever wrote them down or published them. He never became a professional storyteller. They were just for us.

And for Jesus.

Art Lundahl didn't know it, but he was laying the foundations of story creation in the heart of a ten-year-old boy. He was teaching him that it's possible to tell a great story, speak truth and talk about Jesus all at the same time. Every Pete story ended with Jesus and He wasn't just tacked on either. Faith in Jesus was a deep part of Sheriff Pete's life and guided all he did. Art's been in Heaven a long time, but whatever success I have had as a storyteller, that humble man has a share in it.

When I think of humble people, I remember Dave Gibbons. Dave was my roommate at a little Bible college in Dallas. I was 17 and it was my first year. Dave was in his mid-twenties, but he seemed much older than that. I have to say that there was nothing glamorous about Dave. He wasn't good-looking and he was very quiet. Girls showed no interest in him. He might as well have been part of the wallpaper. In a school that was preparing people for Christian ministry, Dave didn't have any great skills to offer.

I was his roommate, so there was one thing I knew that others didn't. Dave spent a lot time on his knees praying. I would come in and there he would be. He prayed for me and I needed it because what I wanted to do was party.

Dave was a terrible public speaker. He could never have been a preacher. There was no punch behind his voice. When he spoke it was just above a whisper. But that wasn't the biggest problem. The biggest problem was that he couldn't talk about Jesus without crying because he loved Him so much. It's hard to preach sermons that way. I want to love Jesus the way that humble man did. His life still speaks to me after half a century.

When I think of humble people, I think of a man whose name I cannot remember. I was thirty years old when my father passed away unexpectedly. It was one of the saddest times of my life. Immediately after his passing, my mother and sister stayed with us for a few days as we tried to comfort them.

As we approached the funeral, one evening I went alone to my parents' home to pick out the clothes we would bury him in. I was looking through my dad's closet, when the doorbell rang. At the door was an older man I didn't know, the friend of a friend of the family. He had stopped by simply to offer his condolences. We sat down for a few minutes and he talked to me. I don't remember what he said, but it was what I needed to hear. He brought the comfort of the Lord to a broken heart. I never saw him again.

When I think of humble people I think of Marie. At the very start of my career in Hollywood, my family and I went through several years that were really difficult. There were times when the pantry was almost bare. We were attending a little church in North Hollywood that was full of humble people of God. They really cared about us and Marie was one of them.

During our financially difficult years, we never told anyone. We didn't ask for help, but people knew. It was hard not to. I was an elder. Several times, people came to our home for counselling. We had to do it by candlelight, because we couldn't afford electricity.

One day Carel had gone out and I was home alone in a back room. Suddenly, I heard something. I went to the kitchen and there was Marie, stocking our shelves with food. She thought since the car was gone, that Carel and I weren't there. The door was unlocked. Instead of leaving bags on the porch, she decided to put the food away. She was very embarrassed. What a wonderful and difficult moment and how humbling it was for me. Marie and her family weren't wealthy. It was a gift of love. The humble people in that little church gave us so many gifts of love and encouragement. Truly, they took us by the hand and led us to Jesus. At the end of that difficult time, the doors to network television opened. But not before I had been given some serious lessons in humility and faith.

When I think of humble people, I think of Clark Mathias. Clark was an old friend from Wheaton, Illinois who had migrated to LA a couple of years before us. Though he was bright man, I'm sure his family and many others thought of Clark as a true underachiever. He had no great career aspirations. He liked cars so he was a car salesman, but wasn't even very successful at that. Though he enjoyed the company of women and was a romantic at heart, women weren't interested in him except as a friend. In LA, who wants to get involved with a guy who isn't driven to achieve?

But there was something very unusual about Clark. He had an uncanny ability to meet people and become their friend.

Lots of people. He had a simple charm and everyone trusted him. He was a good, thoughtful friend who never tried to use anyone to advance himself. Instead of pushing himself forward, he brought people together then stepped back. Clark was a humble man and people responded to that humility. He's been in Heaven for quite a few years. Only a handful of people were at his funeral in Illinois.

It was through Clark that I taught my first Bible study in Los Angeles. It was through Clark that I met Bob Dylan and many others. Was Clark a meaningless person, a failure as far as the world was concerned? Probably. But I will tell you this. *My entire career in network television can be traced back to people I met because of Clark Mathias.* That's right, not because I studied film at USC grad school, not because of agents. Because of Clark. Whatever success I have achieved, that humble man has a part in it.

I could write books about all the humble people of God who have blessed my life, who have taken me by the hand and led me to Jesus. They helped guard me from disaster. They guard me still. Wolves like humble people because they need servants. They are blind to the fact that Jesus Himself is within those people. What the wolf does to them he does to the Lord.

Do you have humble people of God in your life? If not, for the good of your soul, you need to find some to befriend you. I don't believe that it's possible to bear fruit for the Kingdom without them. But if we're in leadership, there is a special kind of humble person that we need.

CHAPTER TWENTY-NINE

The Fool's Prayer

In the old medieval courts of Europe often there was a court jester. He was called The Fool and would dress in a ridiculous costume, but usually he was one of the wisest, bravest and most creative men in the Kingdom. He had a very dangerous job. His task wasn't just to make people laugh, it was to remind the king publicly and sometimes through sarcastic derision, that he was only a mortal and prone to all the foolishness and stupidity of any other person, either high born or low.

The Fool's job was to help the king remain humble. To do it well, meant that he was irritating. He was the only man in the kingdom who could call the king names. He might disagree with royal decisions and present differing viewpoints. Kings would rage at their jesters, sometimes banishing them or worse. But a wise king knew the great value of such a man. This poem, by Edward Rowland Sill, captures it well.

THE FOOL'S PRAYER

The royal feast was done;
The King sought some new sport to banish care,
And to his jester cried: "Sir Fool, kneel now,

And make for us a prayer!"

The jester doffed his cap and bells,
And stood the mocking court before;
They could not see the bitter smile
Behind the painted grin he wore.

He bowed his head, and bent his knee
Upon the Monarch's silken stool;
His pleading voice arose:
"O Lord, be merciful to me, a fool!

"No pity, Lord, could change the heart
From red with wrong to white as wool;
The rod must heal the sin:
But Lord, be merciful to me, a fool!

"Tis not by guilt the onward sweep
Of truth and right, O Lord, we stay;
Tis by our follies that so long
We hold the earth from heaven away.

"These clumsy feet, still in the mire,
Go crushing blossoms without end;
These hard, well-meaning hands we thrust
Among the heart-strings of a friend.

"The ill-timed truth we might have kept—
Who knows how sharp it pierced and stung?
The word we had not sense to say—
Who knows how grandly it had rung!

"Our faults no tenderness should ask.
The chastening stripes must cleanse them all;
But for our blunders – oh, in shame
Before the eyes of heaven we fall.

"Earth bears no balsam for mistakes;
Men crown the knave, and scourge the tool
That did his will; but Thou, O Lord,
Be merciful to me, a fool!"

The room was hushed; in silence rose the King,
And sought his gardens cool,
And walked apart, and murmured low,
"Be merciful to me, a fool!"

Yes, Lord, be merciful to all of us sinful fools.

We need to resurrect the job of Court Jester in churches, schools and other Christian organizations. If you are a leader, has God placed a court jester in your life? If not, for your sake, it would be wise to find one. When you start believing the flattery that pours out about how wise, caring and gifted you are, your jester will remind you that under a thin façade you are a self-centered idiot and only by the grace and mercy of God are you accomplishing anything.

Your jester will remind you that you are the least of the saints and ought to be the servant of all. He will ask you the tough questions that will call into doubt your great wisdom and bloated vision. Encourage that person to tell you the truth and don't get angry when he does. He is a rare gift from God.

Wolves hate court jesters and put them to the sword. Are you seeking a humble, godly leader whose life is fertile ground for the bearing of Heaven's fruit? Find a person who is humble enough to hear brutal, even sarcastic truth and learn from it. Find a man or woman who doesn't hide his arrogance behind a demand for respect. Find a person whose ear is tuned to truth no matter the source. Find a leader who laughs publicly at his or her own foolishness. There is a court jester of God within that soul.

All of this is part of what it means to "not set your mind on high things". When a leader is committed to living a humble life (humble people should feel comfortable and not out of place in your home), that life will be fertile ground. If you see a leader who refuses to live this way, who stands apart from those he leads, who won't listen to criticism and retaliates against those who give it, who wants only praise, who has no sense of his own idiocy, turn on your wolf radar. And watch out for the foul fruit that's going to drop all around you.

But humility alone is not all that is needed to make fertile ground. There is another vital element that goes hand-in-hand with a humble life.

CHAPTER THIRTY

Faithful is Fertile

My father, Dr. G. Coleman Luck, passed away thirty-eight years ago. His death was a great tragedy for our family. As I have written, for most of his professional career he taught the Bible as a faculty member at the Moody Bible Institute in Chicago. He was a very bright, yet humble man. When I think about humility and faithfulness and how they work together, I think of him.

My father was faithful to his wife and loved her to the day that he died. He was faithful to his family and did his best to provide for them, though his salary was small and frugality was necessary. He was faithful to his students, doing the best that he could to teach them God's Word. When he entered the last part of his career he began writing to former students asking them about their lives and ministries and encouraging them as he prayed for them.

Most of all, my father was faithful to God. For decades he commuted each morning from our home into Chicago. He did this with other faculty men who lived in our town of Wheaton, Illinois. They would leave very early to miss the worst of the traffic, which meant that my father had to be up before dawn. Over the years, there were times when I had to be up early as well. Many times, I remember seeing him on his knees in prayer. I know that he was disciplined about praying with lists of people who needed intercession. I know that his prayers for me have blessed my life and have followed me down through the years.

My father's humility and faithfulness manifested in many ways. At his funeral were men who had shared the carpool experience with him for decades. Day in and day out, morning and afternoon, they had spent untold hours with him. At the end, they said that not once had they ever heard him say anything negative about anyone. Not once had he passed along gossip. How I wish the same could be said of me at my funeral. Sadly, it won't be.

Many times I heard my father teach and preach the Bible. Whether the group was large or just a few people in a rather dismal room, his commitment and energy in ministry were the same. I never heard him complain or express disappointment about a group or how his teaching had been received. Always, he was thankful for the opportunities that God gave.

Being faithful means that God can depend on you and me to carry out the assignments that we are given, without complaining, without self-pity and without being influenced by definitions of success that come from this world.

At the end of one of His parables, Jesus said these words:

"Who then is a faithful and wise servant, whom his master made ruler over his household, to give them food in due season? Blessed is that servant whom his master, when he comes, will find so doing. Assuredly, I say to you that he will make him ruler over all his goods. But if that evil

servant says in his heart, 'My master is delaying his coming,' and begins to beat his fellow servants, and to eat and drink with the drunkards, the master of that servant will come on a day when he is not looking for him and at an hour that he is not aware of, and will cut him in two and appoint him his portion with the hypocrites. There shall be weeping and gnashing of teeth. (Matthew 24:45-51)

Notice that when the master arrived, he didn't ask, "Well, how many people did you bring in to eat at the table?" He didn't ask, "How did they respond to the food? Did they enjoy it? Did they spread the word about what a wonderful chef you are?" He didn't ask how the servant's kitchen compared to a kitchen across town. The master was concerned only whether the servant had carried out his assigned duties with what he had been given. Did the servant provide the best food he could, working hard without laziness? Did he treat his fellow servants kindly? Does that describe a wolf? The unfaithful servant that Jesus describes is a spiritual wolf.

The entire Bible flows with the importance of faithfulness. Over and over, God is described as faithful. Over and over, the true followers of Jesus are told to be faithful in the face of great difficulty. In Revelation Jesus tells the suffering church in Smyrna, **"Be faithful until death, and I will give you the crown of life."** (Revelation 2:10b)

Because we have been so corrupted by the systems and values of the world, in America we reward our Christian leaders for unfaithfulness.

In the mountain community where I live, I attended a church that was still suffering from what I would consider an unfaithful ministry. Years in the past they had a very gifted preacher. I can't speak about his abilities from personal experience, I never heard him. But long after he was gone, everyone still talked about his preaching power.

However, many of those same people have expressed the opinion that there was a kind of mystery about the man. Though he was wonderful in the pulpit, on a personal level he was distant and hard to get to know, a man with many invisible barriers carefully erected. Was he a wolf? I don't know, but, from what I can determine, I don't think so. He appears to have been a man gifted with preaching ability, but not gifted with an outgoing personality. And, like most of us, he was controlled by the values of our culture.

What happens when a gifted preacher is in a pulpit? From everywhere Christians flock to hear him. And that's what occurred in this church. Membership boomed. People were being "fed". There was excitement. Soon the congregation outgrew its building. Big plans were laid. They would build a much larger building. They would start a school. And these things they did. They built the first of what was to include several large buildings. They started the school. Needless to say this kind of "vision" costs money and they found themselves with a huge debt. But all would be well...as long as their success continued.

Unfortunately, that success was based on the efforts of one person. Not long after the building was completed and the school had been started, this man "felt the call of God" to go to a more prominent church in another state. When you lose a gifted "pulpiteer", it's hard to replace him, especially in a small community.

As the years passed, many in the congregation did what most modern Christians do when they grow bored and discontented. They found other churches where their "needs" could be more fully met. For years, those who remained have labored under the financial yoke that this "pastor" left on their shoulders. In spite of what he did to them, the people still revere his wonderful "ministry".

Let's be honest. To do this kind of thing to people who have vested all their trust in you is despicable. In any other area of life such lack of concern and commitment would be repudiated. If you are the founder of a business you just don't start something huge, enlist the deep involvement of many trusting souls who quit other jobs to join you, then walk out on them leaving them to suffer the consequences of your grandiose "vision" because a more lucrative offer has come along.

If you were a General and had recruited an army based on your leadership skills, then took them into battle, what would your soldiers think if you abandoned them at the height of the war? But such things don't bother Christian leaders today because they are "Following the Call of God".

Saddest of all, because of our unbiblical understanding of "fruit," evangelical Christians encourage such unfaithfulness. The fact that a pastor is willing to leave a ministry in the lurch should be the first reason another church would refuse to hire him. But we encourage men like this to go on and on. This is because we view our Superstar Pastors like Superstar Athletes. If we can steal one away from another "team", so much the better for us.

Does God lead people to new assignments as they work for His Kingdom? He does. But don't you think it's rather odd that almost always those assignments are a step up in prestige and money and not a serious step down?

I'm not implying that the only definition of faithfulness in ministry is staying in one place for many years. I know a faithful man of God whose primary ministry over many, many years has been to plant churches. After which, he turns them over to people who have been gifted to build them. Also, many times he has been an interim pastor helping struggling churches get through difficult transitions. Some sow, others cultivate and still others reap. Nevertheless, our definition of success and "fruit" has been radically perverted by secular American values.

However, there is an opposite side to frenetic unfaithfulness that spiritualizes upward financial and career mobility. The opposite is lazy selfishness. What Jesus says about faithfulness among His servants speaks to that issue as well. I have known people who stayed in paid positions of Christian leadership for a long time simply because they were comfortable. They had no vision and resented those who did. Those who followed them were just like their leader, sluggards blocking the work of God.

Wolves are drawn to both extremes, whether it's the greed of spiritualized upward mobility or the lethargy of spiritual slughood.

Fertile ground where the fruit of Heaven can grow is humble, faithful ground. It is a life that has set its course, following the King no matter where He leads or what storms may come. So when looking at the ground of a potential leader's life in order to determine the kind of fruit that is growing there look for patterns of faithfulness - faithfulness in love for God, faithfulness to family, faithfulness to friends and faithfulness toward those who are under his care and leadership, whether in business or ministry. Above all, there should be faithfulness in the way he handles the Word of Truth, preaching and teaching the full Counsel of God in simplicity and without apology.

My father is buried in a little cemetery outside Tonkawa, Oklahoma. My mother and sister are beside him. Tonkawa was my mother's hometown. She and my father were married there and early in his ministry he served as interim pastor in the little Presbyterian Church. On his tombstone we placed his life verse.

2 Timothy 2:15 – Be diligent to present yourself approved to God, a worker who does not need to be ashamed, rightly dividing the word of truth.

CHAPTER THIRTY-ONE

The American Evangelical Ministry Metrics of Fruit Measurement

What do so many American Christians consider "fruit"? If we think about it at all, many of us believe it means being busy in church activities and "ministry". If we get serious about our faith, we think fruit is the number of people we "witness" to or even lead to the Lord.

For a professional in ministry, the idea of fruit gets numerically specific. It's how many attend your worship services, "share groups" or other meetings. It's how many hands go up or people come forward in an "altar call". It's how many backsliders you return to the faith and how many you baptize. You may count fruit as the number of people blessed by the quantity of books or videos you sell. You may think fruit is how excited people get by your worship music, how they praise and wave their hands in the air. Fruit may mean how much God has filled your ministry bank account.

In American Christianity we love to place spiritual value on ourselves and others by applying a range of "ministry metrics" which we might call the American Evangelical Ministry Metrics of Fruit Measurement (AEMMOFM). When the positive side of the ledger is growing, we think we are doing great work for the Kingdom of God. We are bearing "fruit". And if the numbers aren't growing or are sinking, it means that God is not blessing and we are not "bearing fruit".

In American Christianity, "fruit unto God" has come to mean some sort of measureable numeric success. The fact that this is true proves that wolves have been in control for a long time hiding a Biblical definition of fruit and implanting a definition that comes straight from Satan's world. Wolves have helped us learn to spiritualize worldly success. In 1 Corinthians 4:1-5 Paul takes a different approach.

Let a man so consider us, as servants of Christ and stewards of the mysteries of God. Moreover it is required in stewards that one be found SUCCESSFUL. (Oh wait, that isn't the word he used. The word he used is **FAITHFUL**. Be found *faithful*.) **But with me it is a very small thing that I should be judged by you or by a human court. In fact, I do not even judge myself. For I know of nothing against myself, yet I am not justified by this; but He who judges me is the Lord. Therefore judge nothing before the time, until the Lord comes, who will both bring to light the hidden things of**

darkness and reveal the counsels of the hearts. Then each one's praise will come from God.

The word Paul uses that is translated "judge" means to scrutinize, to investigate in order to determine value and worth, guilt or innocence. He says that he is not concerned about what people think of him or his ministry. He answers to the Lord who is the Righteous Judge. This doesn't mean that Paul refused true, Godly authority. He was quite willing to account for his work and accept the authority of the Apostles and other church leaders in Jerusalem.

Paul was attacked a lot. All sorts of ungodly people judged and condemned him from Roman courts to false teachers and ignorant Christians. He suffered under those attacks. It would have been easy to have defended himself with a few statistics, yet not once does he apply the American Evangelical Ministry Metrics of Fruit Measurement to the people and churches under his care.

If Paul had applied those metrics he might have written his letter to the Church of Corinth in a very different way:

Letter to the Church in Corinth

Well, congratulations to the C of C. You guys are smokin'. Praise God, it's clear that He is really blessing you. According to the latest stats that Timothy has brought from the Vision Engineering '60 Conference, 598 people are attending your Sunday morning worship and you need to rent a larger lecture hall. That is a 30 percent increase over last year. And what really warms my heart is the fact that you had 80 baptisms. 80! **WOW, all I can say is WOW. On top of that, 39 backsliders have returned to the faith, your Sunday night healing service is packed and your worship team is putting out its first album. I love the title, 'How Do You Feel About Jesus?"**

It just takes my breath away what the Holy Spirit is doing in your city. Keep up the outstanding work. What-ever you're doing, don't stop. By next year God will have blessed you so much that you'll have to meet in the arena. (Oops, probably he wouldn't have said that.) **If you keep grow-ing like this we're going to franchise your system. I've al-ready got Titus working up an outline for a DVD series.**

Your buddy in ministry,

Paul.

If Paul had applied the modern American ministry value system to his churches, the New Testament would have been a lot shorter. No need for all those confrontations, arguments and neg-ativity. Think of the money and time that could have been saved copying and printing Bibles over the past 1900 years. But that isn't how he wrote to the "successful" church at Corinth. He wrote in the way he did because he had a vastly different definition of "fruit".

How do you define a successful ministry? For a long time, what might be called a "business/entertainment" model has con-trolled and defined what the American church calls "ministry".

Good capitalist business methodology is defined as good "steward-ship".

Having worked many years in Hollywood, I am very familiar with the business/entertainment model. Behind all the glitz and glamour of the entertainment business are some of the toughest, smartest, most profit-driven minds in the world. As an executive producer/showrunner in network television, I was responsible for the production of 22 one hour dramatic episodes every year. Even back in the late 80's and early 90's this meant responsibility for a budget of about 1.5 million dollars per episode. And it wasn't like mass producing widgets. You couldn't cut a mold and blast out an endless string of product.

In television, each weekly episode was like creating a new product and sending it out to the marketplace. After it aired, you watched the Nielsen Overnights to see how well your product "sold". It's a brutal way to live. If you do well, there are great rewards. If you do poorly, you'd better turn the situation around fast.

For a long time, that is the way churches, Christian ministries and Christian businesses have been operating. They may spiritualize it with all sorts of holy sounding jargon, but at rock-bottom "fruit" in American Christianity is about numbers and dollars. The dollars may be labeled "offering" or "contribution", but it's all the same. If a leader doesn't bring in the people/bucks, eventually, he or she will be gone.

Several years ago, I had a disturbing conversation with a senior editor at one of the largest Christian publishers in the world. We were talking about Christian fiction. She informed me that the only fiction they were interested in publishing was Christian romance fiction targeted for middle-aged Christian women. Why? Because middle-aged Christian women were the only ones who came into the Christian book section of stores. They were the only ones who bought their fiction.

I asked, "Aren't you interested at all in going beyond that group, for instance trying to reach non-Christian young people who are so lost? And they do read books. Look at the Twilight Series."

The response? "We can't do that."

That was incorrect. The correct response would have been that they could do that, but they didn't want to. Why didn't they want to? Because to make such an attempt would be a risk and they weren't in the business of taking such risks. With all of their high-sounding spiritual advertising jargon, their real motivation was finding the most secure and predictable route to a big bottom line.

This "Christian" publisher is owned by Rupert Murdoch. But they are not alone. Producing "product" for the Christian "ghetto" is big business. You just have to know your market and not try to go outside of it. Give the people what they want, even if it has the life-changing power of dishrag. In our churches "worship" itself has descended to the level of being a product. This mercenary attitude, hidden beneath various spiritualized mantles, has been in control of the evangelical world for a long time.

All the way back in 1970, I teamed with a godly, talented Christian radio personality named Bill Pearce (now with the Lord). Bill was a fabulous musician, at the time one of the greatest trombonists in America. He had a very successful late night radio program in syndication that was ministering to millions. The 60's generation of young people was in full bloom and it was a disaster. We told the large Christian organization where we worked that we would like to create a soft rock version of Bill's successful program to reach non-Christian youth with the message of Jesus. It wouldn't even have to carry the organization's name.

The request was turned down. Why? They were afraid that the donors who supported the non-profit organization might find it objectionable. Did they know for sure? They didn't. But they didn't want to take a risk. This was the god of money in control cloaked under the mantle of "stewardship".

When accountability in the church is the same as in Hollywood, the iron fist of a spiritualized entertainment business model slams down. We want results from our leaders. We want a good spiritual show. Of course, we would never be so crass as to call it that, but that's what it is.

A good spiritual show puts bodies in pews and brings full collection plates. It brings "sales" as measured in numbers of people saved, delivered, healed and restored from backsliding. Count them up each week then turn in the report to the denomination. When "fruit" is defined this way, little wonder that wolves run free and enjoy great power.

CHAPTER THIRTY-TWO

Fruit in the Tsunami

It's very difficult to stand against the monstrous tsunami of cultural goop created by the Hollywood entertainment/ marketing business model that has taken control of American Christianity. It's hard to maintain a correct Biblical perspective about fruit-bearing when people stare around and see a lot of empty chairs in your Sunday morning service, or your books don't sell or the bank account is empty, while the cheesy church and cheesier preacher across town is booming. It's easy to get discouraged when others apply the American Evangelical Ministry Metrics of Fruit Measurement to you. Wolves and tares just love to do this.

What is real "fruit unto God?" What does the Bible say it is? Now I face a problem, because there's no evangelical "dog and pony show" built into answering that question. Worst of all, it can't be measured in this world. You can't report it to the denomination. It won't fit on a power-point for your board of directors. When you are bearing much fruit unto God you can appear unsuccessful, even "fruitless", to everyone around you.

What did Jesus say about fruit-bearing?

"For a good tree does not bear bad fruit, nor does a bad tree bear good fruit. For every tree is known by its own

fruit. For men do not gather figs from thorns, nor do they gather grapes from a bramble bush. A good man out of the good treasure of his heart brings forth good; and an evil man out of the evil treasure of his heart brings forth evil. For out of the abundance of the heart his mouth speaks. (Luke 6:43-45)

The treasure of a heart! What is the treasure in the heart of an apple tree? It is the very principle of its life that ultimately produces apples. Before apples appear, they are born first in the heart of the tree. What comes out on the branches is nothing more than the expression of that tree's genetic heart. The tree naturally produces fruit outside on its branches from what it is inside. Jesus says that good treasure or evil treasure is first in the heart. From there it will spread to the world. What kind of tree are you?

If we think that bearing fruit is the result of what we "do" for the Lord, we have missed the mark. Bearing fruit is the result of what He is doing in our hearts. If we are connected to Jesus what we "do" for Him is the natural distribution of the fruit that He is producing from inside of us. And that is what He said would happen.

"I am the true vine, and My Father is the vinedresser. Every branch in Me that does not bear fruit He takes away; and every branch that bears fruit He prunes, that it may bear more fruit. You are already clean because of the word which I have spoken to you. Abide in Me, and I in you. As

the branch cannot bear fruit of itself, unless it abides in the vine, neither can you, unless you abide in Me.

"I am the vine, you are the branches. He who abides in Me, and I in him, bears much fruit; for without Me you can do nothing. If anyone does not abide in Me, he is cast out as a branch and is withered; and they gather them and throw them into the fire, and they are burned. If you abide in Me, and My words abide in you, you will ask what you desire, and it shall be done for you. By this My Father is glorified, that you bear much fruit; so you will be My disciples. (John 15:1-8)

So bearing fruit unto God *will happen naturally* if we remain connected to Him. He is responsible for it happening. We are responsible to remain connected. That's all. As you remain connected to Jesus, He will feed others with the true food of Heaven that He is growing from out of your life. It's the fruit of joy and suffering and most of the time you won't even know that your life is feeding anyone. Only when you stand before Him, will it be clear what He has done in and through you. That's what Paul is talking about when says that he doesn't worry about people judging him and his work. He can't see the results and doesn't know what they are. Only Jesus knows that. The branches on a vine never count their own grapes.

Do you remember that breakfast on the Sea of Galilee after Jesus' resurrection? It's found in John 21. After providing a meal for His disciples, the Lord takes Peter aside and three times asks him a single, profound question, "Do you love me?"

Each time when Peter responds that he does, Jesus tells him to feed His lambs and sheep. By doing so, the Lord directly linked feeding the people of God with deep, passionate, self-sacrificing love for Him. There will be no "fruit unto God" in your life and mine without that kind of love for Jesus. It is love for Jesus empowered by the Holy Spirit that will keep us connected to Him so that we produce real fruit that will feed others. Anything less is just meaningless activity.

And here is a wonderful and frightening truth. Most often, the fruit that really does feed others grows out of suffering that God allows into our lives. It is what the writer Oswald Chambers calls being made into "broken bread and poured out wine". Our lives are the bread that Jesus breaks and distributes to the spiritually starving. Our lives are the grapes that He crushes into drink for parched souls. *That is what "bearing fruit unto God" really means.*

How Satanic are the systems that have taken control of the church? Of all their hellishness, what is the most hellish thing they accomplish? How do they destroy "fruit unto God" most effectively? Because they spiritualize a worldly definition of success, because the aggressive lies of the wolves have so completely deluded us, suffering is viewed as an embarrassment, an unnecessary and even shameful proof of a lack of faith, evidence that God is not "blessing" the sufferer. We have accepted a worldly definition of strength that is far more from comic books than the Bible. Consequently, suffering is hidden. And as it is hidden, real fruit dies on the vine.

How do we nurture the seed of the Kingdom of God and the plant that is growing from it in our lives so that it will bear much fruit? We do so by nurturing our love for Jesus, telling Him every day that we love Him and asking that He fill us with His Holy Spirit so that we can love Him more. It is asking that His Love for us and ours for Him might transform all the words and deeds of our lives, including suffering, into broken bread and poured out wine to feed the starving.

Good fruit is meant to be eaten. When it dies on the ground, the seeds inside are meant to bear more fruit. Do you really want to bear fruit for the Kingdom? Then ask God to make you into broken bread and poured out wine. Are you searching for a godly leader? Find the man or woman who truly and deeply loves Jesus. Then look for the broken bread. It will be the bread of suffering from a broken heart offered up to God. Look for the poured out wine. It will be God's love crushed-out through a life in love with Him. And the people will be fed.

What is the fruit of the wolf?

A year or so ago, I had a tragic conversation with a very bright young man who holds degrees from a leading Christian university. He sits under the "ministry" of a well known "pastor". There is much evidence from many sources to indicate that over the years this man has become a wolf. My young friend knows the Scriptures well. He can make good Biblical arguments and considers himself a devout Christian. His "pastor" is a skilled Biblical "exegete".

But here is the tragedy. After an extensive conversation, which I found rather disturbing in its emphasis on legalism, I asked this young man a simple question, "Do you really love Jesus?" I don't think he'd ever been asked that question. He couldn't answer. I urged him just to say the simple words, "I really love Jesus." He couldn't do it. He could talk about honoring Him, etc. But love for Jesus wouldn't leave his mouth.

The test of true discipleship has never changed and the question asked by the real Jesus rings down through the centuries, "Do you love me?" Loving Him is the secret to remaining connected to the Vine. If we love Him, it will bring certain results.

"If anyone loves Me, he will keep My word; and My Father will love him, and We will come to him and make Our home with him. He who does not love Me does not keep My words; and the word which you hear is not Mine but the Father's who sent Me. (John 14:23-24)

Obedience to rules without love for Jesus is the fruit of the wolf. Whatever fruit it brings and no matter how impressive it appears, it isn't fruit unto God.

The great pastor and Bible teacher of a previous generation, F.B. Meyer, told the story of a young Scottish woman in the 1800's who applied to a mission board to go overseas as a missionary. During the interview, the men on the board were very unimpressed with her lack of sophistication, particularly in her speech. She had a heavy accent and was not very fluent, so they decided to reject her. When they called her in and informed her of their decision, tears came to her eyes and she replied, "I may not be able to speak very well for the Lord Jesus, but I love Him so much that I could die for Him." The men changed their minds. One wonders what kind of response she would get from a mission board today with all of our modern sophistication.

Lack of real love for Jesus pervades the American Christian church. There are many proofs of that lack of love. A main one is that Christians want to spend so little time alone with Him.

Pastors and other leaders bemoan the fact that so few Christians spend even five minutes a day alone with the Lord praying and reading the Bible apart from other distractions. They struggle to convince people of its value. But their arguments ring hollow. Why don't arguments work? You can't argue a person into love.

CHAPTER THIRTY-THREE

Fortress in the Wilderness

Here in the mountains of central California, if you want to grow a garden you need to build a fortress. Whatever you plant will be attacked from all directions, so you need raised beds surrounded by tall fencing with netting above. If you don't have all that in place, whatever you plant will be food for the creatures, not you. As far as plants are concerned, we live in enemy territory.

Wolves thrive where there is ignorance of the Scriptures. If you don't know the Bible, you will not be able to discern the subtle perversions of wolf teaching.

2 Timothy 3:16-17 says: **All Scripture is given by inspiration of God, and is profitable for doctrine, for reproof, for correction, for instruction in righteousness, that the man of God may be complete, thoroughly equipped for every good work.**

Imagine that the Bible is a collection of giant building blocks. You are in enemy territory and you want to build a fortress that is so impregnable that it will withstand any attack. The huge blocks to build the fortress are stacked in front of you, but you can't just throw them together. They're cut to fit in specific ways.

You need an architectural plan. What Paul calls doctrine is that plan. It shows you where the blocks are to go and how they fit. When the fortress is built according to the plan, it will protect you.

The fortress of Bible doctrine incorporates and integrates the great themes of Scripture. Every true disciple of Jesus who wants to bear fruit for Him and His Kingdom should understand those themes. Here is one list to consider:

1. The Bible: Its Author, subject, purpose and inspiration.
2. God the Trinity: His Person and Deity.
3. God the Father
4. God the Son: His pre-existence, Incarnation, substitutionary death, resurrection, ascension, priestly ministry and His coming for His saints.
5. God the Holy Spirit: His personality, advent, anointing, ministry and baptism.
6. The Covenants of God.
7. The angels.
8. Satan: His personality, work and future
9. Man: His creation and fall
10. Sin: Its character, universality and God's remedy for it.
11. Law and Grace
12. Salvation from the guilt, penalty and power of sin.
13. Righteousness and sanctification
14. The assurance of the believer
15. The Church: Her membership and mission
16. The Sabbath of the Old Testament and the Lord's Day of the New.
17. Love
18. Prayer
19. Service.
20. Thanksgiving

21. Stewardship
22. Prophecy in the Old and New Testaments
23. Judgment of the Believer's works
24. Judgment of the nations
25. Judgment of the wicked
26. Heaven and the eternal state of the redeemed

(Adapted from Major Bible Themes, Lewis Sperry Chafer, The Bible Institute Colportage Association, Chicago, 1937)

Try showing this list to your church home group. See how much they know. All true followers of Jesus should have some understanding of these themes. If you are a pastor and those under your care do not have such an understanding, you are building on sand. When there is no understanding of doctrine, wolves take control much more easily.

In 2 Timothy 3:16-17 the Apostle Paul says that Scripture is profitable for reproof. That's an old fashioned word, what does it mean? Reproof is a warning meant to save someone's life. It means to stand against wrong thinking and destructive actions by convicting a person of sin so he doesn't damage himself and others.

The Apostle Paul says that Scripture is profitable for correction. That means to straighten up a person, to re-form him. Imagine a deformed sufferer who can barely stand, much less walk. Suddenly, you pull him up straight so he is able to stand and walk as never before. He has been "re-formed". Or imagine a man wandering in the dark on the edge of a precipice and you pull him back, correcting his course so he doesn't kill himself.

Scripture is profitable for instruction which is disciplinary correction that leads to righteousness. Righteousness is a life set apart in love for God. Unrighteousness is slavery to sin and Satan. Without righteousness there is no Heaven for you and me. Romans 6:20-23 is clear:

For when you were slaves of sin, you were free in regard to righteousness. What fruit did you have then in the things of which you are now ashamed? For the end of those things is death. But now having been set free from sin, and having become slaves of God, you have your fruit to holiness, and the end, everlasting life. For the wages of sin is death, but the gift of God is eternal life in Christ Jesus our Lord.

The King James Version translates it "fruit *unto* holiness" which leads to everlasting life. So if true fruit unto God is growing inside you or anyone, it will result in a holy (set apart) life ready to enter the Kingdom of Heaven and work for that Kingdom on earth. As far as our life in this world is concerned, Paul says that the Word of God is *necessary* for a man or woman of God to be complete, thoroughly equipped to do the work of Jesus' Kingdom here and now.

So what happens when the integrated teaching of Scripture is neglected or when wolves strip it of its power? Turn those verses in 2nd Timothy on their head.

Correct instruction about Truth will not be available, therefore error won't be refuted so people won't be convicted of sin and turned from destruction.

They won't be straightened up or reformed. They will keep on staggering.

There will be no chastening that leads to righteousness. Consequently, people will lead unholy lives.

They will not be equipped to do the work of the Kingdom and will not bear fruit for that Kingdom. The fruit they will bear is for darkness and destruction.

When all of this pervades a church, what is left is a congregation with hearts that will not stand for sound teaching. Wolves are quick to enter, replacing the Holy Spirit with the spirit of this world. In so many churches, instead of love for Jesus and evidence of a transformed life, all that is required is a nod to a "statement of faith". Wolves nod very well.

Deep study of Scripture should be an expression of love for Jesus and a desire to know Him better, but it isn't always. The Spirit of Darkness is the Spirit of Legalism. Satan is an expert on the Bible. He's been studying it for thousands of years.

One of the most frightening and heartbreaking things I have ever seen is a man who is an "expert" on the Bible, who has studied it for many years and has published books about it, yet by the evidence of his personal life and the destruction he has brought to the people closest to him, it is clear that he knows nothing about repentance, forgiveness and the Love of God. He knows nothing about righteousness. All he knows is self-love, self-pity and legalism. With all of his knowledge, he is spiritually blind and the fruit of his life proves it.

Satan uses wolves and tares to stop the accurate, integrated, powerful preaching and teaching of God's word. This can happen in many ways. Beware when the simple teaching of the Bible is plastered with a whole system of marketing-style jargon and cutesy slogans supposedly designed to help people understand

Scripture and "do church". This could be part of an elitist system designed to protect the wolf, promote his message and coalesce people around his leadership.

Wolves stop the preaching of the "whole counsel of God" through a subtle application of their own paranoia. A wolf will be very anxious that his followers listen only to him or to his approved leaders who teach exactly what he desires, men and women who share his heart and have been programmed with his jargon. The wolf may present his paranoia as a simple concern for accurate Bible teaching. It isn't. He wants his followers to be indoctrinated into his system of thought and resents any other strong, gifted voice that might arise with a Biblically faithful point of view.

A key mark of a wolf is his paranoia about competition. Under his leadership, no one can be elevated to teach or preach without his permission. All such individuals will be carefully vetted to assure that only what is in agreement with wolf-teach will reach the congregation or his constituency. Darnel people and weak believers are anxious to comply. Once they have committed their self-image and self-respect to him and his system, they will defend him even when irrefutable evidence appears of his evil duplicity. Often with rage, they will attempt to refute the irrefutable.

If a strong voice speaking Biblical truth arises that disagrees with the subtle lies of the wolf, there will be hell to pay. The attacks against that person may begin as "gentle guidance" from the wolf supposedly meant to keep him or her from going "sideways". If that "guidance" is not accepted, attacks will escalate to public vitriol and worse. Even if the wolf's "guidance" is accepted, the offending individual will no longer be trusted. Soon they will be marginalized.

Here let me restate the warning that I have given throughout this book. A wolf doesn't have to be the pastor or the president of an organization. He can be the chairman of the board of elders or some other leader. There are many pastors who have lost their pulpits because a powerful wolf among the elders didn't like their preaching. A wolf can arise in the congregation accusing a godly leader of being a false teacher as he gathers a pack around him. If others in the congregation don't really know the Scriptures, they will have no ability to judge.

Never before has there been a greater need for believers who love Jesus to be serious students of the Bible. Wolves flourish because of our laziness and ignorance. The Sword of the Spirit is the Word of God. God's Word is a fortress in the wilderness. The American church is entering a time of great darkness and it is entering with nothing more than ignorance, platitudes and emotion. These are not weapons.

CHAPTER THIRTY-FOUR

Wolves of the Secret Knowledge

Where is wolf leadership and wolf fruit taking us? Where is all of this going? The Apostle Paul tells us:

For the time will come when they will not endure sound doctrine, but according to their own desires, because they have itching ears, they will heap up for themselves teachers; and they will turn their ears away from the truth, and be turned aside to fables. (2 Tim 4:3-4)

What does Paul mean when he says people won't "endure" sound doctrine? He means that they won't stand for it. They won't put up with it. They won't be able to bear it. Listening to it will bore them to death or drive them crazy and infuriate them. So they choose teachers, preachers and spiritual leaders who will tell them what they want to hear. And these wolf "ministries" will bear horrible forbidden fruit.

What do people want to hear? According to Paul they want to hear what appeals to their desires. The Greek word translated desire means longing, especially for what is forbidden. They are living in sinful, immoral ways, doing forbidden things, but they want to be told that it's perfectly all right. God loves them and that's all that matters. Everyone is going to Heaven. Don't worry about hell. This is the message of the charming wolf who hugs people straight into damnation.

But there's another implication in Paul's words. He says that these wolves will turn their followers away from truth and toward "fables". The word that is translated fable is the Greek word from which we get our word myth.

Clearly, Paul isn't talking about little stories populated with fantastical creatures. Resonating in his use of the word is the idea of mystery, false teaching that takes people ever deeper into the secrets of darkness just as it did in Thyatira so long ago. Because of Satan's skill as an illusionist, these dark teachings can appear to be the Light of God.

Satan has been doing this kind of teaching since the Garden of Eden. From that day to this, humans have lusted to know secret paths that lead to transcendent power – power over supernatural forces, power to coerce the unseen world to give us what we want, power to know the future. That is the heart of the occult. And the occult has entered many of our churches.

For most of us, the word "occult" conjures up images of Ouija boards, witches, Tarot cards and Halloween. These are cheap distractions designed to keep us from understanding the real darkness that is overwhelming us. That darkness is far more subtle. It is "occult" in the original meaning of the word which is "hidden".

Hidden secrets of darkness have breached the church in a number of ways. Sadly, the Pentecostal movement has played a significant part in this. Because of its historic weakness in expository Bible teaching and preaching, and its emphasis on "signs and wonders", the occult, packaged as the "Anointing of the Holy Spirit," has taken control of many in the church, introducing evil spirits who present themselves as the Spirit of God.

For too many, the Baptism of the Holy Spirit has become an initiatory rite meant to lead the novice into power with no thought about repentance from sin, love for Jesus or obeying Him in discipleship. Due to general naivete, Biblical ignorance and Satanic illusion, there is no thought about the true source of the power that is being received. If it feels good and exalts a person it must be from God. If a miracle really happens, it must be God who did it.

Many ignorant people are so anxious to share the initiatory rite and the power that they think goes with it, that they are willing to force "speaking in tongues", urging neophytes to just start babbling in order to "prime the pump". At best, this is foolishness, at worst, such people are unwitting accomplices of darkness.

A few months ago I was in a morning worship service where a man got up to lead communion. There was no time for serious spiritual self-examination and repentance. Instead, with a great emotional rant, he informed the congregation that if anyone was ill that person should eat the bread in faith and it would heal them. After the service I confronted him. I have studied the occult for decades. Though I think he was ignorant of the fact, what that man was doing could have come straight out of ritual magic.

I believe that there has been direct occult Satanic influence in the charismatic church. And I want to suggest that there was a specific time when it entered. Could it be possible that it began in Southern California during the late 1960's and focused on the Jesus Movement, inserting itself into that movement from the very start?

Let me be quick to say that all of the Jesus Movement was not Satanic. God was at work in much of it. However, I believe that the Powers of Darkness inserted themselves in amazing ways. And I will ask a controversial question: Could they have entered through a single man named Lonnie Frisbee?

Frisbee was a hippy who claimed to have met "Jesus" on an LSD trip. During that experience, he said that "Jesus" had given him "Holy Spirit Anointing" for power and had told him that he would reach many thousands.

Frisbee entered the ministry at 17 years old in the late 1960's. He continued using LSD for spiritual illumination for a period after his purported salvation experience. Though, publicly, Frisbee condemned homosexuality, secretly he was a practicing homosexual who continued in that lifestyle during his entire "ministry". Tragically, later in life, he died of AIDS. For a time Frisbee was married to a woman he had met before his conversion experience, but they divorced in 1973 because of her infidelity with a pastor.

Lonnie Frisbee had tremendous spiritual power and he had a deep influence on important Christian leaders of that time. It was Frisbee who led many into the so-called "signs and wonders" ministry. Later, when the truth about his life came out, some of these men disavowed and separated from him.

For years, Lonnie Frisbee's activities and "power" caused people to be misled and brought division in the Body of Christ, especially in the churches where he personally ministered. He had real "spiritual" power and many Christian leaders wanted that power. Later Frisbee complained that they had used him. All they had cared about was the "stuff that he could bring".

And he did deliver the "stuff". Many, many times Frisbee would stand before congregations and simply wave his hand. Instantly, huge numbers of people would fall to the floor babbling in "tongues", barking and laughing. From various reports, real healings took place. Many thousands claimed to have "accepted Jesus". But the focus of his "revival" ministry was on the power of experience.

While few leaders from that period want to talk about him, Frisbee's influence on the charismatic movement has been deep. It can be seen in counterfeit revivals in Toronto, Pensacola, the so-called Kansas City prophets and elsewhere. The difference between real revival and Satanically influenced revival is very, very great. We are fooled by Satanic power and revival because we are ignorant of both the Bible and church history. When people with no discernment want to see "Power", Satan's wolves are ready to oblige. In this way, Lucifer has been welcomed into many churches and homes and continues to reside there.

At Lonnie Frisbee's funeral, a leading charismatic pastor described him as a tragic "Samson-like" character with great power and even greater weaknesses. This is delusion. It was a sad attempt to excuse lack of discernment and lust for spiritual power among those leaders who chose to place themselves under Frisbee's influence.

Where do we see a "Samson model" for Christian ministry in the New Testament? Precisely nowhere. No Christian leader is perfect. All are sinners saved by Grace. All must lead lives of daily repentance. But to live a life of secret sin, constantly saying one thing and doing another without any public repentance, displaying strange power that focuses on the one wielding it instead of Jesus, a power that brings false revival that has nothing to do with repentance from sin and everything to do with self-centered experience, all of this describes a wolf and his or her occult "ministry". When ecstasy and "signs and wonders" are the measure of truth, wolves will run free, glutting themselves on the sheep and the Pentecostal/Charismatic movement has an abundance of such wolves.

I believe in the power of the Holy Spirit. I believe that He does miracles of healing today. I have experienced such a miracle myself under the ministry of a humble man of God. I believe there are people who have the gift of tongues. But to assume that all miracles and spiritual gifts are from God is naïve, Biblically ignorant and dangerous.

However, Satanically empowered signs and wonders are hardly the only way that the occult is entering Christian churches. Recently, I learned of an evangelical church in San Francisco that has incorporated the teachings of eclectic, esoteric occultist, G. I. Gurdjieff into their counseling ministry. This church utilizes what is called the Enneagram of Personality developed by Oscar Ichazo and Claudio Naranjo, two South American new-age occultists who created this model as a means of self-development and self-understanding. It was based on the work of G.I. Gurdjieff and Fritz Perls (founder of Gestalt Therapy). The key word is "self". Gurdjieff prided himself on having discovered a short-cut to enlightenment.

The Enneagram of Personality, though debunked by traditional psychology and banned by the Roman Catholic Church, has gained a foothold in the evangelical world through the teachings of Father Richard Rohr, a self-proclaimed "mystic" who has been a great influence on former mega-church pastor and best-selling author, Rob Bell and Emergent Church leader Brian McLaren, both of whom are probably ignorant of the occult influences of their mentor.

Obviously, this is not the only way that the occult is entering churches. (No, I don't believe for a minute that when a church has a Halloween party that a door is opened through which the occult enters in. When we think in such simplistic ways we are blind to the real darkness.) Many will find what I'm going to say next very controversial. It is my opinion that one way the occult - defined as strange, hidden powers that are not of God - can enter a church or Christian organization is through sexual immorality of every kind among church leaders.

For instance, within various ancient shamanic traditions, it has been considered highly desirable for a homosexual to be the shaman. It was believed that a homosexual combined both the male and female principles and, therefore, would provide a much stronger conduit for spirit power. These traditions did not embrace such a philosophy lightly and neither should we.

But the issue is not just about homosexual immorality. For thousands of years there has been a clear sexual component to much ritual magic. Coitus by a man and woman was the symbolic act of joining the male deity with the female deity in order to gain power on Earth. We see it from the worship of Baal and Ashtoreth to the temple prostitutes of the Apostle Paul's day, straight down to ours with the ceremonial magic of Aleister Crowley, L. Ron Hubbard (before he founded Scientology) and Jack Parsons (pioneer rocket fuel scientist and one of the founders of JPL). In 1946 Parsons and Hubbard did a series of magic rituals designed to open the supernatural door in America to a powerful feminine evil spirit that they called Babalon (sic).

The Second Principle of Hermetic philosophy is the Principle of Correspondence. "As above, so below; as below, so above." As far as sexual union is concerned, this means that fornication by a man and woman can represent the fornication of "gods". In the physical linking, a conduit is created for "heavenly" power to come to Earth.

Child molestation is a form of child sacrifice, which has been at the center of some occult systems for eons. Demons are at the heart of it because Satan hates children. When a Christian in leadership enters into any kind of illicit sexual union, whatever that union might be, it is very likely that such acts have a much deeper meaning than we have imagined. There is every possibility that they create conduits for dark powers to enter straight into a church or organization. By such acts, the authority that has been vested in the individual is given over to Satan. The person becomes a slave along with all those who follow him.

Based on this understanding, I believe that when spiritual wolves sexually abuse their followers the spiritual darkness around them grows exponentially. We have been so programmed by Hollywood to think that frightening occult power appears in certain physical ways, that when we don't see those expected manifestations we are blind to the subtle soul enslavement that is actually taking place.

For a long time Satan's power has been manifest through wolves who belong to him, but are so self-deluded that they are unconscious of the fact. Very likely, Lonnie Frisbee was deluded in this way. A false Jesus gave him real power. However, as we approach the End of Days, we will see a new and far more dangerous variety of wolf arise among the Perfectly Possessed.

CHAPTER THIRTY-FIVE

Reward and Punishment

Hollywood is a strange place to work. It goes without saying that it isn't like working in a church or Christian organization. You hear things that you wouldn't hear in other places. People tell you things that they don't feel free to share with others because they fear being labeled insane. Probably they think anyone who works in Hollywood is insane already, so what's the danger?

Over the years, I have received disturbing reports. They haven't come with information that could be verified, but they have come from people I trust who have been Christian leaders. Based on these reports, I believe that for decades, men and women have been established in the evangelical Christian church, its schools, businesses and ministries, who are willing, dedicated servants of the Prince of Darkness. (They are in the Roman Catholic Church as well, but others have written about that, particularly Father Malachi Martin.)

These wolves are true occultists in the sense that they are perfectly possessed initiates into the profound depths of Satan. They believe that Lucifer is the giver of all wisdom and have experienced his power. They view the human race as a race of slaves. They think that because they follow Lucifer, they are destined for greatness and to be the rulers of the earth. They hold true follow-ers of Jesus in contempt, because they view Jesus as a weakling.

These wolves pervert the truth, not through the razzle-dazzle of a Holy Spirit Show with babble, barking and laughter, but through the subtlety of their secret perversions and worldli-ness. They worship their Dark King. Like Balaam, who guided Israel's enemies to pervert God's people through lust leading them into idolatry, these Masters of the Hidden Arts of Darkness care-fully weave the idolatrous lying values of Satan into the Church. With great subtlety, they have turned whole schools, universities, organizations and churches away from following the Lord.

The false God they consciously present to the world is the Serpent himself cloaked as an angel of wisdom, light and healing and given the name "Jesus" or "Holy Spirit". In this way, many false "christs" are being worshipped. (In some so-called "contem-porary" church services with contemporary "worship" it is possible to go through an entire service without ever hearing the Name of Jesus.)

Who is the God of the Bible to these occultist wolves? He is a minor deity who will be overcome, a lesser power who by his niggling laws, has destroyed the true freedom and knowledge that their god, Lucifer, has always wanted to bestow upon the human race. They are actively preparing for the Final Confrontation, which they believe their side will win. They are deluded, but don't think for a minute that they have no evidence of Satan's power. In their positions of authority, these wolves are enjoying the tangible benefits of his rulership right now.

Does Satan really reward people? There have been books and plays about the glittering rewards given to those who consign their souls to him, but is there any reality behind such stories? Is there any proof?

I have a friend who was a huge film star in the 1960's. Successful as he was, he was miserable. At a certain point he gave his life to Jesus Christ. Let's just say that it didn't help his career. He came to realize that he had been a servant of darkness. My friend told me about some of the "benefits" that he had received while he was an enslaved "celebrity".

One day he was on a flight to a particular city. Of course, he was flying first class. Serving on the plane was a beautiful flight attendant. When the plane landed and they got off, he and this flight attendant went straight to a hotel where they had sex. Amazing as it may seem, during the entire time they were together they never spoke a single world to each other, not from when they were on the plane until it was all over and they parted. There was no invitation to the hotel, no pretense at a romantic evening. Without speaking, they left the airport together, had sex, then went their ways, never to see each other again.

My friend told me that while he was unknowingly living for Satan, he experienced a number of these "benefits", which included great professional success in Hollywood. But the memories of such "benefits" have haunted him. He has received the forgiveness of God, but he can't forget those women and the kind of influence he had in their lives. He prays for them.

Satan rewards those who follow him and his rewards are real. It is a form of payment. Ultimately his rewards lead to hell, but for the moment the wages of sin are sweet. Satan knows the people who belong to him and those who don't.

A number of months ago, I received an email from a Christian man who told me a strange story. For some insane reason, his teenage son, who is also a Christian, decided to experiment with dimethyltryptamine, one of the most powerful hallucinogenic drugs in the world. It is also produced naturally in the human brain. DMT as it is known, is an essential ingredient in the brew called ayahuasca that has been used by Amazonian shamans for centuries to open the door to other dimensions for the purposes of divination and healing. Those who have used it say that it brings an experience of a reality like no other.

Upon taking the drug, this young man found himself in a terrifying world surrounded by strange beings. They told him that he was a Christian and demanded to know what he was doing there. When he couldn't give an answer, they attacked and severely beat him. When he came out from the drug he was terrified by the reality of the horrible experience. He had entered a dimension of evil and the beings that attacked him were like creatures described in centuries-old myths.

In confronting wolves, not only are we dealing with human antagonists, but with the principalities and powers of the spirit world that subtly guide and strengthen them. The ultimate Day of the Wolf is yet to come.

CHAPTER THIRTY-SIX

The Fruit of Life and Death

I'd never met anyone like him. He was the first man I'd ever known who appeared to me to be totally committed to subtle evil. Was he a criminal? No, not as far as the law was concerned. He was the sleek and wealthy owner of his own company. He had private planes, a trophy wife, businesses overseas and a beautiful home in an LA suburb. To pay for graduate school, I took a job working for him as marketing director. I didn't know what I was getting into.

Very soon I came to understand what kind of man he was. He was shrewd and cared nothing about other people. He was a decorated WWII combat veteran, a former officer, who had created a male dominated company to the point of having a club room for his execs, complete with bar, pool table and pictures of naked women on the wall. From the start, we didn't get along well. I worked there for only a year and hated every minute of it.

This man enjoyed finding weaknesses in people and subtly exploiting them. He was a charming manipulator who could become abusive in a split second. Everything from the products he sold to his personal life was a fraud and a lie.

When you entered his building a kind of oppressive pall would settle over your spirit. He claimed to be highly successful in the import export business. He wasn't. He had made his millions selling a virtually worthless set of expensive books that purported to tell poor people how they could make millions in import/export.

His trophy wife had been his mistress when he was married to his first wife. Since he had divorced number one and married that mistress, he had established a new mistress and wife number two hated it. She came into the company almost every day and almost every day when she arrived, she had been drinking. I had never met an angrier woman.

This man was the perfect example of what the Apostle Paul meant when he wrote, "The wages of sin is death..." A dozen years after I left the company, his trophy wife murdered him. He is the best example in my experience of a person who was a Born Wolf. Soil, seed and plant, that man belonged to Satan and the fruit of his life was lies and destruction.

If you are following Jesus, what kind of fruit will appear on the vine of your life? The Bible is very specific about the fruit that comes from Heaven.

Galatians 5:22-26 says: **But the fruit of the Spirit is love, joy, peace, longsuffering, kindness, goodness, faithfulness, gentleness, self-control. Against such there is no law. And those who are Christ's have crucified the flesh with its passions and desires. If we live in the Spirit, let us also walk in the Spirit. Let us not become conceited, provoking one another, envying one another.**

238

Based upon this passage, we can understand what wolf fruit will look like. Just turn the list upside down. Satanic fruit will be the opposite of what the Holy Spirit gives.

Instead of self-sacrificing love (agape) which is the first element of the fruit of God's Spirit, there will be love for self and the willingness to use and sacrifice others to achieve selfish goals.

Instead of joy, there will be periodic moments of hilarity usually at the expense of others, coupled with an endless hunger for satisfaction and personal fulfillment, which are never found.

Instead of peace, there will be constant fear and insecurity, which will be communicated to everyone unfortunate enough to be inflicted with the wolf's presence.

Instead of longsuffering patience, there will be an ever-unpredictable short fuse that triggers episodes of bad temper that might be expressed in anything from brutal sarcasm to denigrating verbal abuse and even physical violence.

Instead of kindness, there will be harshness with little or no praise or reward for the work and sacrifice of others. When people fail there will be no real mercy. At best, a wolf will wait for the opportune moment to use their failures against them.

Instead of goodness (which is virtue), there will be self-serving meanness that takes satisfaction in the stumbling mistakes of those who are considered weaker.

Instead of faithfulness, there will be untrustworthiness in word and deed. Promises and commitments will be made and broken. The breakage will be overlooked, excused and justified or blamed on others.

Instead of gentleness, there will be the heavy hand of authority that inflicts stifling control.

Instead of self-control, there will be addiction to the fulfillment of lusts.

The Satanic fruit that grows from a wolf-vine is fed to the people closest to the wolf. Following the guidance of their father, Satan, wolves exalt the flesh with its passions and desires.

I have never met a spiritual wolf who was not conceited. The Greek word that is translated conceited could also be translated "desiring vainglory". Vainglory is empty glory, glory that you give yourself and expect others to give to you, though you haven't earned it. Due to their exalted self-image, wolves are quick to challenge anyone they think isn't giving them proper respect. Because of their insecurity, they are deeply envious of others.

Those who live and walk in the Spirit, those who are experiencing the true fruit of the Spirit, will not manifest the fruit of wolves. The fruit of the Spirit goes hand-in-hand with humility and faithfulness.

Take a good look at the people closest to a leader. What condition are they in? Are they damaged and fearful? Are they silent, afraid to say anything? Is there a spiritual cloud over them, or do you sense the love and joy of Jesus? Are they angry? This is the first place where fruit should be examined. If there isn't some good fruit apparent in the lives closest to a leader, don't fool yourself into thinking that you will find it elsewhere.

But as you do your examination, keep some facts in mind. Look at long-term patterns of behavior. Individuals and families can have bad days, weeks and even years. There are many faithful men and women of God, true servants of Jesus, who are brokenhearted and struggling because of attacks that have taken place within their families and attacks from outside by wolves. With the best efforts and sacrificial love, children walk away from the Lord, husbands and wives prove unfaithful and trusted friends become traitors. Also, through no fault of their own, some faithful leaders are surrounded by unfaithful staff. *Do not jump to conclusions based on wrong evidence. You will add to the suffering of a saint and God will hold you accountable for that.*

Remember that God has a broken heart over the sins of his children and a broken heart is a gift from Him that can bring great fruit for His Kingdom. So don't stand in judgment over the tragedies in the lives of others. Be careful that your concern about wolves doesn't destroy the mercy and compassion that God wants to show through you. In the way that you judge others, you will be judged. If you are harsh and doctrinaire, you shouldn't be in a position to lead or make decisions about leaders. Very likely you will reject God's true servants. And there is every possibility that you are a wolf.

Is the fruit of the Holy Spirit being manifest in your life? If it isn't, you will have no ability to discern wolves. As you search for a godly leader, look first for the eternal fruit that counts, the fruit of Galatians 5:22-26. Only in that context should you examine his or her various publicly acknowledged gifts and external accomplishments. Remember that God's strength is made perfect in weakness. Very often the Fruit of Heaven grows from a broken heart.

CHAPTER THIRTY-SEVEN

All That's Fine, But...

...HOW do we measure success?

The question came from a good friend who truly loves the Lord. We had been talking about what the New Testament means by fruit and how it should apply to Christian leadership. My friend is retired after many years in business management and has served on church elder boards. He has a lifetime behind him of measuring success and failure in quantitative terms.

In our discussion about wolves, I've tried to give a fairly extensive view of what failure in ministry looks like. And too much of it looks a lot like what many people call success. The New Testament says that some of Jesus' servants plant seeds, others nurture and cultivate them, while still others reap the harvest. Everyone wants to be in on the harvest. Planting and nurturing isn't nearly as glamorous. Part of our problem is that, because of selfishness and impatience, we insist on demanding immediate harvest results from the entire process.

Stepping away from measuring spiritual success using quantitative methods is difficult when you have to figure out how many bulletins to print and how to create a realistic budget based on projected contributions, etc. It's difficult when *everybody* is *watching* and *counting everything*. It takes a lot of courage and discipline to step away from the business model as a measuring stick while still using it for practical necessities. It takes faith to keep on going when the chairs and offering plates are empty. It takes faith and maturity not to trust in the measurements (whether they are large or small) when you have to report those measurements to various governing bodies.

We've brought most of this on ourselves because of our passionate belief that buildings with mortgages and all of the accoutrements and religious infrastructure that goes with them are necessary for ministry. The greater the investment, the more courage it's going to take to free your mind from the metrics of fruit measurement.

How does Jesus measure success? I think He gave us a very specific statement about that. It's found in Matthew 25:31-41:

"When the Son of Man comes in His glory, and all the holy angels with Him, then He will sit on the throne of His glory. All the nations will be gathered before Him, and He will separate them one from another, as a shepherd divides his sheep from the goats. And He will set the sheep on His right hand, but the goats on the left. Then the King will say to those on His right hand, 'Come, you blessed of My Father, inherit the kingdom prepared for you from the foundation of the world: for I was hungry and you gave Me food; I was thirsty and you gave Me drink; I was a stranger and you

took Me in; I was naked and you clothed Me; I was sick and you visited Me; I was in prison and you came to Me.'

"Then the righteous will answer Him, saying, 'Lord, when did we see You hungry and feed You, or thirsty and give You drink? When did we see You a stranger and take You in, or naked and clothe You? Or when did we see You sick, or in prison, and come to You?' And the King will answer and say to them, 'Assuredly, I say to you, inasmuch as you did it to one of the least of these My brethren, you did it to Me.'

Wouldn't you say that's a rather clear statement of priorities? It fits in perfectly with Jesus' statement about who He was and what he came to do found in Luke 4:18-19:

"The Spirit of the Lord is upon Me, because He has anointed Me to preach the gospel to the poor; He has sent Me to heal the brokenhearted, To proclaim liberty to the captives and recovery of sight to the blind, to set at liberty those who are oppressed; to proclaim the acceptable year of the Lord."

Those words describe His whole ministry. They describe the ministry of the 70 disciples that He sent out into Israel. They describe the ministry of the Apostles that He sent out after His resurrection. They delineate the message and the means – going out. So to the question, how do we measure success, the first answer is that success looks like "going into all the world". Somewhere in the past, the church changed the word from "go" to "come". This shift in emphasis gives us an excuse to live in our comforts and go nowhere.

So how do you measure success in a leader, a church or a ministry? Is the "view" of that person or group directed outward or inward? Is a church, a school, a ministry, even a mission board, truly oriented outward? How do they spend their money? How much of it is oriented to reaching the world both far and near outside the church doors? Does a church care about its immediate community? Does it have any idea about what that community needs physically as well as spiritually? Wolves really don't care about anything beyond the foyer…unless there's money and fame in it.

Many years ago we were members of a large inner city church that was quite old. Over the decades the neighborhood had changed dramatically. In the 1950's it had been a bedroom community and the church was filled with young, white families. When we were there the neighborhood was dangerous. Most members had moved away and commuted from their homes in safe suburbs.

The church had an excellent basketball court. Some of the younger members wanted to reach the at-risk youth of the neighborhood. They wanted to start an afternoon basketball ministry. The church leaders refused. Too much risk, insurance problems, etc. The truth was that they had absolutely no interest in their immediate community. They were a suburban club with an inner city location.

My wife is a fine artist, a painter. Her heart was for the fine art community of Los Angles. She helped establish a group for painters, some were believers in Jesus and many were not. The purpose was to be an outreach to those who didn't know the Lord. She arranged for small art exhibits in one of the outer rooms of the church that bordered on the street. She had approval from the pastoral staff and, of course, she was very careful about the kind of art that was hung to make sure it wasn't offensive. The Sunday School class that met in that room once a week hated this use of their space.

A Christian artist came in for a special exhibit. He had painted Jesus on the cross. The class felt that the image was far too violent. They covered it. Also, the kind of people who were coming onto the campus for these exhibits didn't look like good Christians. They were artists from the LA community. Some were dressed in leather. They had piercings and wore odd metal decorations. Soon the art exhibits were no longer allowed and the outreach ended.

What does success look like? It looks like leaving the safety of the building and taking risks for the sake of the Good News about Jesus. "GO into all the world..."

But there is a second measurement that I propose in determining success within a church or ministry. Is real discipleship taking place?

Discipleship! That word has become a cliché, hasn't it? Has there been any period of church history where there has been more talk about discipleship and less of it actually happening? Jesus told His Church to go out and make disciples to Him. A disciple is much more than a simple believer. A disciple has committed his life in absolute surrender to the King to obey and follow Him forever no matter what happens and where He may lead. It means following Him into increasing spiritual maturity. But how does that happen?

To make a disciple means to teach and instruct. In a Biblical context it implies a unique relationship. In the Old Testament there is Elijah with Elisha. In the New, we see Jesus with His disciples, Paul with Timothy and Titus, Barnabas with John Mark, etc. I believe that these offer a pattern for how discipleship is supposed to work in the Body of Christ.

A believer who has followed Jesus for years in absolute surrender commits to being involved in the life of a younger believer for an extended period of time in order to help that person grow in wisdom and knowledge into a mature relationship of love and trust with Jesus so that there is fruit for the Kingdom of God. It means a commitment of time, the commitment of one life to another. While groups and group teaching play an important part, Biblical "discipling" happens one on one.

Also, for discipling to work it requires a range of ages and spiritual experience. Can a younger person disciple an older person? Certainly, when that older person is newer to the faith. But generally speaking, older more mature Christians should be discipling those who are younger. Is this happening? I have had many wonderful teachers, but in my whole experience in the church since childhood I don't remember seeing this kind of one-on-one discipling except in a few isolated cases. Sometimes an older pastor will disciple a younger person just entering the ministry, but within the congregation this is rare.

Why isn't it happening? Perhaps there are several reasons. First, people are just too busy. Spending time in a discipling relationship isn't important to them. They depend on church ser-

248

vices, programs and various media to teach them what they need to know. Second, people are too mobile to be discipled. Many of us don't stay in one place long enough to develop any deep relationships. And even if we do, we lead physically isolated lives. So-called "social media" has increased this physical isolation. Nothing can replace sitting across from a person talking face-to-face.

But there are other reasons that discipleship isn't happening that are even more serious. The sad reality is that many people who are older in years with long attendance in church, who ought to be discipling others, have never matured in their faith. After decades as Christians, they are still selfish babies who need discipling themselves.

But perhaps the greatest barrier that stands against discipling today in American evangelical Christianity is the almost total isolation of age groups. This is largely due to Hollywood and pop culture that thirsts for control of the youth market. With great diligence and massive investment, they have stripped young people from the larger society and re-formed them into a homogeneous youth subculture for the purpose of selling products designed specifically to appeal to the immature and insecure and then to perpetuate that immaturity and insecurity as long as possible.

Marketers define the prime subgroup as those who are 18-34 years old. In centuries past, adulthood was expected of a person by their mid-teens. In our segmented society, adulthood is often never reached and certainly not within the 18-34 year-old category. This same rigid market segmentation and the purveying of products to a homogeneous youth subculture has taken control of the church. In many churches very few gray heads are visible and this is by design, while in other churches few young people attend after they are old enough to leave home.

It is not by accident that many young people leave the church altogether when they reach the 18-34 year old bracket. The impact on Biblical discipleship and ultimately on ministry has been devastating. As far as Satan is concerned, the strategy is logical. Divide the mature from the immature. Isolate the age groups based on what is fashionable at the moment in music and teaching style. Further isolate young people by destroying their families. Discipleship programs, books and dvd's are fine, but if that is the only "discipleship" taking place it will fail. And, clearly, by the spiritual and moral state of the evangelical church it has failed.

So I propose that the second measure in determining whether a church or leader is successful is the commitment of that group or individual to true discipleship. Is a church actively helping young believers find mature Christians who will walk beside them, leading them closer to Jesus and out into the world in service to Him? Is a leader committed to establishing and overseeing that kind of discipleship ministry under the Power of the Holy Spirit? Is a church or ministry truly multi-generational? It needs to be in order to accomplish the work that Jesus assigned. When you find a person or organization committed to this kind of ministry, it is a mark of spiritual success.

Above all else, look for love for Jesus and each other. Look for love for a world lost in such terrible need, love not just in words, but in actions.

PART THREE

Wolves – The Confrontation

In this final section, I'm going to spend a lot more time discussing the preparation to confront a wolf than I will about the actual confrontation. Every situation is different. There is simply no way to give guidance that will cover every case. But there are principles that will hold true no matter the situation.

A confrontation with a true spiritual wolf is spiritual warfare against the Powers of Darkness. We need all the wisdom, strength, maturity and Holy Spirit empowerment that is available to us. Therefore, preparation is just as important as the confrontation, because it deals with our spiritual lives.

If you are carrying wounds, preparation can be the beginning of healing. All of us are wounded in this world. How we deal with our wounds is what counts. They will either destroy us or God will use them for His glory. We can't control what a wolf does. Only God can do that. But we can control what we do, including how we go into and come out of a confrontation.

The U.S. Navy SEALs spend months getting ready for operations that will take minutes. They do everything possible to know the enemy and his fortifications. They may build models.

Over and over, they do run-throughs of the attack until every man is prepared to accomplish what is expected of him.

Yet, with all of that meticulous preparation, the SEALs know that what ultimately happens in combat will be unpredictable. Though they have studied what they consider to be every possible configuration, it's likely that something unexpected will happen. Consequently, they have fallback plans. But the preparation of a SEAL is not for a single mission. It's a lifestyle of being ready to face the unknown.

Should less be true of servant warriors who walk through this world following our King?

CHAPTER THIRTY-EIGHT

Of Giants and Wolves

We think of it as a children's story. But we leave it in childhood at our great loss. Buried in it are important facts that we need to understand as we prepare for a confrontation with a spiritual wolf. Please take out your Bible and read that story again right now. It's found in I Samuel 17. It's the story of David and Goliath.

Did you read it?

The facts of the case are simple. The entire Israelite army, which included trained soldiers led by King Saul, was totally stymied by one man. Granted, at almost ten feet tall, covered with metal and armed to the teeth, Goliath was a human war machine, a walking tank. Every day when he rumbled out onto the field and started raging, it was an effective form of psychological warfare. It was terrifying.

Then came David.

Goliath was a wolf times 100 and standing behind him was an entire army of wolves. And what was standing behind David? Cowards and more wolves. His brothers were cowards who resented him. The rest of the Israelite army were cowards too. And they were led by a wolf-coward, King Saul. That Saul would let a teenager go out and face a giant alone, speaks to his utter coward-ice and stupendous lack of Kingly leadership. The fact that David was willing to go alone should have shamed Saul into doing it himself, but it didn't.

So the situation was somewhat grim. Based on any objective assessment, David was worse than alone. Does that feel like your situation? He found courage and so can you. Let's look at the six sources of that courage.

The first source: Knowing God.

David had spent years alone in the wilderness tending his father's sheep. But there were many shepherds in Israel who had spent years alone. The difference was that David had used the time to seek God's Presence, desiring to know Him, talking to Him and singing songs to Him. (By the way, the right music is extremely important to warriors.) In all of his loneliness, David got to know God. To know our loving God is the greatest source of courage, but you have to spend time alone with Him to do it. Is that what you are doing?

The second source: Knowing God's Word.

It's clear from the songs that he wrote that this young man knew the Scriptures as they existed during his time. He had so little compared to what we have today. Nevertheless, God's Word impacted his life on the deepest creative level. This led him to struggle with many issues in his poetry, applying His knowledge of God and the Scriptures to crisis issues with great spiritual maturity and creative sophistication. He was a student of God's Word. In that Word, He could see the history of God's faithfulness to those who trust in Him. Are you a serious student of God's Word?

The third source: Passing smaller tests.

In his solitude, David had faced dangerous tests where his life had been at stake. He didn't run from them as many shepherds had. Why? Two reasons: He saw God's Hand and Presence in the middle of them and he had deep compassion for the vulnerable flock. David considered himself a sheep of God's flock, following Him through the wilderness of this world. He knew where his strength had come from to defeat the lion and the bear and gave God the glory. He was a humble young man who could look back on God's faithfulness in trials. As you look back, do you see God's faithfulness in the trials of your life? Do you really care about His flock, the Body of Christ?

The fourth source: Holy Spirit anointing.

David was ready to confront Goliath because at his anointing by the prophet Samuel (in chapter 16), the Holy Spirit had come upon him. David was called to the battle with Goliath by God Himself. When he walked out onto that field, saw the monster and heard his blasphemy, he knew that this battle was assigned to him. Have you experienced the anointing of the Holy Spirit through absolute surrender to Jesus' Lordship and Will? The evidence is not found in any particular spiritual gift. The evidence is love, humility and obedience, which is the mind of Christ being formed in you. Nothing less will prepare you to face a giant. Without it, you will lack wisdom and lurch into conflicts that are not meant for you.

The fifth source: Concern for God's reputation more than his own safety.

David was angered by the way God's Name was being dragged in the dirt by this gigantic wolf. He was angered because God's people were letting it happen. That righteous anger empowered the strength of faith. David's statement to Goliath rings down through history as one of the great statements of courage and faith.

"You come to me with a sword, with a spear, and with a javelin. But I come to you in the name of the LORD of hosts, the God of the armies of Israel, whom you have defied. This day the LORD will deliver you into my hand, and I will strike you and take your head from you. And this day I will give the carcasses of the camp of the Philistines to the birds of the air and the wild beasts of the earth, that all the earth may know that there is a God in Israel. Then all this assembly shall know that the LORD does not save with sword and spear; for the battle is the LORD's, and He will give you into our hands." (1 Sam 17:45-47)

How could David say such outrageous things and be sure of them? It sounds like a boast and that's exactly what it was. But he wasn't boasting about himself and his own abilities, he was boasting about his God. He was boasting about God's greatness and power. He was giving all glory to the King of Heaven. That is the only way to begin the confrontation with a wolf.

Many Christians are quick to take offense when a non-Christian uses Jesus' Name inappropriately. But they let spiritual wolves take His Name in vain in the most hellish ways week in and week out and never say a word. Do you understand the difference?

The sixth source: He understood and
accepted his weakness.

David knew the secret that Paul wrote about many centuries later when God told him, **"My grace is sufficient for you, for My strength is made perfect in weakness. Therefore most gladly I will rather boast in my infirmities, that the power of Christ may rest upon me. Therefore I take pleasure in infirmities, in reproaches, in needs, in persecutions, in distresses, for Christ's sake. For when I am weak, then I am strong."** (2 Corinthians 12:9-10)

David went into the battle with Goliath knowing that he was utterly weak, that there was no strength in him to accomplish anything. Compared to that giant, as far as armament was concerned, he was naked. And he was willing to face Goliath naked. I'm sure that he had to lay down his staff to put a stone in his sling. As he rushed forward, his whole life depended on a single throw. There was no backup plan. One small turn of Goliath's head at the last moment and David would have been doomed. In absolute weakness, it was all or nothing.

This is the secret to facing the giants and the wolves that God allows into our lives. It is the secret to victorious spiritual warfare and it's all through the Bible. We see it in Gideon who had to face an army of 120,000 with 300 men because God wanted him to be weak enough so he didn't depend on human strength. We see it in Daniel's three friends when they refused to bow to the golden statue of Nebuchadnezzar. In utter weakness, for the glory of God, they were willing to be bound and thrown into the fire. We see it in Esther who, all alone, risked her life for her people. Most of all, we see it in Jesus who made Himself weak so that we could be made strong forever.

Here is the most important point: When David faced Goliath, he wasn't just facing a very angry giant. He was facing Satan himself. The raging that came from Goliath's mouth against God and his people was the raging of the devil that had possessed him. His desire to destroy God's people was and is the desire of Satan. In thousands of years, that has not changed.

That day in ancient Israel, David's battle with Satan was the Lord's battle. It was the Lord's pleasure to show His Glory by defeating a monster and all of his hosts with a single stone. It was His pleasure to use a very young man who was not afraid to be weak. Your battle with a spiritual wolf is the same. Are you willing to be utterly weak and naked so that God's Power can be manifest through you whether in life or in death? It is the bottom line of absolute surrender.

Remember the lessons of David.

CHAPTER THIRTY-NINE

Why Do It?

Confronting a spiritual wolf is the last thing that most people want to do. Personally, I hate confrontations of any kind, even minor ones. I will avoid them if at all possible. Confrontations take energy and if the issue is important, they take special preparation. Always, there is emotion involved, which can include deep hurt and anger. Confrontations can be dangerous.

To make a confrontation with a spiritual wolf even more distasteful, you may feel certain that it will do no good. Very likely, you know the wolf and think you can predict the response that you are going to receive. As you consider a confrontation, it's clear that you could be hurt even more, while the wolf may not be damaged at all.

Goliath just seems too big. That's why most Christians choose either to remain enslaved in the agonizing situation, doing and saying nothing while they grow more and more depressed and angry, or they disengage and walk away in silence. This is why so many wolves continue unchallenged. When they are never confronted, their sense of empowerment grows and their attacks will become more vicious. What if David had not appeared on that battlefield? God's people would have been destroyed. This very day, God's Name is being dragged through the sewer and His people are being destroyed for lack of a David.

Be clear about this. Your fear and despair, your sense of futility, are temptations of Satan. He wants you to see a mirage and think that it is real. He wants you to believe in his mirage more than you believe in the Power of God. It is his way of trying to gain control of your life. As you watch the wolf, he wants you to do nothing, while your hurt and anger increase. In this way he will strip you of all strength and usefulness for the Kingdom of God.

God allows wolves into our lives. Dealing with them is a test on many levels. Is Jesus' Name and reputation being dragged through the dirt by the on-going actions of a leader? Does that anger you? Are the sheep of Jesus' flock being wounded and led away from Him? Does that break your heart? Are you called to do what you can to confront the situation? Does that frighten you? Will you accept the risks and responsibilities of a confrontation? Does that weigh heavy on your soul? All of these are the normal feelings of a warrior for Jesus who faces a confrontation.

Your Goliath may not come down with a single stone. It's likely that you will get many stones hurled back at you. In a local church, confronting a wolf can mean that the congregation ostracizes you. This may include rejection by old friends. You won't be attacked by the wolf alone, but also by the pack that surrounds and protects him. You will be slandered.

In a Christian business or para-church ministry, confronting a wolf can cost you your job. You may become an instant pariah to those who are fearful and weak. They may justify their cowardly support of the wolf by attacking you. Some kinds of confrontations may present legal issues. What has happened may re-quire the involvement of law enforcement. You may be viewed as a traitor.

None of this matters, compared to obeying the Lord, de-fending His Name and reputation and standing up for the wholeness and purity of His Body, the Church. None of it mat-ters if you are called to risk your life in defending Jesus' flock.

Confronting spiritual wolves is a vital act that should be taking place in the church today. It doesn't happen because of ig-norance and fear. Most of all, it doesn't happen because of lack of faith. If false teaching, lies and abuse are being perpetrated by a person in spiritual authority and you choose not to confront the wolf because you are afraid, you need to deal with that before the Lord.

James 4:17 says: **Therefore, to him who knows to do good and does not do it, to him it is sin.**

Confronting wrong in the Power of the Holy Spirit is an act of faith, because when you confront a spiritual wolf, you may have only one Person standing by your side, but that Person will be Jesus, the King.

Having said all of that, remember that every battle is not your battle. God will give wisdom about which ones have been assigned to you. If you have a volatile personality and a "short fuse", you need to be especially concerned about your choice of battles and how you fight them. With the best of intentions, you can do great damage.

The wrong kind of confrontation at the wrong time can set back the work of the Lord and empower Satan and his wolves even more. But if God has brought you to a battleground and given you the responsibility, He will strengthen and protect you in the middle of whatever you must face. You belong to Him and He will provide what you need both now and after the confrontation.

All of this assumes that you have time to consider and prepare. There are many wolf attacks that arise in an instant and must be dealt with in that instant. To watch them happen and do nothing makes you complicit in the evil. I have faced several of those situations. They are always shock attacks meant to manipulate and control through surprise and fear. Because they are so shocking, most of us are unprepared to deal with them.

CHAPTER FORTY

Shock Attack

Years ago, a TV production company associated with MGM Studios contracted with me to help develop and produce a new television series. It was a fairly large company run by three partners with several series on the air and several more in development. One of the partners ran their television operations while the others took no active role in that side of the business.

The partner in charge was known as a bully. While he had this reputation among all the TV staffs that worked for him, when I joined the group I had no difficulties with him at all. He was charming and friendly and I tried to be the same.

The relationship went along well for a number of weeks. He was complimentary about my work. My assignment was to write a pilot script and guide other writers who would be writing the episodes that followed. I employed several professionals and we began working on stories. These had to be approved before we went into the scripting phase. Story creation is always a lot of work. In developing a story for a TV episode, you strive to be thorough enough so that writing the script will not be difficult.

Finally, after several weeks of meetings and multiple drafts, the first story was ready to submit for approval. The writer was an old friend who had worked for me in the past. Together, we had pounded out every detail and I was satisfied that it would make an excellent episode. After submission, we waited.

Several days later the executive I have mentioned sent word that he wanted to meet with the writer and me. The meeting took place the following day in my office. The writer walked in. A few minutes later, the executive arrived with the multiple pages of our story in his hand. I introduced them and they sat down in front of my desk.

We were barely seated when, without warning, the executive literally threw the pages at the writer and began cursing at him. Using the foulest language he knew, he execrated our story and the writer. The attack was shocking in its viciousness. Though I had spent years in Hollywood and dealt with many abrasive (and even abusive) people, never had I seen such a performance.

Psychologists tell us that when we are confronted with danger we must choose either "fight or flight". Most people in Hollywood choose flight. They cower and run. Wolves assume that their victims will cower. That's what this executive expected, but it was not to be.

While he was yelling and cursing, I stood up and bent across my desk toward the man. I am not a small person and he was not a large person. Staring at him with a kind of deathly calm, I told him to *STOP*. Then I told him that never again was he going to act that way with one of my writers. I was responsible for everything they did. He could scream at me and throw things at me all he wanted. But he wasn't going to do that to them.

It was a horrible moment. The man shriveled into silence. He left my office without saying another word. It was reported that from that day, he was terrified of me. Though I told no one what had happened, the word got out to his company personnel and all the show staffs. A dozen years later at a Hollywood party, a writer who had been on one of those staffs came up to me and told me how much he appreciated what I had done. No one else had ever stood up to the man.

The problem with such confrontations is that they change everything. Afterward, I tried to be friendly and continue the professional relationship that we had developed, but it was impossible to return. When a wolf is frightened of you, he will attack from behind. A few weeks later I left the company because of things the man was doing behind my back. Several years later, he was fired from his own organization due to financial malfeasance.

When you confront a wolf, there is a price that must be paid. David's defeat of Goliath earned him a dangerous enemy, another wolf who made his life miserable for years, King Saul. After a wolf confrontation, you can expect to carry wounds of various kinds that may last a long time.

Many years after my confrontation with the executive, the young man who had been his assistant became president of a major cable network. (That's the way things are done in Hollywood.) He was a person whom I had liked. We had never had the slightest problem. He must have been bullied himself during the time he was employed by that man. Yet years later, he refused to meet with me to discuss new TV series. Why? There's only one reason that I can imagine. Fear. He was one of the lesser wolves surrounding the alpha wolf. While I don't know that he had attacked anyone, I'm sure that he had facilitated his superior's viciousness. When you confront the alpha wolf, the lesser wolves will not forget.

Because our faith is in God, every believer in Jesus should have the courage to confront wolves when vicious attacks take place against innocent people. And if the situation warrants it, that defense must be immediate.

But what if the attack is against us? What if that television executive had done to me what he did to my writer? (Of course, though it was indirect, the attack was intended to establish his superiority over me through intimidation.) The alternatives are not just "fight or flight". There is a third choice. When you are under vicious attack you can stand your ground and take it without giving back in kind. (This does not apply to physical attacks. They are a separate issue. But spiritual wolves in leadership are not fools. Rarely are their attacks physical.)

In the army, I learned to stand my ground. During training there was a lot of yelling and verbal abuse. This was done for our good, but it wasn't pleasant. I learned to stand firm in the face of it, remaining silent with no visible reaction. I have come to believe that this can be a form of "turning the other cheek" that Jesus instructed His followers to do.

In November of 1967 I arrived in Vietnam. I was what was known as a "butter bar", a green second lieutenant with a gold bar on my collar, just eight months out of Infantry Officer Candidate School at Fort Benning, Georgia. Several weeks after I arrived, I turned 22 years old.

My first two weeks "in country" were spent at a reception station where all of us got some additional training while we ac-

266

climated to the heat and the time change. Finally my orders came to go to a unit. They arrived late at night and instructed me to report immediately to an infantry battalion that was flying out the next morning to back up a division that was in a huge battle in the Central Highlands. Needless to say, my stomach was churning.

Close to midnight, I arrived in the battalion area. My first duty was to report to the battalion commander, a Lieutenant Colonel. I was told that he was in the officers club (just a large tent with a makeshift bar) with all the other officers of the unit. I thought that probably they were having a tactical meeting in preparation for the next day's assignment. Not quite. When I entered, I discovered that they were all getting drunk. Considering that we might be in combat the next day that was a bit disturbing.

I reported to the battalion commander. He ordered the bartender to get me a beer. That's when the difficulty started. I thanked him, but told him I'd take a Coke instead. (At the time, I didn't drink alcohol of any kind.) The battalion commander stared at me. Then, he *ordered* me to drink a beer.

It was hard to imagine a more surreal situation. What weird dimension had I entered? As politely as possible, I declined his order. I knew it was illegal, but I really, really didn't want to offend the man. That's not a good way to go into combat with a superior officer.

Lieutenant Colonel Baldwin (I will never forget his name) proceeded to "lock my heels", standing me at attention and for the next hour in front of all the other officers of the battalion, berated me for not drinking, for being married (yes, that too) and for being a second lieutenant. (Drunks are such pleasant folk.) Over and over, he ordered me to drink and over and over, I politely de-

267

clined. (At a certain point, I would have sucked acid before I drank one of his beers.)

I didn't announce that I was a Christian, but that was rather obvious because back then about the only people who didn't drink were evangelical Christians and Mormons. After an hour or so, I just wore the man out. Finally, he gave up. Several weeks later the chaplain took me aside and told me that he admired the stand I had taken against the bully. But neither he nor any other officer stood up for me that night.

What I had learned in the army applied well in Hollywood. Without either confrontation or cowering, it is possible to let the abuse fall around you with no response either visual or verbal. After it passes, you can deal with it in a reasoned manner. While it is taking place, pray for the abuser. (In the army, I'm afraid I wasn't mature enough to be praying. It was just basic stubbornness.) There are other situations where you need to answer the abuser and sometimes strongly. God must guide.

Followers of Jesus should have the strength from Him to deal with attacks without striking back. According to the Apostle Paul in Ephesians 6:10-13, spiritual armor and weapons are available. It is our fault if we don't use them.

Our responsibility is to be watchful and ready to stand for the truth. An essential part of being ready is to cultivate the right attitude and sense of purpose. Choose your battles wisely. The Apostle Paul described this kind of spiritual readiness in one of his letters to Timothy.

"But avoid foolish and ignorant disputes, knowing that they generate strife. And a servant of the Lord must

not quarrel but be gentle to all, able to teach, patient, in humility correcting those who are in opposition, if God perhaps will grant them repentance, so that they may know the truth, and that they may come to their senses and escape the snare of the devil, having been taken captive by him to do his will." (2Timothy 2:23-26)

CHAPTER FORTY-ONE

Preparation: Understanding Your Purpose

God loves spiritual wolves, even the psychopathic Born Wolves. He loves the person who has done damage to you and to others. He loves that bullying TV executive and his assistant who rejected me. He loves the Lieutenant Colonel who made my life miserable that night in Vietnam. Understanding that God loves wolves, no confrontation should take place out of vindictiveness, anger and a desire for revenge. This is not easy when you are hurt.

The first purpose in confronting a wolf is so that he or she may have the opportunity to repent, to stop damaging people and, perhaps, to come to know Jesus Christ in reality. It is God's deep desire that this enslaved individual be released from the control of Satan. Your overriding desire should be for all of that to happen.

But is it possible for spiritual wolves to repent? According to what Jesus said in Revelation 2 in His message to the church in Thyatira, the answer is yes. In His letter to that church, Jesus says that He has given the woman called Jezebel time to repent but she has refused. If He gave her time to repent, though she was very deep into Satanic evil, it must be possible. So the first reason to confront a wolf is to offer the opportunity for repentance and deliverance. We may believe that we are dealing with a psychopathic leader who never feels guilt or remorse. It doesn't matter. That leader's heart is in God's Hands.

The second purpose is to defend the weak and broken-hearted, to set the captives free. For whatever reason, there are many people who just aren't able to defend themselves against spiritual wolves. Often, they are blind to their own enslavement. Maybe they have been wounded too many times and are deeply fearful. They need healing in order to become strong enough and wise enough to see the truth of the situation. The lies of the wolf keep them weak, unable to heal and susceptible to destructive leadership.

The third purpose in confronting spiritual wolves goes hand-in-hand with the first two. It is to stand for truth in the face of lies. Truth needs to be spoken for its own sake. It is the Truth of God that brings His Light into darkness. It is His Truth that sets people free and destroys the lies and illusions of Satan. Of course, speaking His Truth means "speaking the truth in love".

In Ephesians 4:15 when the Apostle Paul tells us to speak the truth in love, the word translated "love" is agape. It is a self-sacrificing love. That is the heart of all such confrontations. In the right spirit, they are a form of self-sacrifice done in the Name of Jesus and for His glory. Such acts of truth-speaking are for the good of both the victim and the attacker.

The political philosopher Dr. Thomas Sowell has stated it well. "When you want to help people, you tell them the truth. When you want to help yourself, you tell them what they want to hear." Wolves hate hearing the truth. Being under the control of

Satan, they are the most deluded. They surround themselves with people who tell them what they want to hear. In the history of the Church, no one ever became a martyr by telling those in authority what they wanted to hear. There is no self-sacrificing love in lies and flattery. Truth always comes at a price.

Speaking the truth in love under the Power of the Holy Spirit does not always mean being gentle and nice. Jesus and His apostles spoke with great gentleness, except when they were dealing with demons and human servants of darkness. Then they spoke with power and their words were like swords. No matter how wonderful and gifted they may appear, the spiritual wolves that Jesus warned about are servants of Satan. When you speak truth to them, know that you have become a member of a unique group of warriors that stretches back for thousands of years.

When King David sinned by having an adulterous relationship with Bathsheba, then murdering her husband to cover it up, he was well on his way to becoming a spiritual wolf. God sent the prophet Nathan to deliver a terrible message. It's found in 2 Samuel 12. The confrontation began with great subtlety, the simplicity of a story. But it ended with brutal truth and a severe warning. The result was David's repentance. Read that passage. Guided as it was by God, Nathan's approach provides one model for a wolf confrontation. There are others.

How wonderful it would be if you were used by God to bring repentance and transformation into the life of a "Christian" leader who is on his way to destruction and taking many others with him. It is vital that you believe such an outcome to be possible, even as you are willing to accept any outcome that is in God's Plan.

But let me give you the most serious warning. Satan knows what you are preparing to do. During your preparation to confront a wolf, expect attacks to come from many directions that will not seem to be associated with the wolf at all. During the year that it has taken to write this book, all sorts of attacks have come. Some have been heartbreaking. All have been designed to stall and distract by creating frustration. Most of all there has been the on-going attack of discouragement, the sometimes overwhelming sense that I had nothing to say and no authority to say it, not enough faith, not enough knowledge, not enough holiness. Often, I have forgotten the very principles I am presenting to you. Though I should expect attacks, in the middle of them I forget that's what they are.

One of the most important principles in this book is that Satan understands us and knows how to create illusions. He uses whatever is available, adding his dark twists to the normal adversities of life and piling more onto those.

In your preparation, do not stop. Keep walking, though it may be slowly and in pain. The Lord will give you strength. The battle is His.

So let's get ready for the confrontation.

CHAPTER FORTY-TWO

Preparation: The Iron Discipline

Little boys dream about being warriors. But dreaming is not the same as being and doing. Christians may dream about being spiritual warriors. But dreaming means nothing if there is no daily preparation. That preparation involves spiritual discipline. And there is one discipline beyond all others that must be part of your life if you are going to confront a wolf. Because it is such a challenge, I've called it The Iron Discipline.

The Iron Discipline is forgiveness.

What is the proof that there is so little real love for Jesus in the church today? Lack of forgiveness, both getting it from God and giving to others. Spiritual wolves feast on flocks of delicious, backbiting, unforgiving sheep. Instead of real forgiveness there is a lot of fake forgiveness among Christians. But the truth of what is actually in the heart will not stay hidden.

Many years ago, I knew a Christian woman who blamed a doctor for a particular medical procedure that she had experienced. As time went on it became scientifically clear that he had done nothing wrong, but evidence didn't matter. She had made a decision about the man and her heart was full of deep hatred for him. Though she had no contact with him from the time of the procedure, for decades his name could not be mentioned without rage spewing out. Her hatred grew with the years.

As the trials of life accumulated, which they always do, her anger generalized to include each new negative situation and each new person whom she considered responsible. While she could be charming and very sweet and gave much to her family, anger was always just under the surface and it was expressed in many different ways. Ultimately, her rage and vindictiveness blinded her to reality and helped bring sorrow and destruction to her own family, a family she truly loved.

Unforgiveness guarantees that we will fall victim to evil delusions that are temptations of Satan. As we view any negative situation we will seek to justify our anger, bitterness, and self-pity. In doing so, often we reconstruct what we think others have done to us to vindicate our sinful attitudes and actions. Partial truths become "memories" and we will fight to the death in our belief that they are all 100 percent accurate. We will compound the effects of any negative situation by demanding that others accept our view as reality. When they refuse, it offers a new opportunity for hate, rage, bitterness, self-pity and a desire for revenge. Do not be fooled. Satan will be happy to cover all of this in a lovely, spiritual wrapping.

To have a congregation full of unforgiving and unforgiven people is very possible in the modern evangelical church where everyone is invited to "say 'yes' to Jesus" with no serious preaching about sin and its deadly eternal consequences. Unforgiving and unforgiven congregations grow from shallow preaching about the Cross. Unforgiving and unforgiven congregations do not experience the true work of the Holy Spirit who, according to Jesus in John 16:8-11, came first to convict the world of sin, not just to help us speak in tongues or "worship".

Without the humiliation that comes with true conviction of sin there is no sense of need for repentance. When our understanding of God's forgiveness is shallow, our forgiveness of others will be shallow. We forgive in the same way that we have experienced the need to be forgiven.

An *unforgiven* church is an *unforgiving* church. Pastors and spiritual leaders who refuse to preach and teach about sin and repentance because they don't want to offend people and drive them away, deserve the vicious, gossiping, backbiting, divisive congregations they will get. If they think they can ease people into an understanding about sin in a way that guarantees no one will be offended, they are foolish and do not understand the New Testament. Though they may not be wolves, they shouldn't be in leadership.

Spiritual wolves are master legalists in part because they are masters of unforgiveness. What may appear to be forgiveness in them is simply waiting for the right moment to exact revenge or execute a quid pro quo. They'll "forgive" if the offender does something for them. Wolves do not forget the weaknesses and sins of others. They catalog them for future use. In this, they are like their father Satan.

Satan uses his wolf attacks to bring wounds that he hopes will never heal, taking away all joy and leaving nothing but bitterness and self-pity. In that state, we are susceptible to even deeper wounds and greater delusions. We are in danger of becoming spiritual wolves ourselves.

Are you carrying a spiritual/emotional wound? Whether it has come from a wolf attack, from some other source such as bereavement or another kind of loss or misunderstanding, left untreated it will destroy your life and your effectiveness as a servant-warrior for Jesus in this world. The only healing for such wounds is real forgiveness. But I'm afraid many Christians don't have the slightest clue about what that is.

CHAPTER FORTY-THREE

What Does Forgiveness Look Like?

In 2012 there was a striking interview on the U.S. television program 60 Minutes. It was with a most unusual man. He had been released from prison after serving 18 years for a crime that he didn't commit. He had been wrongly convicted of murdering his wife. The Innocence Project had spent five years trying to get the courts to re-examine his case based on new DNA evidence that proved conclusively that he was not the killer.

Far worse than the long, unjust battle to reopen the case, it was discovered that during his trial the district attorney, in a criminal act, consciously withheld exculpatory evidence that very likely would have kept him from being convicted.

So an innocent man full of horror and sorrow over his wife's murder went to prison due to a false accusation and conviction. But that wasn't all. His little son had been three years old at the time of his mother's death and had witnessed the terrible crime. He had told what he saw, at that young age even accurately describing the real murderer. But his testimony was part of the evidence that had been withheld. To add even more sorrow, as the years passed and the little boy became a teenager, he wrote to his father telling him that he didn't want to visit him in prison anymore.

The 60 Minutes interviewer asked this poor man, "How did you deal with all of that? So much was taken from you. It seems more than a person could bear." The man replied that he had spent years brokenhearted, enraged, full of hate, wanting revenge. But one day he woke up and realized that carrying this awful burden was destroying him. He couldn't live with it any longer. He didn't want to be the man that he was becoming. There was only one answer. He had to forgive all of the people who had done such terrible things to him. Apparently, he came to this conclusion before there was any hope that he would be exonerated and set free.

So he did it. He told the interviewer that when he forgave everyone it was as though a giant weight had been lifted off his heart. As the camera came in close, it was very clear. His eyes were filled with peace.

I call forgiveness The Iron Discipline because it does not come naturally to us and must be applied over and over, sometimes with great difficulty, throughout our lives. When someone does something bad to me or my loved ones what comes naturally is stoking my anger until it turns into rage soaked with bitterness. What comes naturally is the desire for revenge. I want to hurt the person who has hurt me or those close to me.

What does it mean to forgive? Here is a dictionary definition: Forgiveness means to excuse a fault or offense, to pardon, to renounce anger and resentment, to absolve from the payment of a debt.

A spiritual wolf has attacked you. (Or someone else has hurt you in some way.) You have determined that the person has sinned against you. That sin could be anything from besmirching your character to something far worse. In your mind, you have sustained real injury. Perhaps it was to your reputation or your sense of peace and security. Perhaps you are living with the hell of false accusations that everyone believes. Perhaps it was physical abuse that has polluted your memory and emotions. Or maybe it was done to someone you love. There are many possibilities, but what was taken was important.

There are people who think forgiveness is based on emotion. "I can't forgive until I feel forgiving." Since they never feel forgiving, they never forgive. And let's be honest. It feels good not to forgive. I get dark satisfaction from nursing the anger that comes with evil memories and desires. To give that up takes the very Power of God. I have heard people say, "I'm just not ready to forgive." That may be honest, but it's just as foolish as saying, "I'm not ready to give up the cancer that is killing me. I'm going to enjoy it awhile longer."

True forgiveness starts by realizing and accepting the fact that it is not based on emotion at all. It is an act of the will. The spiritual wolf owes you a debt because of the injury that he has inflicted. He hasn't admitted it and maybe he won't. You are preparing for a confrontation with him. Spiritual failure is guaranteed if forgiveness is not an essential part of your preparation.

But what does forgiveness require? It requires kneeling before God in prayer and placing a person into His Hands, trusting Him to be the Righteous Judge. It requires giving up your right to

281

exact payment for the emotional debt that a person owes you. It means renouncing your right to be angry any longer.

Though deep emotion is involved, true forgiveness is a judicial decision. Like all judicial decisions it is made once. But very likely, you will have to remind yourself of that decision many times. When memories return, hurt returns and anger with it. Each time, you choose to remind yourself of the decision you made and give that person to the Lord. Though it may be reaffirmed many times, the act of forgiveness is accomplished once.

Imagine that you are a judge in a court. The prisoner, the person who has sinned against you, stands shackled in the dock of your mind. Forgiveness is setting that person free, letting him walk out the door unchained. A year later, you don't run after him, dragging him back and chaining him up again for the same offense. You may want to do that, but when you do, you remind yourself of the decision that you made. You recommit him into God's Hands, *praying blessing upon him.* In a sense, the person who has sinned against you is a prisoner that you are holding in the dungeon of your mind. As you set him free, you are freeing yourself, because as long as he is kept in that dungeon you are imprisoned with him.

In the middle ages, a terrible justice was exacted on murderers. The dead body of the victim was strapped to the murderer's back to rot until it killed him. When we do not forgive, it is as though the dead body of the one we hate is strapped to our soul. As it rots, it kills us with anger, bitterness and self-pity. The most horrible reality is that Satan can make that rot actually taste good to a soul on its way to hell.

But even knowing all of this, there are many who will say, "I have a right to my anger and desire for revenge. Why should I give it up? My anger protects me. If I give it up, I'll just be hurt again. Doesn't the Bible say an eye for an eye? And the one who did this to me hasn't asked to be forgiven anyway, so I don't need to forgive him until he does. Isn't that what the Bible teaches?"

Many times this leads to disastrous confrontations. Because we believe that we don't need to forgive until the perpetrator asks to be forgiven we decide, "I've got to get this individual to acknowledge and accept what he has done to me. Then he'll ask to be forgiven. Unless that happens, my wound will never heal and I don't have to forgive."

Wrong.

This puts forgiveness and healing into the hands of another person who may never want forgiveness and who may even be dead. As long as we believe this lie our wounds will never heal. Could Jesus have taught something that would put us into such a bind? He didn't. So what did He really teach about forgiveness?

CHAPTER FORTY-FOUR

Vertical and Horizontal

As we deal with the damage done by spiritual wolves, it's vital that we have a clear understanding of what Jesus taught about forgiveness. He taught two kinds and both work together. To misunderstand either one is to misunderstand what forgiveness toward others means in the New Testament. The teaching of one kind to the exclusion of the other has been disastrous in the church.

The first kind that Jesus taught has been called "Vertical Forgiveness" and it's found in Mark 11:25-26.

"And whenever you stand praying, if you have anything against anyone, forgive him, that your Father in heaven may also forgive you your trespasses. But if you do not forgive, neither will your Father in heaven forgive your trespasses."

This kind of forgiveness is between you and God, that's why it has been called "vertical". In your opinion, someone has done something that damaged you. You hold something against that person. From your viewpoint, the individual has caused you palpable loss. Notice that Jesus doesn't say that your view of the situation is accurate. Maybe it is and maybe it isn't, but that doesn't matter.

The person who did these things to you may never ask to be forgiven. He or she may be dead. They may not believe that they have done anything wrong. Maybe the wrong done to you was intentional, as in the case of a spiritual wolf, or maybe it wasn't, but you thought it was. It may be people in a faceless institution. There are endless permutations. Whatever the case, in your mind with your view of the circumstances, you believe that you have a right to be angry and, if possible, to require justice of some sort. At the very least, you believe that you are owed a serious apology.

However, in obedience to Jesus' command in Mark 11, in humility and faith, you give up what you consider to be your right to require justice. In prayer you unconditionally release the offender into God's Hands, forgiving him once and for all, for the debt that he owes to you. You set him free.

This is done in dependence on God's Justice knowing that He is the only one who understands what happened. You release the individual to God not with the angry hope that He will punish that person, but that God will work in his life to bring him to repentance so that he can receive eternal forgiveness and blessing. It acknowledges that you do not know the whole truth and if you are wrong in any way about what happened, you want God to do what is right.

This act of forgiveness acknowledges that all sins are really against God and He is the One who has the right to judge and punish the wicked. Based on the sacrifice of His Son, Jesus, who died to the pay the penalty for the sins of the world, God's Justice has been satisfied and He can forgive.

This act of forgiveness on your part acknowledges one overwhelming fact. Whatever is owed to you, you owe *much more* than that to God. Whatever sins have been committed against you, you have sinned *much more* against Him. Whatever it costs you to forgive, it cost God *infinitely more* to forgive you. It cost the death of His Son. Since He has forgiven you for so much at such a price, you *must* forgive others.

This is clearly taught in Jesus' parable found in Matthew 18:21-19:1.

Then Peter came to Him and said, "Lord, how often shall my brother sin against me, and I forgive him? Up to seven times?"

Jesus said to him, "I do not say to you, up to seven times, but up to seventy times seven. Therefore the kingdom of heaven is like a certain king who wanted to settle accounts with his servants. And when he had begun to settle accounts, one was brought to him who owed him ten thousand talents. But as he was not able to pay, his master commanded that he be sold, with his wife and children and all that he had, and that payment be made. The servant therefore fell down before him, saying, 'Master, have patience with me, and I will pay you all.' Then the master of

that servant was moved with compassion, released him, and forgave him the debt.

"But that servant went out and found one of his fellow servants who owed him a hundred denarii; and he laid hands on him and took him by the throat, saying, 'Pay me what you owe!' So his fellow servant fell down at his feet and begged him, saying, 'Have patience with me, and I will pay you all.' And he would not, but went and threw him into prison till he should pay the debt. So when his fellow servants saw what had been done, they were very grieved, and came and told their master all that had been done. Then his master, after he had called him, said to him, 'You wicked servant! I forgave you all that debt because you begged me. Should you not also have had compassion on your fellow servant, just as I had pity on you?' And his master was angry, and delivered him to the torturers until he should pay all that was due to him.

"So My heavenly Father also will do to you if each of you, from his heart, does not forgive his brother his trespasses."

Notice at the end Jesus doesn't say anything about the trespassing brother coming to ask to be forgiven. In the Lord's prayer there is nothing about it. When He was dying on the cross and forgave those who were killing Him, they hadn't asked to be forgiven. Those who believe that you can't forgive until someone asks to be forgiven are making a terrible mistake.

What is the end result of vertical forgiveness? Where should it lead us? We pledge to God that we will deal with the one who has offended us in sacrificial love.

The Apostle Paul described what our attitude should be in Romans 12:17-21: **Repay no one evil for evil. Have regard for good things in the sight of all men. If it is possible, as much as depends on you, live peaceably with all men. Beloved, do not avenge yourselves, but rather give place to wrath; for it is written, "Vengeance is Mine, I will repay," says the Lord. Therefore "If your enemy is hungry, feed him; If he is thirsty, give him a drink; For in so doing you will heap coals of fire on his head." Do not be overcome by evil, but overcome evil with good.**

Many people misunderstand what Paul meant when he said "give place to wrath". They think it means that it's all right to be full of anger toward an enemy. But that isn't what it means at all. It means to give up your anger. Set your anger aside and give place to God's wrath if He chooses to exercise it because all vengeance belongs to Him. In the meantime, insofar as it is possible, do nothing but good for your enemy.

When someone does something that hurts us it is normal to feel angry. God knows that we are going to get angry. That's part of being human in a fallen world. If you don't ever get angry about anything, something is wrong with you. There is a place for anger, but it must be strictly limited. The Apostle Paul writes in Ephesians 4:26-27:

"Be angry, and do not sin": do not let the sun go down on your wrath, nor give place to the devil.

After a brief period of being angry, set it aside. Don't even hold it overnight. One form of holding on to anger is the carrying of grudges. How destructive that has been in the church!

During the 1940's in my mother's hometown of Tonkawa, Oklahoma, all of her family went to the little Presbyterian Church that is located there. This was during the great modernist/fundamentalist war that raged in the major denominations. Her family in Tonkawa split. One brother-in-law and his clan left the church to start a new non-denominational church a few blocks away. Another brother-in-law and his family stayed Presbyterian. The rancor between these families became so intense that they rarely spoke to each other, though they lived only two miles apart in that little town. The brothers-in-law never spoke. When my family would come down from Chicago to visit in the summer, we would bounce back and forth between the warring clans. It broke my mother's heart.

Finally, that generation began to die off. One brother-in-law passed away in 1967. In the mid-1980's my wife and I visited Tonkawa and spent time with the other aging brother-in-law. In my presence he said, "If Ernest is in Heaven, I don't want to go there." I hope he repented of that. He's been dead now for years.

The second kind of forgiveness that Jesus taught has been called "horizontal". It takes place between people and it's found in Luke 17:3-4:

Take heed to yourselves. If your brother sins against you, rebuke him; and if he repents, forgive him. And if he sins against you seven times in a day, and seven times in a day returns to you, saying, 'I repent,' you shall forgive him."

Horizontal forgiveness is *conditional* forgiveness. Conditional? But wait, didn't we just say that real forgiveness is unconditional? Horizontal forgiveness is conditional in the sense that we verbalize it when the offender asks to be forgiven. After the individual acknowledges his sin against you and asks for forgiveness you can speak the words of release, "I forgive you."

But preparation to forgive in this way has already been made through vertical forgiveness between you and God. In prayer you have forgiven the person so you are ready to complete the action when he asks for it. That's how the two types of forgiveness that Jesus taught work together. But be cautious, serious mistakes have been made by well-intentioned Christians who rush up and forgive someone when that person hasn't asked to be forgiven and may not want it.

There are times when we should tell someone they are forgiven though they haven't asked for it. Often, those are times when the perpetrator is filled with so much sorrow for his actions, is so humiliated or is so damaged, that he can't imagine you could ever forgive, yet you do. This can be the most powerful witness to the reality and Love of Christ. The Holy Spirit will guide.

In horizontal forgiveness, the request to be forgiven should be real. How do we know that it's real? There is some kind of honest attempt to make things right or to change. This comes from a humble attitude of the heart. Watch for the smallest change and desire to make things right. That may be in the request for forgiveness itself. The very request may be a major step for that individual. When you see it, accept it as evidence.

In Jesus' parable about the servant who was forgiven a huge amount by the king then refused to forgive someone who owed him only a little, the man's actions proved that there was no real gratitude or repentance in him. But in watching for true repentance, we should never stand over a person waiting for him to fail. This is not forgiveness and proves that "vertical forgiveness" has not taken place.

After asking to be forgiven, if your brother or sister does fail and asks to be forgiven again you are to do so. As Jesus told His disciples, a person may stumble many times a day and if he repents, he must be forgiven. There will be no strength to do this if the judicial act of real forgiveness isn't taking place between you and God.

Over and over, Jesus gave the most serious warning possible about forgiveness. If we refuse to forgive others, our Father in Heaven *will not forgive us*. This is echoed in the Lord's Prayer. "Forgive us our debts *as we* forgive our debtors." We might read that "in the same manner" in which we forgive our debtors.

How would you like for God to forgive you? Would you like for Him to say He's forgiven you, then years later or maybe when you die, shove all your sins back in your face? Do you want Him to forgive you conditionally? "I'll forgive you as long as you never do anything that hurts Me again?" Is that what you want? If not, then as you pray to the Father, forgive others in the same way that you want God to forgive you, unconditionally and completely. That means no strings attached.

Forgive others as though your eternal life

depended upon it.

CHAPTER FORTY-FIVE

Was Jesus Serious About Rebuking?

I'm afraid so. The horizontal (conditional) forgiveness that Jesus teaches in Luke 17 assumes that we are going to rebuke the person who has sinned against us. The Greek word that is translated "rebuke" means to censure and/or admonish. Those are strong words. Censure is to vehemently express disapproval about the thing that was done. Admonish means to strongly urge someone to do something that he should do to make a situation right. That is the heart of confronting a wolf and is an essential part of working toward forgiveness, reconciliation and healing.

What kinds of rebuking are Biblical? None of them are easy. First, there is the kind that Jesus taught when dealing with a brother or sister who has sinned against you. We'll talk about that kind of personal confrontation in the next chapter. The rebuking that takes place there is done after vertical forgiveness has been declared and is never done in anger or with vindictiveness. The wrong kind of "rebuking" is not of God and will do great damage. Satan loves such rebukes because they bring destruction to everyone involved.

But there is another type of godly rebuke.

In the introduction to this book, I wrote about the New Tribes missionary who had been convicted of creating and distributing child pornography, photographing little girls in the Amazon, children to whom he had been sent to minister in the Name of Jesus. After being caught by federal authorities, he repented. There are Christians who believe that such a person shouldn't be rebuked publicly by the church. The state should do its job, while the church simply should love this man and assist in his healing. To rebuke him would be "piling on". While this sounds loving, is it Biblical?

The rebuke that takes place first between two people alone is designed to re-establish a relationship that has been broken due to a private matter. There are two other purposes for rebuking within the church. The first is to end a sin that is taking place and bring about repentance and the second is to instill righteous fear in others.

There is no doubt that the church should love an individual and accept his or her repentance. However, the New Testament is clear about publicly rebuking those whose sins are not private and that affect the entire body. When the sin has been public and has affected many people, the rebuke and the statement of repentance should be public.

Our problem with rebuking is the manner in which we imagine it being done. We imagine that the only way to rebuke is harshly with cold eyes and cold hearts. After Peter denied the Lord three times, all it took was a single look from Jesus. I'm sure that in that look was the deepest sorrow and love. Not a word was spoken, but it was the heaviest rebuke he could ever have received and it was without condemnation. Peter's repentance was real and came with tears.

Any kind of rebuke in the Body of Christ should be given with deep sorrow, deep love and without condemnation. In particular, this should be true of a public rebuke. Such a rebuke is a statement of the facts and how the sinful actions have damaged many. Then there is the call for repentance and, if possible, restitution. After the rebuke and public repentance, the person who has sinned should be shown public forgiveness through the love of Christ and acceptance by the entire body. This is the beginning of real healing. Such a public rebuke and repentance calls on all who have witnessed it to examine their own lives as they forgive.

But caution should be exercised. What the young man did in the Amazon to little children who were under his care are the actions of a spiritual wolf, a vicious predator, and, possibly, a psychopath. After he returns to society from prison, the church should watch him with great loving care until his repentance is confirmed by godly actions over a very significant period of time. Born wolves, psychopathic personalities, are quick to "repent" even with tears, but it's all an act. There is no change of heart and they will attack again.

Clearly, the Apostle Paul believed in the proper role of rebuking within the church:

2 Timothy 4:2 **Preach the word! Be ready in season and out of season. Convince, rebuke, exhort, with all long-suffering and teaching.**

Titus 1:10-14 **For there are many insubordinate, both idle talkers and deceivers, especially those of the circumcision, whose mouths must be stopped, who subvert whole households, teaching things which they ought not, for the sake of dishonest gain. One of them, a prophet of their own, said, "Cretans are always liars, evil beasts, lazy gluttons." This testimony is true. Therefore rebuke them sharply, that they may be sound in the faith, not giving heed to Jewish fables and commandments of men who turn from the truth.**

Titus 2:11-15 **For the grace of God that brings salvation has appeared to all men, teaching us that, denying ungodliness and worldly lusts, we should live soberly, righteously, and godly in the present age, looking for the blessed hope and glorious appearing of our great God and Savior Jesus Christ, who gave Himself for us, that He might redeem us from every lawless deed and purify for Himself His own special people, zealous for good works. Speak these things, exhort, and rebuke with all authority. Let no one despise you.**

In dealing with false teachers and their followers, Paul commands the most confrontational form of rebuking. He wanted their mouths stopped. But there were proper times for that kind of rebuking and times when other approaches should be used.

Paul tells Timothy: **Do not rebuke an older man, but exhort him as a father, younger men as brothers, older women as mothers, younger women as sisters, with all purity.** (1 Timothy 5:1-2)

The Greek word that is translated "exhort" means to call near, to invite, to implore, to entreat and beseech. It includes strong pleading. These people are not false teachers/spiritual wolves, they are doing things that are wrong and need correction. If Biblical exhorting and rebuking were taking place today perhaps there would be far fewer wolves in church leadership and more believers growing toward maturity.

What most of us want is for those who have sinned against us to realize what they have done and ask to be forgiven without our doing anything except, perhaps, forgiving them before God and praying for them. Forgiving a person and praying for him is meant to prepare our hearts for the important step of rebuking.

No one likes to be rebuked. No spiritually healthy person enjoys rebuking others. But where it is possible (and there are situations where it isn't possible) godly rebuking with love and sorrow is essential. The purpose is to bring repentance which means a change of life direction. Godly rebuking is an act of self-sacrificing love. Godly rebuking cannot be accomplished without God's Love working in us. Do we love someone enough to take the risk of confronting and rebuking that person when he has sinned?

When I was a young man, during the time that I was Supervisor of Production and Talent at the Christian radio station,

WMBI in Chicago, one of our most gifted freelance writer/producers began having an affair with a woman who was also a free-lance writer for us. The writer/producer's wife was part of our freelance talent team as well. These three people were all my friends. I looked up to the man who had instigated the affair. I didn't want to offend him or be rejected by him, so in the face of his sin I was silent. I even went to a party hosted by this "couple".

Sadly, I wasn't the only one who remained silent. In fact, there was only one man at WMBI who knew about the situation who cared enough and had the courage to confront our adulterous friend. The confrontation was a step toward his repentance. Later he asked why no one else had cared enough to confront him with the truth. I was silent. All I could do was repent.

I had convinced myself that the adulterous situation really wasn't my business. None of these people were fulltime employees of the Moody Bible Institute. I came up with all sorts of reasons to say nothing. But as members of the Body of Christ, what happens to one of us affects us all.

CHAPTER FORTY-SIX

Confronting Leaders

The most difficult and painful confrontation that I have ever experienced took five months to bring about. The individual lived in another state and I knew that the meeting had to be face-to-face. Our schedules didn't bring us together for almost half a year. During those five months I prayed constantly for wisdom. He had been a leader and a Bible teacher. He knew the Scriptures. I was deeply concerned that I bring only God's message to him. The months of preparation were really a form of agony.

When the evening finally came, I took the individual to dinner and, after a long conversation, gave the message that I believed was from the Lord. It was a most serious warning and a call for repentance. It was heartbreaking to give it and I tried so hard to form every word with the love of Jesus. The message was completely rejected and eventually mocked. Tragically, the person continued on the same path, deeply damaging himself and others. That was over a decade ago. The years since have proven that the warning was true. This has brought great sorrow, but as I continue to pray for the individual, I have peace that God is still at work.

Such confrontations are part of spiritual warfare. In them we are fighting for souls that God loves. Confrontations with wolves fall into this category. But as I have said, not all confrontations in the Body of Christ are spiritual warfare and we should not try to view them as such. I'm talking about disagreements of a personal nature between two people. Another member in the Body of Christ does or says something that offends you. It isn't known by everyone. Awareness of the offense is limited. Jesus gave us specific instructions for handling situations of this sort. They are found in Matthew 18: 15-17:

"Moreover if your brother sins against you, go and tell him his fault between you and him alone. If he hears you, you have gained your brother. But if he will not hear, take with you one or two more, that 'by the mouth of two or three witnesses every word may be established.' And if he refuses to hear them, tell it to the church. But if he refuses even to hear the church, let him be to you like a heathen and a tax collector.

Jesus' instruction focuses on private sin and hurt between two people. The entire local Christian body is not involved. The hope is that the sin can be dealt with and resolved between those two alone. Only when that isn't possible does the church need to be informed so that it can act appropriately.

Not only does Matthew 18 assume that the nature of the sin between two people is a private matter, it assumes that the people involved are both believers in the Lord. Confronting a potential spiritual wolf who is damaging many people isn't dealing with a private matter and if the individual is a spiritual wolf, he or she isn't a believer at all no matter how "Christian" that person may appear. When sin is public affecting many people, a different model from Matthew 18 is presented by the Apostle Paul. The first example is found in I Corinthians 5:1-5:

It is actually reported that there is sexual immorality among you, and such sexual immorality as is not even named among the Gentiles -- that a man has his father's wife! And you are puffed up, and have not rather mourned, that he who has done this deed might be taken away from among you. For I indeed, as absent in body but present in spirit, have already judged (as though I were present) him who has so done this deed. In the name of our Lord Jesus Christ, when you are gathered together, along with my spirit, with the power of our Lord Jesus Christ, deliver such a one to Satan for the destruction of the flesh, that his spirit may be saved in the day of the Lord Jesus.

There is no record of the Matthew 18 "process" being implemented in this account. The situation was known by everyone in the church and the sin was against the Lord and the entire body. For this reason, Paul calls for it to be dealt with publicly.

Why don't we see Paul's process of direct, public confrontation in use today within the church? Fear! First, the fear that the church will be sued if sin is confronted publicly and dealt with in the way Paul, through the Holy Spirit, instructed. Second, there is the fear of being considered judgmental, unloving and legalistic.

Often, Jesus' words in John 8:7 are misapplied. This is the story of the woman caught in adultery and brought to Him for judgment. In the passage He admonishes the one who is without sin to cast the first stone at her. The religious leaders who had brought the poor woman were hypocrites. They cared nothing for her. All they wanted was to destroy Jesus. This is very different than the motives expressed by the Apostle Paul in his letter to the Corinthians. His goal for public confrontation was repentance and reconciliation, which happened. To let people continue in public sin brings destruction to all involved.

The second example of a different process than Matthew 18 is found in Galatians 2:11-21. The Apostle Paul is speaking:

Now when Peter had come to Antioch, I withstood him to his face, because he was to be blamed; for before certain men came from James, he would eat with the Gentiles; but when they came, he withdrew and separated himself, fearing those who were of the circumcision. And the rest of the Jews also played the hypocrite with him, so that even Barnabas was carried away with their hypocrisy.

But when I saw that they were not straightforward about the truth of the gospel, I said to Peter before them all, "If you, being a Jew, live in the manner of Gentiles and not as the Jews, why do you compel Gentiles to live as Jews? We who are Jews by nature, and not sinners of the Gentiles, knowing that a man is not justified by the works of the law but by faith in Jesus Christ, even we have believed in Christ Jesus, that we might be justified by faith in Christ and not

by the works of the law; for by the works of the law no flesh shall be justified.

"But if, while we seek to be justified by Christ, we ourselves also are found sinners, is Christ therefore a minister of sin? Certainly not! For if I build again those things which I destroyed, I make myself a transgressor. For I through the law died to the law that I might live to God. I have been crucified with Christ; it is no longer I who live, but Christ lives in me; and the life which I now live in the flesh I live by faith in the Son of God, who loved me and gave Himself for me. I do not set aside the grace of God; for if righteousness comes through the law, then Christ died in vain."

The instant he saw this public sin take place, Paul knew that Peter's religious elitism would bring disaster to the entire church. The implications were both deeply theological and relational. What he had done had happened publicly and had to be dealt with publicly.

How would such a situation be handled between "Christian" leaders today? Because of institutionalized spiritual elitism and not wanting to offend such a powerful leader as the Apostle Peter, if anything would be done at all it would be done privately. Gently, Peter would be taken aside. Very carefully, it would be suggested that he not "dis-include" (that's the non-word they would use) any particular groups of Christians. Perhaps he could shift back and forth between the groups, having lunch one day in a

305

room with the gentiles where the Jews couldn't see him and in another room the next day with the Jews. That way no one would be offended and everyone would feel "special".

In the elitist act of bowing to Peter's status, the public offense would not be dealt with publicly and the very serious sin of legalistic elitism, which was the heart of the curse brought by the Judaizers, would be established by Apostolic action within the church through all the ages. The very work of Jesus on the Cross would be nullified.

The offenses in Corinth and Antioch were public from the start, but they were not with wolves. When the sin is against the entire body and/or involves the leadership, a public confrontation is vital. The Apostle Paul instructs Timothy about dealing with sinful leaders in this way:

Do not receive an accusation against an elder except from two or three witnesses. Those who are sinning rebuke in the presence of all, that the rest also may fear. (1 Timothy 5:19-20)

That's about as clear as it could get. So often the focus is on the issue of the "two or three witnesses", with no attention paid to the public rebuke. If you are going to confront a spiritual leader about an issue of public sin, the truth about that sin must be established by more than one person. This implies that the sin may represent a pattern of behavior. Also, it attempts to assure that it isn't a false accusation designed to retaliate.

At least two or three people from the offended group should confront the leader together and more if possible. Evidence of sin should be gathered including Biblical undergirding that shines God's Light on what has taken place. There should be agreement about what the group will ask the leader to do in response to the evidence. (Personally apologizing to a small group about a public sin is not adequate. Public sin calls for public repentance and restitution.) One person should be selected to speak for everyone. That person (and the entire group) should be respectful, direct and fiercely loving.

How the words "in the presence of all" are defined may vary. It depends on the case. Paul intends that "the fear of God" come upon all who witness the rebuke to keep others from falling into sin. Isn't it implied that, if there is no public rebuke, others may fall into sin more easily?

As disturbing as it is to write these words, it's important to remember that if you are dealing with a true spiritual wolf, you are not dealing with a brother or sister in the Lord. Ultimately, whether the individual is a spiritual wolf or not will be determined by his or her response to the evidence and the rebuke. If the sin is proven and the response is one of true humility, sorrow, love and repentance, you are not dealing with a wolf, just a misled and sinning brother or sister. Remember, such people can look like wolves when they aren't. The response of a spiritual wolf will be very different. You can expect some disturbing tactics including, in the case of some wolves, false repentance and false sorrow. Be prepared for the unexpected.

When I was in my mid-twenties, Carel and I were living in the Chicago area with our little family. During my teenage years, I had performed magic shows for church groups and others. I considered it a ministry and tried to present the truth of the Lord to every group. Most of those groups were children and teenagers. After the army, I lost interest in doing magic tricks. It was 1969 and fascination with the occult was sweeping the country. I had known about an area of magic called mentalism. The principles of trickery were the same, but the equipment was different and the effect on an audience was amazing. With simple secrets you could make people believe that you really could read minds and predict the future.

We developed a program called Beyond Reality. For the first half we would do illusions of the mind apparently demonstrating everything from telepathy to telekinesis. During the second half we would tell the audience that all of it was trickery and talk about how easily humans are fooled. Then we would present the truth of Jesus and how it destroys the lies and supernatural power of the occult. We took Beyond Reality into many churches and other groups around the mid-west.

After one program, we were approached by a Christian PR representative who thought he could get us onto some TV shows in Chicago. Soon thereafter, he booked us onto a local talk show. I taped one program, discussing with the host the trickery behind many so-called "psychic" manifestations. The host enjoyed it and booked me for a second program. In this one, he wanted me to confront a leading Chicago area psychic named Irene Hughes. Ms. Hughes was well-known throughout the mid-west for her astrological guidance and psychic lectures. She had been on television many times. As part of our research, Carel and I attended one of her large, group presentations.

When we arrived on the set, it was obvious that Ms. Hughes was on edge as she looked at me. The taping began. I laid out the first piece of evidence in my confrontation with her. I thought I was prepared for anything. I was sure that this lady was capable of a lot of rage. However, I was totally unprepared for what she did. She was enraged all right. But instead of blasting me, she started sobbing. Instead of dealing with the evidence she turned her fury on the host. In tears, she told him that she couldn't believe what he had done, how he had treated her after all she had done for him, being a guest so many times in the past. She said that if this was ever put on the air she would never come back. The coward was utterly intimidated. The taping was stopped and he asked me to leave.

Irene Hughes was a true spiritual wolf and I was unprepared to deal with her. Being young, I thought the only approach to take was straightforward confrontation. I expected anger, not sobbing emotion.

The truth is that I deserved to be blindsided. While quite a bit of preparation had taken place, there had been almost no prayer. I didn't care about her soul. It didn't occur to me that God loved Irene Hughes and I should do my best to show her that love even in a confrontation. My approach was all about me and my knowledge. It was a total failure. Needless-to-say, I would do it very differently today.

As you prepare for a confrontation, be deeply concerned about the true needs of the person you're going to confront. That will involve prayer for his or her soul. Only the Holy Spirit understands that individual. He will give you wisdom.

As you look toward the meeting, expect the unexpected. In such confrontations, I have seen the range from blistering rage to the good-old-boy wolf I wrote about earlier. Confronting him was like trying to nail Jell-o to the wall. No matter what you said he would just keep on smiling. I'm sure he was seething, but he hid it well. And afterward, he would attack from behind. By the way, the good-old-boy was always very concerned that people not gossip in his congregation.

As you prepare for a confrontation and when you are in the confrontation, very likely, you are going to be accused of gossiping. We might as well deal with that issue right now.

CHAPTER FORTY-SEVEN

Beware of the Whisperers

Did your grandmother ever tell you this? "If you can't say something nice about someone, don't say anything at all?" Now there is a lot of truth in that statement and it's so well known that many people think it's in the Bible. It isn't. Of course, at its heart is a very Biblical idea. Do unto others as you would have done unto you. To put it a different way, say about others what you would like said about you. But, while there is truth in the old adage, there is also a lot of danger. Certainly, while we are to do everything possible to speak well about people, especially those who are attacking us, it's very important for truth to be spoken at the right time and in the right way.

I know a wonderful Christian lady who loves the Lord. As faithful servants and church members, she and her family suffered under the "ministry" of a wolf for years. Her family was deeply damaged by the man, yet she refused to listen to any negative reports about him because, no matter how truthful and proven they were with firm evidence, she considered them "gossip" and gossip is sinful.

Gossip! We hear that word a lot, don't we? The tabloids live on "gossip". There are TV talk shows based on nothing but gossiping hosts lounging in chairs. It's meaningless babble and falls under the warning that the Apostle Paul gave in I Timothy 5:13.

"...And besides they learn to be idle, wandering about from house to house, and not only idle but also gossips and busybodies, saying things which they ought not."

In this verse, the Greek word that's translated "gossips" could also be translated "silly babblers", lazy people who wander around sticking their noses into other people's business and waste time blathering about meaningless things. Often they hurt others with their babbling.

In church, we're warned not to "gossip". But what is gossip? It's one of those common words that we think we understand. Unfortunately, I'm not so certain that we do. Silly, nosey babbling is one kind of "gossip". But, as bad as it is, there is a far more dangerous kind of hellish, destructive talk and a different Greek word is used for it. Some Bible versions translate that word as "gossip" as well. A good example is II Corinthians 12:20. The New International Version renders the verse this way:

"For I am afraid that when I come I may not find you as I want you to be. I fear that there may be quarreling, jealousy, outbursts of anger, factions, slander, gossip, arrogance and disorder."

Compare this to the way the New King James Version (which I have used throughout this book) translates the same verse:

"For I fear lest, when I come, I shall not find you such as I wish, and that I shall be found by you such as you do not wish; lest there be contentions, jealousies, outbursts of wrath, selfish ambitions, backbitings, whisperings, conceits, tumults;"

It's a little stiff to read, isn't it? But it's much more accurate and I prefer the accuracy. Instead of "gossip" it uses the word "whisperings". To me, this says a great deal. The meaning of that Greek word becomes clear. A whisperer is someone who goes around secretly and pointedly trying to destroy a specific person's reputation and relationships through slander and innuendo. It's a private, one-on-one activity. It isn't just nosey blathering. He pretends to have important information and gives evil hints. A whisperer always says that what he tells you must remain "just between the two of you", while knowing and hoping that it will be spread everywhere. He consciously lies and twists the truth in order to destroy someone.

Notice that in the New King James Version there is another word that precedes whisperings. It's backbitings. This is from a different Greek word. While a whisperer operates secretly in a conscious attempt to destroy a person, a backbiter goes public. He speaks lies about another person in front of a group with no concern for hiding it at all. But he does it while that person is absent and can't defend himself. What is it that both of these evil individuals speak? Slander.

To slander someone is to make false or damaging statements about him, to blacken his name, to smear his reputation and spread scandal and to do so consciously. Let's be clear. You can also slander someone by speaking things that aren't true about him, but that you *think* are true. Out of ignorance, laziness and disobedience you haven't taken time to find out if they are true or not before you blather them. But we have to add in another element. It's possible to mercilessly whisper things that *are true* with the goal of destroying a person.

So what is a whisperer? A person who is merciless and who consciously wants to destroy another person through slander and vicious talk. Often such whispering is sugarcoated and presented as "spiritual concern". Wolves and tares are expert whisperers and backbiters. While accusing others of gossiping, slander is their stock in trade. It is a primary way in which they deal with their enemies.

Now notice something. What is it that gossip *doesn't* include? It doesn't include honest, first-hand reports, given with sorrow, anger and pain, but without malice or a desire for revenge, of damage, destruction, malfeasance, suffering, illegality, sexual and psychological abuse, false teaching and lies perpetrated by wolves. When such reports come in from reliable sources, *they are not gossip and must be taken seriously.* To label them gossip and disregard them because you "don't want to hear bad things", is to share in the sin that is taking place. Don't try to hide behind a convenient wrong definition of gossip.

If a negative report comes in about someone and it is second or third hand information, it is your responsibility to stop the passing of such information until you can get clear, first-hand evidence. This will mean that you talk to the person who actually observed or experienced the damage. If the report is confirmed, you don't keep on passing the information to everyone and anyone. You make a determination about what steps need to be taken and who needs to be informed in order to deal with the crisis.

There are those who think that automatically this should begin the Matthew 18 process. Go alone to the offender and confront him. If there is no resolution bring someone else along, etc. But as we have said, this process is not for use in every case. To attempt it when it shouldn't be used can cause great damage.

For instance, if there is clear evidence of the sexual abuse of a child you do not use the Matthew 18 process. You go first to law enforcement. After that, you go directly and publicly to those above the perpetrator within the church or organization. If there is clear evidence of embezzlement, you do not use the Matthew 18 process, etc. When you are dealing with such wolves the Matthew 18 process *will not work*. It will be nothing more than a warning shot giving them the opportunity to hide evidence, solidify their cover stories and sometimes even physically escape.

In Matthew 12: 35-37 Jesus said this:

"A good man out of the good treasure of his heart brings forth good things, and an evil man out of the evil treasure brings forth evil things. But I say to you that for every idle word men may speak, they will give account of it in the day of judgment. For by your words you will be justified, and by your words you will be condemned."

The word translated "idle" could also be translated "barren", which means lifeless, incapable of bearing fruit. Another translation of the word could be "pernicious" which means causing insidious harm or ruin. This describes the words of backbiters

315

and whisperers who are wolves. Their slanderous words create a kind of living death that spreads like a plague. We must stand against it by fearlessly speaking the truth in love and doing it publicly when that is necessary. Certainly, that is part of the good treasure that comes from the heart. And don't accept the accusation of gossip from slanderers, the cowardly and those who don't know what the word means.

Remember...

An ungodly man digs up evil,

And it is on his lips like a burning fire.

A perverse man sows strife,

And a whisperer separates the best of friends.

(Proverbs 16:27-28)

CHAPTER FORTY-EIGHT

Going in Victorious

In retrospect, the most serious mistake I have made in spiritual confrontations has been a lack of prayer, both prayer for the individual and self-examination before the Lord. Also I have failed to enlist the prayer support of trustworthy Christians. Consequently, I went in much weaker than was necessary. Nothing can take the place of the unified prayer of God's people for Jesus to be glorified and good to come for His Kingdom out of a very bad situation.

You are about to deal with a person who is under the deep influence and, perhaps, total control of Satan. Beyond personal preparation, there needs to be unity between the spiritual warriors involved and the full empowering of the Holy Spirit.

This means prayer and fasting. This means applying the Blood of Jesus to the wolf and the spiritual territory that he has taken. It means applying the Blood of Jesus to the souls the wolf has enslaved. It means crying out to God for His deliverance. It means lifting up to God His promises in Scripture. It means praying for a mighty work of love and healing to be done first in you as warriors and then in all those who are being led to destruction under evil leadership. The battlefield must be bathed in prayer and consecrated with the Blood of Jesus that cleanses from all sin.

In preparation for the battle, the power of Satan must be bound. This is in accord with Jesus' promise in Matthew 18:18-20:

"Assuredly, I say to you, whatever you bind on earth will be bound in heaven, and whatever you loose on earth will be loosed in heaven. Again I say to you that if two of you agree on earth concerning anything that they ask, it will be done for them by My Father in heaven. For where two or three are gathered together in My name, I am there in the midst of them."

Here I would give a warning. If you do not really believe in the full Power of the Holy Spirit that came upon the church at Pentecost and has been at work down through the centuries in and through God's people, you are defeated before you begin. Don't waste your time with a confrontation. There are many evangelical Christians today who have been far more influenced by Enlightenment rationalism, which they have baptized and made to sound "Christian", than by the Word of God. When they speak about the miracles of God and the Holy Spirit's Power always it is either historical (as in the days of the Apostles) or vaguely theoretical. This is one reason that spiritual wolves are thriving among evangelicals.

Satan's wolves are just as happy to feast on coldly "rational" evangelical sheep who spiritualize their disbelief in the Holy Spirit's Power as they are on Pentecostal/charismatic sheep who accept any fake or satanic miracle that is presented to them. Based on these hellish extremes, Satan's wolves further divide Jesus' flock by establishing elitist groups on both sides that look down each other. When will we stop being fools and learn to have real faith and discernment? Until we do, the wolves will prevail.

As you go into a confrontation with a spiritual wolf you can't afford to be a fool. Without the Power of the Holy Spirit you are just as lost as David would have been if he had fought Goliath in his own strength. Like all the rest of the soldiers in Israel's army, he would have been overcome with fear and defeated.

What Holy Spirit empowerment should you pray for that will take away fear and give the Peace of God in spiritual battle? May I suggest that you should ask to be filled with...

Gratitude.

The Apostle Paul wrote in 1 Thessalonians 5:16-18: **Rejoice always, pray without ceasing, in _everything_ give thanks; for this is the will of God in Christ Jesus for you.**

That is a frightening and wonderful statement. I can hear a thousand objections. "Are you insane? You want me to be grateful that I have to go and confront a wolf? I'll do it, but God can't expect me to be thankful about it."

The Greek word that is translated "everything" is what is known as a primary word. It is fundamental, foundational. This primary word means "all manner of", the "whole", "whatsoever" and "whosoever". Everything means _everything_. There's no wiggle room.

Rejoice and be grateful that you have been found worthy to take on this task in Jesus' Name and for His Glory. In the middle of a terrible situation it is a wonderful discipline to ask God for the wisdom and power to be thankful. I think most people (including me) don't want to make that request of God. Just forming the words is so difficult when you are dealing with overwhelming sorrow and pain. But the willingness to do so is an important test of whether our forgiveness and repentance, yes, even our salvation, are real. It's a humbling test of true discipleship.

We live in a cursed day when emotion rules everything. "Feelings" are all that matter. If I "feel" something it must be real and if I don't "feel" something it isn't. Like forgiveness, rejoicing gratitude does not depend on feelings. Empowered by God, it is a decision of the will. As we choose to rejoice and be thankful, the energy and emotion will come. Sing songs of rejoicing like David learned to do.

"In the face of all that has happened to me, in spite of everything, I rejoice and am grateful to God for His mercy. I stand in faith. Though I cannot see how what has happened is for my best, I trust that God will make it so. And I thank Him for the fact that all things work together for good to those who Love God and are called according to His purpose. I thank Him for the thousands of blessings that He has poured out on me. Praise you, Lord, I'm suffering, but in faith I thank you for this person or circumstance that has hurt me so much. I trust You to heal my broken heart and I pray that out of this pain You will be glorified. And now I thank you for giving me this opportunity to speak your truth in love to someone who is damaging many people. May Jesus be lifted up. May this person's heart be changed."

Rejoicing gratitude of this kind is a walk through the fire, but Jesus is walking with you. It is the key to the healing of many wounds in this dark world and it gives strength to face many giants and wolves.

The spiritual discipline of gratitude applies far beyond the wounds inflicted by wolves. A number of years ago my pastor was the Reverend Doctor Lloyd John Ogilvy. Lloyd went from being pastor at the First Presbyterian Church of Hollywood to becoming Chaplain of the U.S. Senate. After moving to Washington, his dear wife grew desperately ill. Finally, she died. Lloyd wrote to the many people who had been praying for them. In that letter he said that the only thing that gave him strength, that made it possible to go on day after day, was gratitude. He was so thankful to God for all that he had been given, especially the many wonderful years with his wife. Gratitude was the only healing antidote to overwhelming sorrow.

Paul tells us in Ephesians 6 that the Sword of the Spirit is the Word of God. I believe that one sharp edge of that sword is gratitude. The Bible is filled with thankfulness, praise and gratitude. Often that rejoicing gratitude is expressed from a broken heart. Gratitude is essential to healing from wolf attacks and gaining strength for confrontations. Fear vanishes when gratitude fills your life.

CHAPTER FORTY-NINE

What to Expect

You are ready. The group that is with you is ready. All of you have examined yourselves and are exercising the Iron Discipline of forgiveness. Your hearts are rejoicing in gratitude to God. You have prayed much and others are praying with you. You are empowered by the Holy Spirit. Your case is ready to present. The necessary evidence is at hand and organized. The facts are clear and one of you will present them. What you are asking the offending leader to do in response is specific and Biblical. The meeting is as public as required by the circumstances or that you have been able to establish. What might you expect?

When confronted, spiritual wolves will use a variety of tactics. All are tried and true methods of counter-attack, defense and manipulation. Here are a few possibilities:

The Charm Initiative.

Because it has worked so well in the past, very often this is the first ploy of a wolf caught in sin. He will appear to be gracious and humble, even grateful that you cared enough to bring your "concerns" to his attention (though he would have preferred that you do it in private). While not agreeing with your accusations and disavowing your evidence, he will be deeply conciliatory. Then in the most gentle and disarming way he may:

Appeal to His Own Authority.

The wolf may remind you of his "anointing" or "call" by the Lord to the position that he holds and the confirmation of that call by many people. He will speak about how seriously he takes his responsibilities and how much he prays for wisdom before each decision. He will remind you that God has given him the authority to make decisions and everyone isn't going to agree with them. Beyond that, he has other spirit-filled leaders who assist him. Nothing is done without accountability (his type of non-accountable accountability).

If the sin is of a sexually immoral or illegal nature expect anything from outright rejection of the evidence to various excuses that it's all just a misunderstanding. There may be an...

Appeal for Your Sympathy.

This could include tears. If the evidence is unequivocal, he may agree that what he has done was a "mistake", a lapse of judgment in a moment of weakness, like David who fell with Bathsheba. But God restored him and did not take his leadership away. In the admission, there will be the cloying odor of self-pity. For spiritual wolves it is the air they breathe. He may "share" with you that, in his position, things are so difficult. He grows so tired and is under constant spiritual attack. It's easy for people to stand in judgment. What he needs are people who stand with him, helping to "hold up his arms" in the battle.

While not taking full responsibility, he may admit to having stumbled, but he will assure you that the Lord has forgiven him and is "lifting his head". He may request your prayer, telling you how much he needs people like you as he fights against the Powers of Darkness that are constantly trying to destroy this Great Work of God.

Don't be fooled. This is nothing but gaseous flattery. It's flattering to have someone of his importance appear to include you in his inner circle of "prayer warriors". Fake humility can be so appealing. Many Christians have been taken in by it. If an appeal for your sympathy has no effect, he may try...

Shifting the Ground of Guilt.

Expect a blizzard of words in which he will attempt to distract you from the importance of your allegations by redirecting your attention to all the wonderful things that he is accomplishing for the Lord. With masterful convolution, he will wend his way around to the point where you are the problem. If you continue with your negativity you will impede the Spirit's work. (Negativity is the only mortal sin of modern evangelical Christianity. It is negativity that brings disunity and disunity takes money from the offering plate.) The wolf will urge you to lay aside less important things and get with his program. The work of the Lord cannot move forward if people go "sideways" and become stumbling blocks to the ministry.

If the wolf knows you and your weaknesses and if he senses the slightest lack of resolve, he may try a ploy called:

In for a Penny, in for a Pound.

This will begin with him listing all the areas where you have agreed with his decisions in the past. Then he will lead you into "grayer" areas where you have agreed and supported his decisions. The argument is that if you have agreed with all of that, why do you have a problem with this? If he hits something that you agreed to in the past and shouldn't have, it's important to say so, to admit that you were wrong and have repented of it.

If this doesn't work he may move to more direct confrontation with a tactic called...

If I'm One, You're Another.

"Let the person without sin cast the first stone." Yes, he may not have handled things quite correctly, but his intentions were good. And what are your motives? How have you handled this? You should have come to him privately in Christian love as Matthew 18 instructs. Not only have you not done things Biblically, he's not sensing much love coming from you. Such public accusations as you have made are sinful. How much gossip has been fed by what you have done? He may bring up things he knows about you and cast them in a negative light to make you feel guilty.

Finally, in a supreme act of magnanimous condescension, the wolf may suggest that it's time to "reboot" the relationship and start over. (Of course, "starting over" will not include any change on his part, only yours.)

If none of these tactics work, at some point the gloves will come off completely. He will get angry. Very likely you will experience...

Veiled and Unveiled Threats.

These can be everything from ostracism to legal action if you continue with your public accusations. Threats may include using Bible verses to attempt to browbeat you into silence. If it gets to that point, you can be sure of one thing. Not only is the wolf angry, he is afraid. But remember that wild animals are at their most dangerous when they are cornered. He or she may end the meeting abruptly and even throw you out. If there is no repentance, this may be the most preferable conclusion. At least it is clear.

However, the wolf may end the meeting by promising that he will seriously consider all that you have said. You must remind him of the Biblical response that you expect and give him a very short time-frame for his "consideration". Then follow up to see what actions he has taken. One of the most disturbing aspects of dealing with the Good-old-boy wolf I wrote about in a previous chapter was the fact that you could have a serious meeting with him about a significant problem that needed prompt attention. He would listen intently and appear to agree. He would assure you that the problem would be dealt with. Then, absolutely nothing would happen. It was as if the meeting had never taken place at all.

If you are dealing with a psychopathic personality, things could become very difficult.

Be extremely cautious of false repentance.

The Born Wolf will think nothing of lying. It is in his blood. He will know what you desire to see – true and deep repentance. He knows that you want to see a miraculous, transforming work of the Holy Spirit in his heart. You want to feel the Power of God in that room. Being a consummate actor, he may give you an Academy Award winning performance, complete with sorrow, tears and promises accompanied by hand-holding, heart-wrenching prayer. Do not let your emotions and desires blind you and keep you from requiring specific, Biblical, public acts of re-pentance and restitution, not simply emotional words said in front of a relatively small number of people.

In all such confrontations, the wolf knows that he has dis-tinct advantages. First, very likely the meeting will take place on his ground, in his office or some other location where he feels comfortable and you don't. Second, he knows that you have re-spected and perhaps even loved him in the past. Believing the best about him, you placed yourself under his authority. Given that this is true, you will be somewhat emotional and uncomfortable in confronting him. (It's one thing to imagine confronting a leader about sin and quite another to actually do it.)

A Christian leader stands in the position of a spiritual fa-ther or mother. The wolf knows this and uses it. Many who are drawn to follow authoritative leaders come from homes where they have not had good relationships (or sometimes any relation-ship) with fathers or mothers. Consequently, there is a deep desire for acceptance by this surrogate parent.

In a face-to-face confrontation, many old desires and emo-tions can come into play influencing attitudes and outcomes. The wolf knows that it is easy to manipulate his followers' love. He does it naturally. This is why it is very important to have people with you in the meeting who are in agreement and to prepare your case in advance even in writing. Then, no matter what is said or done in the meeting, stay focused on your facts and objectives. Do not let your deep desire for a positive outcome and reconcilia-tion blind you to reality. Christians are capable of the most dan-gerous fantasy thinking.

Never forget that Satan is a master debater. Following Satan's lead, a spiritual wolf may attempt to draw you into an argument. He will make false accusations against you. Do not argue with him or try to defend yourself. If you argue, he will have you in his power. Stay focused in prayer.

It is sad, but very realistic to warn, that, in a confrontation with a wolf, everything you say will be held against you in many different ways. Be careful that apparent kindness and concern do not draw you into agreeing about things with which you shouldn't agree. Do not be shocked when your own words are later twisted and quoted out of context in an attempt to discredit you. Because this is true, it's important to have witnesses to the confrontation and even a recording of what transpires. If you choose to record, be aware that in some states it is illegal to record a conversation without the consent of all parties.

Does all of this sound paranoid? It isn't. If you go into a confrontation with a spiritual wolf unprepared and with fantasy expectations, you will come away either more enslaved or even more disillusioned and damaged.

Two final warnings: First, if you are certain that you are dealing with a spiritual wolf do not pray with that person. Public prayer can be a great manipulative tool. Jesus didn't hold prayer meetings with the Pharisees. He prayed for them, but not with them.

Second, it is not impossible to imagine that in these days and the dark years ahead, a confrontation with a spiritual wolf might become a direct confrontation with an evil spirit, a demon that is hidden in that leader's life. While such a face-to-face, demonic confrontation may not be likely, it must be considered as part of your preparation for all possibilities.

As the author Neil T. Anderson writes, confrontations with evil spirits are truth confrontations. The more truth you speak about who Jesus is and His authority, the more truth you speak about the Blood that He shed to destroy the power of sin and Satan, the more enraged a demon will become. Indicators of its presence can include sudden, vicious, unreasoning rage and hate, foul language, horrible accusations, a significant change in the voice and demeanor of the individual, the supernatural revealing of past confessed sins of members in the confronting group, and even manifestations of occult power over physical objects. If such arise, the confrontation must become an exorcism.

In the Name of Jesus Christ and with His Authority, the evil spirit must be bound, silenced and forced to give its name. Then, the Blood of Jesus that was shed to destroy the power of sin and set the prisoners free must be applied. The demon must be cast out never to return and to go where Jesus sends it. This is direct spiritual warfare. The deliverance may not happen quickly. It may take time and will be brutally exhausting. But Jesus will win.

If you do not believe that such confrontations could be possible, if you are not prepared to set a prisoner free by the Authority of Jesus and by the Power of the Blood under the direction of the Holy Spirit, it's time to grow in faith and knowledge before you confront someone that you are certain is a spiritual wolf. (In a previous chapter, I recommended the work of several authors in dealing with the occult and deliverance from evil spirits. I would add to that the work of Neil T. Anderson and his book, The Bondage Breaker.)

CHAPTER FIFTY

The Aftermath

If a spiritual wolf repents it must be public because his or her sins have damaged many people. If possible, restitution should be made. It is difficult to imagine that such an individual could remain in the same position of leadership. It would be like leaving a repentant drug addict in charge of a pharmacy. But if there is true repentance, God will give wisdom about all such matters.

For our discussion, we will assume that there is no repentance. If that's the case, expect a firestorm. The wolf will draw together his forces and counterattack. Depending on the situation, tremendous pressure may be applied to you. If you are employed by the organization, you may be fired. No matter what is said or done, trust in the Lord and remain faithful to Him. His message is always the same, "Fear not for I am with you, neither be afraid."

As this book is being written, the truth about a well-known evangelical leader is becoming public. The amazing thing is that it has taken over 30 years for that truth to be revealed. But that isn't for lack of trying on the part of brave individuals. This wolf was confronted years ago by godly evangelical leaders who saw through his sheepskin suit. His response was to disavow the sin and sue his accusers in court. He has been so powerful, with such a strong and utterly blind constituency, that, decades ago, he managed to fire one board of directors who wanted to stop him and institute a new one.

This evil man has spent his career giving Christians "biblical" guidance. Thousands have been his passionate followers. And what was he doing "behind the scenes"? He was grooming young teenage girls who came to his organization as unpaid interns, then, molesting them in his office.

The tragedy is that when some of these girls reported the abuse to their own families, they were disbelieved and even called liars. Such parents are blind, foolish sheep whose heartless ignorance damaged their daughters even further and allowed the wolf to continue mauling and destroying for decades. They need to repent before God and, on their knees, beg the forgiveness of their children.

After a confrontation, what actions you should take next in publicizing the situation must be guided by the Holy Spirit. The Lord may give you a sense of peace and release you from further actions. But He may not. Most importantly, no further action should be taken out of hurt, vindictiveness and a desire for revenge. If you remain engaged in the crisis, this is going to be a great challenge. Making it far more difficult will be the fact that many people, even former friends, will accuse you of bad motives.

Do not succumb to the temptation to constantly defend and explain yourself. Don't be distracted by false accusations. Do not slander others. Remain focused. Let the Lord and others defend you.

If the Lord guides you to remain involved, the next step is bringing the facts of the crisis to the entire church or organization, including leaders who are above the wolf such as denomina-tional supervisors and boards of directors. This is where hardball is played. Before you take further steps you should consult an attorney. (This may be a wise thing to do before the confrontation.)

Incredibly, there are some Christian organizations and churches that have begun demanding that employees sign non-disclosure and non-compete agreements. This is a very great indicator of wolf leadership, but if you have signed such an agreement it may preclude you from "going public" outside the organization. However, it may not apply to disclosure within the organization which includes the board of directors. In such situations, seek legal counsel.

Various groups and individuals have confronted wolves publicly in a variety of ways. Some have gone to the press. The Internet and social media have opened avenues of communication that didn't exist just a few years ago. Some groups have created entire websites to present their evidence and track the activities of a wolf. This is not a recommendation that you should take such actions. I give these as examples of ways that others have held a wolf and his pack accountable. If there has been financial malfea-sance you may want to look at the resources available at the Evan-gelical Council for Financial Accountability. (http://www.ecfa.org/) In dealing with sexual abuse you might find help at http://www.together-we-heal.org/ or http://netgrace.org/

Whatever you do, prepare to be vilified.

After the situation has become public, very likely others who have been wounded will be drawn to you. This is your op-portunity to minister to them so that they can find forgiveness and healing. It is *not* an opportunity for gossip, shared self-pity and angry commiseration. As always, continued prayer for all involved is vital.

And remember, this too shall pass.

CHAPTER FIFTY-ONE

What Does Victory Look Like?

A pastor friend asked the question after reading an early draft of this book. In a confrontation with a wolf, how do you determine whether you have been successful or not? Before the confrontation, you set objectives and were looking for specific outcomes. You presented the truth. Most of all, you wanted the individual to be reconciled to God and the people he or she had injured through repentance and, perhaps, restitution. Probably not quickly, but over time, you will learn whether those goals were achieved. If they are not, does it mean that you have failed? If the wolf continues on as though nothing has happened and there's nothing more you can do, does that mean you wasted your time?

As we have said, American Christians love measureable success. When we don't see it, we become depressed and discouraged. But even if you do succeed in measureable ways, is that ultimate victory?

Vietnam was a very strange conflict. American soldiers won every battle, yet we lost the war. As you decide how to measure success, don't look at the outcome of a single conflict. Take the long view of your life and work. That's what the Apostle Paul did.

Do you not know that those who run in a race all run, but one receives the prize? Run in such a way that you may obtain it. And everyone who competes for the prize is temperate in all things. Now they do it to obtain a perishable crown, but we for an imperishable crown. Therefore I run thus: not with uncertainty. Thus I fight: not as one who beats the air. But I discipline my body and bring it into subjection, lest, when I have preached to others, I myself should become disqualified. (1 Cor 9:24-27)

What mattered to the Apostle Paul? How he ran the race, how he fought all the battles of his life and kept his body with its temptations and hungers under control was all that mattered, not whether he had won or lost by the measure of the world. Paul was a disciplined spiritual warrior and he had only one fear, that after the long race, he might be disqualified. The Greek word that is translated "disqualified" is very strong. It means unapproved, rejected, found to be worthless. If Paul, the greatest missionary of all time, had such a strong concern, perhaps that should be our concern as well. Finally, at the end of his life, he wrote:

I have fought the good fight, I have finished the race, I have kept the faith. Finally, there is laid up for me the crown of righteousness, which the Lord, the righteous

Judge, will give to me on that Day, and not to me only but also to all who have loved His appearing. (2 Timothy 4:7-8)

To Paul, success meant faithfulness, running the race and completing it with joy. He took the long view. It wasn't about any one battle, though each was important. It was about the faithfulness of his whole life.

No matter what the outcome of a wolf confrontation, if people have been warned, if you have spoken the truth courageously and with love, if you have been faithful to the King in every way that you knew, you are victorious. Leave the ultimate outcome in Jesus' hands. That is all that is required of a servant warrior.

Victory looks like faithfulness. But you can be absolutely certain of one thing. Though it may not happen quickly, in His time, Jesus will deal with the wolf. Watch and pray.

CHAPTER FIFTY-TWO

A Final Question: Are You a Wolf?

Does the question irritate or anger you? If it does, I urge you to stop and take a careful look at your life. Don't look at all the "evidence" that you show to the world to prove your great spiritual depth and power. Don't look at the flattery you receive or how much your ministry "blesses" people. My friend, look inside. Who are you really? What kind of fruit is growing from your heart? What is it doing to those who are closest to you? How much is the love of power and control taking hold of you? Wolves and those who are becoming wolves, lie to themselves more than they lie to anyone else.

As you have been reading this book, has God been speaking to you? Are there things that you are doing, ways that you have been dealing with people that you know are wrong? Many wolves don't appear overnight. They grow into the role.

If you are a charming, gifted, intimidating person it's not easy to find people who will tell you the truth. Though you appear to be warm and open, you keep people at a distance, especially those who disagree with you. Most people know only your carefully manicured public persona. The people close to you may be lesser wolves who are living off you. You may be covered with weeds. Tares may be clinging to you. Some may be afraid of you, others may be too damaged to speak. But God will tell you the truth about yourself if you are willing to listen.

My friend, do you really know Jesus? Do you really love Him? I don't care if ten thousand people have "come to Christ" through your ministry this week. The question is for you, not them. If you really know Him and love Him, that witness will be in your heart and your outer life. If your heart is cold toward Him, if it is cold toward the people around you, if you are unforgiving, if you have done things that you know are wrong, it's time to repent. Your eternal future is at stake.

Is there someone who really knows you who will tell you the truth? Maybe that person has tried in the past and you have rejected it. Maybe you've gotten rid of him or her. The place for truth to be found and repentance to start may be with that individual. Don't let pride and fear destroy the work that Jesus wants to do in you. Don't let it destroy your future. And that's what will happen if you continue in the direction you are going.

Luke 17:1-2, Jesus said:

"It is impossible that no offenses should come, but woe to him through whom they do come! It would be better for him if a millstone were hung around his neck, and he were thrown into the sea, than that he should offend one of these little ones."

The Greek word translated "little ones" is mikros. Do not think that this just means children. It means all those who are un-

342

important or without dignity. It means the little people that you disdain and use and abuse. The word translated offend means to entrap, to trip up, to entice to sin and apostasy. Is that what you have done? Have you talked a lot about Jesus, yet led His sheep away from loving and obeying Him? If so, for the salvation of your soul and those you have led away, it is time for the most serious repentance before the Lord and before those who have suffered under your leadership.

But be assured of one thing. In spite of all, God loves you more than you could imagine. While the path you may have to walk will be difficult and humiliating, God will use it to open doors of blessing for you and others such as you have never experienced. Don't be afraid. Give your heart to Him in a way that you have not done before.

If I can be of help to you, please contact me:

coleman@colemanluck.com

CHAPTER FIFTY-THREE

A Letter to Young Christian Leaders

Dear Brother or Sister,

As you have read, most of this book has been directed to lay people who are dealing with false spiritual leaders in churches, schools and ministries. But right now (and much more so in the future), if you are in fulltime ministry you're going to deal with more wolves and tares than at any period of history. It is true servants of the Lord, struggling to be faithful shepherds, who are experiencing the bloodiest attacks. And it will get much worse.

You are entering a raging battlefield that is littered with bleeding casualties. It is good that you can't see beneath the surface into the souls and spirits of the people around you because you would be overwhelmed. The church is filled with broken, angry children of every age.

In the years ahead, as a young Christian leader on this battlefield, you are going to face many dangers and temptations. Some of them will be blatant, but many will be very subtle. Traps have been laid for you by one who knows you better than you know yourself. Do not underestimate him.

How you view who you are and what you have been sent to do is of utmost importance. May I suggest a way to view yourself? I suggest that you think of yourself as a servant warrior of the King, sent with the Power of the Holy Spirit to set the prisoners free. And as a warrior you expect to be in battle the rest of your life. Does that sound brutal? I don't think there is any other way to live victoriously through the dangerous period ahead.

The United States military spends a lot of time and money getting young men and women to stop thinking like civilians and to view themselves as warriors. In America, a civilian lives day-to-day without any expectation of battle. Imagine someone like that being placed on a battlefield with war crashing all around them. Yet, that's the way most young people go onto the battle-field of ministry, with only the vaguest idea that they have a vicious, implacable enemy waiting to attack and destroy by breaking their hearts and sapping all faith, hope and love from their lives until they become useless to the Kingdom of God. Or worse, they become wolves.

With that in mind, would you allow me to give you some specific warnings about this war? Some of the things I'm going to tell you may go against what you want to believe and how you have been trained to live in modern evangelical culture. Be that as it may, this advice is for your spiritual protection as you live through the Day of the Wolf.

Warning: Beware the Inner Rings.

In a little book entitled, The Weight of Glory, C. S. Lewis included an important essay that he called, "The Inner Ring". I strongly suggest that you read it. I want to talk to you about the "inner rings" that will present themselves throughout your life, because how you deal with them will have everything to do with the kind of a leader you become.

What do I mean by an "inner ring"? I'm sure that you've been experiencing them since grade school. By high school they are full blown. An inner ring is a tightly knit group of people. I don't mean a group of friends who like to "hang out" together. Neither do I mean a group that has gathered to carry out specific tasks using the varied abilities of its members. Such rings are necessary for the functioning of society and meet the legitimate needs of individuals.

I'm talking about an inner ring that is established for no other reason than to advance the selfish interests of its members, a group that excludes people they don't think "quite fit in" and controls the lives of those they allow in. In high school, it was the clique of "popular kids". If you were not in that group, you were very aware of it. Usually, it wasn't by overt rejection. You just weren't included. If you were on the periphery, you did what you could to be included. If you had no hope of entry you may have grown cynical and angry. Such inner ring rejections in high school can influence a person's whole life, building a deep desire to be accepted by *some* inner ring later on. Does that describe you? If so, beware.

If you are old enough to have gone back for a high school reunion and weren't among the "popular kids", did you look around to see how successful those people are today? If they aren't successful and you are, did it give you a little gleam of satisfaction? Many of the powerful people of Hollywood experienced rejection by an inner ring in their early years and it has defined their lives.

Everyone wants to be accepted by an inner ring somewhere because acceptance marks a new level of success. That doesn't necessarily mean more money or career advancement, though often it may. At a minimum, it means the security of being in a group, access to information and a certain amount of added prestige, but rarely is an inner ring a formal group. It exists and maintains its power outside organizational charts and formal structures.

Piercing an inner ring doesn't mean that you like the people in the group. You may dislike them intensely. But this isn't about friendship. They represent an objective to be achieved and are a means to an end. Strangely, as Lewis points out, once a ring has been pierced and you are an accepted member, very quickly membership loses significance. You become focused on the next ring and how to break into that. And there is always another one ahead.

Being accepted by an inner ring, means that you must accept the worldview of its members, including their definition of success and morality. You must accept their view of the people outside the ring and why they aren't worthy to be allowed in. You must listen to their gossip and smile at their attitudes though you may find them repugnant. Whether it's a clique in the neighborhood or at the highest levels of government, business, industry, politics and, yes, ministry, to stand against an inner ring is very difficult. If you stand against it long enough you will be rejected and that can have a devastating effect on your career and personal relationships. If you aren't even given the opportunity to join an important inner ring, that can be the worst of all. Most people can't handle such rejection.

Hollywood is an industry with many inner rings and many gatekeepers. You face them when you try to enter. At the start, while I was in grad school, the first ring for a writer was "breaking in", which meant getting an agent and selling a script to a recognized company. This would allow me to become a member of the Writers Guild, for a writer, the first mark of acceptance in Hollywood. (In reality, it gave me the privilege of paying an agent ten percent and the Guild an initiation fee of several thousand dollars followed by 1 ½ percent of everything I made as a screenwriter for the rest of my life.)

As soon as I passed through the gatekeepers into that ring, there was another staring at me. I've sold one script, but can I sell more? (According to an old friend who is an executive at the Writers Guild in charge of statistics, the average length of a writing career in Hollywood from first script sold to the last, after which you never sell another, is just five years.)

After I passed into the ring of multiple sales, there appeared the ring of television writing. Could I become a staff writer on a network TV series? (Once you're established as a TV writer, it's easier to build a career.) After that ring, could I keep working on shows and become a producer? Then, could I get an "overall deal" with a studio where I would be exclusive to them and they would guarantee a steady income? After that, could I become a senior writer/producer? (They have much more control over the production of their scripts.) After that, could I become a Showrunner, the person in charge of entire series? After that could I become a series creator/showrunner? After that... Well, there were many other rings, but for me there was no "after that". You get the point. The rings never end. There were organiza-

349

tional structures involved at every level, but it was inner rings with their gatekeepers that controlled them.

In facing inner rings, moral choices are always involved. How much do you want to pierce the next ring? Do the gatekeepers like you? Are you willing to give them what they want in order to be accepted? As a Christian, how far will your witness let you go?

You may say, I'm in a church or Christian school or ministry. It's not Hollywood. Sadly, I'm afraid you will discover that whatever professional Christian endeavor you choose, it isn't that different and there are several reasons why. First, inner rings exist because we are insecure sheep and they offer security. Second, we like to think we are better or more successful than others and inner rings give us that opportunity. Third, we don't like people who disagree with us or whose personalities we find abrasive. (Be honest.) Inner rings allow such people to be shut out. (Obviously dangerous, because truth is often shut out with them.) Fourth, like rings outside ministry, they can be means of advancement. Very often, control of organizational structures is in the hands of ring members. Beyond these, there is another reason why inner rings exist within the world of Christian ministry. They are natural points of power and control for wolves.

Invitations to join an inner ring will be subtle and flattering, a word or two here or there, an invitation to a special lunch with "the group" where your peers aren't invited. You may be told that someone important has "noticed" you. Your work has impressed him or her. Whatever. All of this may be quite innocent, an honest opportunity for well-earned advancement. But be on your guard.

For a servant warrior trying to follow the Lord, over and over, the question will be, who do you really serve? It's easy to make spiritualized excuses for doing what you feel you need to do to pierce the next ring of success.

If you are a young pastor what rings exist in your denomination? Who needs to accept and like you in order for you to advance from church to church? Who do you need to impress and how do you go about doing it? Once you've pierced that ring, how do you move beyond the denomination onto a larger stage? What are you willing to do to get there? What compromises will you make? Recently, it was reported that an "emergent" church megapastor wanted to pierce the inner ring of hugely successful authors. So to make his recent book a national bestseller, he used church funds to buy up many thousands of copies, thereby achieving his goal.

After great successes in publishing, another former emergent church pastor has tried desperately to pierce the inner ring of Hollywood, so far without success. What he has been willing to do and teach to pierce the inner rings and gain public notoriety has taken him into heresy. He has become a false teacher, a wolf.

Inner rings exist in Christian schools and para-church ministries. There are national and international "Christian" inner rings operating today. Politics is rife with them and many Christian leaders thirst to be accepted in those.

I'm convinced that it is the lust for worldly success, which entails being accepted by an endless series of inner rings, that destroys many Christian leaders. As they pass into each ring, the things they have done to get there accumulate into a crushing weight of selfishness and sometimes false teaching, done to appeal

351

to the gatekeepers. They may not have done anything overtly wrong to enter a ring, but the motivations and elitism that have taken control are straight from Satan's world system. In this way, the Powers of Darkness have entered many churches, schools and Christian ministries. Facilitating this incursion are Satan's wolves. Spiritual wolves are waiting to mentor young leaders into the next ring. Remember, there is no end to those rings. There is no "There" there.

So be on your guard, especially against the subtle flattery and temptation to be part of a small group that a leader has chosen to receive his personal attention. It is flattering when a successful man or woman, someone you respect and who might hold a glowing future for you in their hands, subtly communicates that others aren't quite ready for their attentions, but you are. That is flattery. Watch for a hidden wolf.

As Lewis points out so clearly, as long as you are controlled by the desire to be accepted by an inner ring, you will never get what you want. It will always be just out of your reach. When "ring lust" controls you, your ability and authority to speak truth to everyone, including powerful people whom you respect, will vanish. Jesus refused the inner rings of Satan and his wolves. Those who follow Him must do so as well.

Warning: Beware of volunteer "mentors".

One of the strangest stories in the Bible is found in I Kings 13. A young prophet is sent by God to cry out against the idolatry of King Jereboam. God tells him that when he has finished his prophecy he is not to stop for anything, not even to eat and drink, but to go straight home by a different way than he came or he will die.

After giving his message and being used by God to perform a miracle, he is on his way home, when an older prophet meets him and invites him to come to his house to eat and rest. When the younger prophet says that God told him not to, the older man uses his authority and speaks a lie, telling him that God sent an angel with a new message. Stopping and eating is all right. The younger man disobeys God and it costs him his life.

Why did the old prophet do this? Was he jealous that God had chosen one so young to speak to the king? After years of faithful ministry, had he become a spiritual wolf? Or was he a wolf all along in sheep's clothing. Clearly, he must have looked and sounded like a true servant of the Lord. Perhaps in the past he had spoken messages that really had come from God. Certainly, he spoke a true one condemning the young prophet after he had rested and eaten in his house. Little wonder that God hadn't seen this older man as spiritually fit to carry a message of repentance to Jereboam.

Just because a person is old with a great reputation for past ministry and appears to speak with the authority of the Lord, doesn't mean that he or she is right with the Lord at this moment. Before you place yourself under the guidance of an older spiritual leader, make certain that this is a man or woman of true faithfulness and established humility, not simply a leader who is successful by the measurement of our evangelical metrics system or the flattering group that is around him.

Do you want a mature spiritual advisor, someone who will tell you what you need to hear, not just what you want to hear?

Most likely you will have to approach such a person, because he or she won't approach you. Beware of those who offer their mentoring services. If you feel the slightest qualm, no matter what benefit you may receive from such a relationship, don't do it. While it may open the door to an inner ring, such "mentoring" could be the beginning of destruction for you and your ministry.

Warning: As you beware of wrong leaders to follow, also beware of raising up wrong leaders.

In this day when emotion rules everything, terrible mistakes can be made in choosing leaders because you really "like" someone. Remember wolves and tares in the church are always spiritually charming. No matter how much you think you need a particular individual to assist in ministry, no matter how much he or she is a friend, no matter how gifted that person is and how much the church or organization may need his or her help, take your time, think and pray. And enlist a few other faithful people to pray with you.

The Holy Spirit does not speak with a loud voice. If there is the slightest sense of disquiet in your spirit about an individual or if mature, trusted men and women of God express the slightest qualm, wait. Mature Christians are not quick to be negative about an individual. If they feel a sense of disquiet, they may be reluctant to voice it. Gently probe...and listen carefully.

I know a pastor who decided to raise up a man into leadership who was charming, talented and appeared to be spiritually mature. He seemed to have all the qualifications for Christian leadership and he could teach the Bible. But in a church vote, a significant percentage of the members voted against him. It wasn't a majority, but it was large enough to demand some serious reconsideration. He disregarded the negative votes.

It wasn't long before the man became a source of terrible division and personal attack. In retrospect, that pastor wished he had listened to the disquiet that was registering. He brought the man into his personal circle and deeply regretted it.

Recently, Reverend Ed Dobson who "mentored" the nationally known false teacher Rob Bell at the start of his ministry, gave an interview to The New Yorker Magazine. In it he recalled the selection process whereby Bell was chosen to join their ministry and lead their Saturday night young adult service. According to Dobson, some of the elders had reservations about Bell. They had doubts about his inexperience and knowledge of the Word of God. Dobson told them, "Look, he can communicate. He really doesn't know the Bible, but if we can add the Bible to his communication skills, we'll have a winner." His view won the day and a false teacher was projected into great success, leading many people away from the truth.

It is quite clear that, with the best of intentions, Dobson used a standard of success measurement that is straight out of the world. Knowledge of the Bible was just another "skill set" to be added. With these kinds of priorities in the minds of major evangelical leaders, it is little wonder that we have a serious wolf problem. Dobson appears to regret his decision. Don't make the mistake he did in choosing your leaders.

As this book was going to press, it was announced that Rob Bell, who has struggled to find success in Hollywood, is now the "spiritual advisor" to Oprah Winfrey and apparently is traveling with her on a tour of live shows. Satan does reward his wolves. But beware of his "gifts".

Warning: Familiarity breeds contempt.

What I'm going to say here may go against everything you think you know about Christian leadership. Those three words represent an age-old principle. The military understands it. That's why they don't want officers to "fraternize" with the enlisted personnel whom they must lead. The principle holds true in every form of leadership from the home to major corporations. They apply to Christian leadership as well.

We live in a day when everyone wants to be a "buddy" to everyone else in the church and in other Christian ministries. We want to be accepted and loved, especially by the people we lead. We hate elitism (while allowing it into the church or ministry on many subtle levels). In their desperate desire to be "accepted" by everyone, many young Christian leaders give up all sense of dignity.

What is dignity? It's an old-fashioned word that means proper self-respect in bearing, conduct and speech. It means having a strong sense of what is both proper and improper in all human relations. A Christian leader treats others with dignity and he or she should act with dignity. That doesn't mean that you can't have fun or real fellowship. It means that you know the dangers and the lines that you should not cross, because to cross them will bring disrespect or worse.

There is an easy example. If a Christian leader is in a group where someone gets drunk, he or she shouldn't get drunk with him or approve of his drunkenness by not taking it seriously.

Though people may joke and appear to think such a leader is "cool" in his progressive openness, respect will be lost and never regained. Far more important, God will see that leader's unfaithfulness and hold him accountable. (Also, in this day of social media, he or she may be held accountable by a video that someone shoots that goes viral. Live your life and make your choices as though the whole world were watching.)

Using the principle of Christian dignity, Billy Graham and his team of men determined early on never to have one-on-one closed door meetings with women and always to treat them with Christian dignity and respect. Do you think this is an outdated concept? Look around at the disasters taking place due to adulterous relationships or false accusations about such in churches and Christian ministries. The system in place now is killing us. Apart from underestimating human weakness, it is an open door to wolves of both sexes. It doesn't take much for Satan to spring that trap. Don 't be caught in it.

The heart of Christian dignity is found in the Apostle Paul's guidance to Timothy: **Let no one despise your youth, but be an example to the believers in word, in conduct, in love, in spirit, in faith, in purity.** 1 Timothy 4:12

In a church or Christian organization, there needs to be the right kind of loving respect between a leader and those whom he or she must lead. You are not required, neither is it wise, to bare your soul to the people either above or below you in the structure of organizational responsibility. There should be Christian dignity in all your relationships so that familiarity will not breed contempt.

Many years ago, I left a small church of about 100 members to help establish a new congregational ministry. A couple of years after I was gone, I got a terrible report. A young pastor had come in just out of seminary. The people liked him and he was doing well. The chairman of his elder board was a man about ten years older. They became fast friends and regular prayer partners, spending a lot of time together.

One day the young pastor shared with his friend a spiritual battle that he was fighting. He told him that he was struggling with lust for a woman in the church. He was happily married. He and his wife had several children. There was not slightest intent on his part to act on the lust. Neither had the woman done anything toward him to encourage the situation. It was just a personal temptation that was distracting him and he needed prayer.

His "friend" reported it to the elder board and it went straight out to the whole congregation. Very soon, the young pastor was gone. When I heard about it, he was working as a used car salesman. Though I hadn't known him, I invited him to lunch. I just wanted to offer some encouragement. He was a devastated soul, struggling with great anger and bitterness. Was the chairman of the elder board a spiritual wolf? I had known the man and I don't think so. He was just a rigid, doctrinaire individual who was charming, but lacked compassion and spiritual maturity. He had been elevated to a position beyond his capacity. Such people are in leadership in many places.

Spiritual immaturity is rampant in the church today. As bad as that is, also there are wolves (including psychopathic personalities) in congregations and ministries who will do whatever is necessary to become your close, trusted friend. Ultimately, whatever you share with that person will be twisted and used against you.

Am I suggesting that you close yourself off and not share with the people you lead anything deeper about who you are? No. In fact, I urge the opposite. In speaking, teaching and writing, it's very important to share yourself. I have done it in this book. But you are not called to parade your deepest doubts, fears and temptations in front of everyone while you are going through them. And every leader battles such thoughts and emotions. When those battles are long over, *perhaps* the stories will make good sermon illustrations.

A word that is in use today is "transparency". Christians, including Christian leaders, want to be "transparent" with each other. If transparency means being lovingly honesty in interactions, no double-dealing, no hidden agendas and always treating others the way you want to be treated, transparency should be our goal. If it means baring your soul to someone else because it feels emotionally right at the moment, beware.

Deep sharing is important. Have a true friend and prayer partner who is distant from your ministry and knows no one in it, someone who will tell you the truth, a sort of praying court jester in your life.

The people within your ministry can and should be praying for you, but there is a line of familiarity that you should not allow them to cross. As the years pass, some of your heartaches and failures will become public. Share what is necessary to deal with them. Remember that you can never satisfy public curiosity, so don't try. The longer you are in ministry, the more you can expect to be attacked by wolves and tares. You don't need to help them.

In particular, maintain dignity in dealing with the opposite sex. To be a leader is lonely. You must accept that loneliness. If you can't, then do not accept a leadership position. It is in that loneliness that traps for you are waiting. So many leaders have fallen by the intimate sharing of their needs and loneliness with members of the opposite sex who are close associates in ministry. Satan, the ultimate wolf, is waiting with a trap designed to meet your needs. You don't have to step into it. That means, with the strength of the Holy Spirit, accepting and carrying loneliness and pain, knowing that Jesus is carrying you.

Warning: Expect a broken heart.

There's a good chance that you have one already. With the state of the family today, young people enter the ministry with broken hearts. Over the course of your time serving the Lord, your heart will be broken again and again. Friends you trusted may prove to be traitors, spouses may prove to be unfaithful, children may turn away and treat you with great disrespect, father and mother figures in ministry whom you have loved and respected may prove weak, sinful and false, your hopes and dreams may never come to fruition, people you love and need may be taken from you in death, wolves may attack at times of great vulnerability. There are many ways to get a broken heart. The only certainty is that, if you don't have one already, one is coming.

But there is another certainty that is greater than all. If you give your broken heart to Jesus, forgiving those who may have caused it, He will use it in his redemptive work in the world. He feels what you feel. What is done to you is done to Him. Trust Him with your broken heart and the very pain will bring His Glory.

Warning: In a day of scintillating lies, for the good of your own soul, be a faithful witness to God's Word.

You are ministering in the wolf-ridden church of Laodicea that does not want to hear the Truth and will punish those who speak it. Do not be a slave to the soft, comfortable lies of this Age. At all costs, preach and teach the Good News of God's Love and forgiveness based only on the Cross and the Blood of the Son of God that was shed there. Preach and teach the Narrow Road of true discipleship. Clearly warn people that hell awaits those who do not accept God's message of salvation in Jesus. Tell them without equivocation, that Jesus is the only Way. And give your warning with a broken heart. Many, many in the church who believe they are going to Heaven, will not be there. As a leader, it is vital that you take seriously Jesus' words in Matthew 7:13-14:

"Enter by the narrow gate; for wide is the gate and broad is the way that leads to destruction, and there are many who go in by it. Because narrow is the gate and difficult is the way which leads to life, and there are few who find it."

Remember these words by the great pastor Charles Haddon Spurgeon, "If sinners be damned, at least let them leap to hell over our dead bodies. And if they perish, let them perish with our arms wrapped around their knees. If hell must be filled, let it be filled in the teeth of our exertions and let no one go unwarned and unprayed for."

Warning: Do not fail to watch for the

unexpected Return of the King.

In Luke 18:8 Jesus asked a haunting question: **"Neverthe-less, when the Son of Man comes, will He really find faith on the earth?"**

Could He have been serious? That sounds so impossible. There are millions of Christians. Don't they all have faith? What kind of faith was He talking about then? Faith that He was actual-ly going to return at all, faith that was watching and expecting His return. The implication of Jesus' question is clear. That kind of expectant faith could vanish from the earth. We are in that day.

Never in my lifetime have I seen fewer Christians watch-ing for the return of Jesus. And He told His followers to watch diligently. Why aren't we obeying? There are several reasons: First, the very idea of it is mocked in popular culture, making many weak, immature Christians embarrassed to talk about it. The mockery and embarrassment grow every time Satan raises up a deluded person who decides that he knows when the return will take place. When he is discredited, the entire subject goes down with him. It is an effective ploy to keep people's minds away from the soon-coming King.

There is another reason: Biblical preaching and teaching about the Lord's return have been relegated to specialized studies of prophecy, the domain of professional scholars and the popular-izers that follow them. As they present the minutiae of their ar-guments in various forms, prophecy becomes divorced from any practical application to spiritual life. Rather than watch for His return, sophisticated Christians prefer to defend their chosen eschatological positions.

For the average Christians, the weeds are just too thick. Their controlling view is that people have been waiting for His return for centuries and it hasn't happened, so let's just not think about it. This keeps their eyes on the world, exactly where Satan and his wolves want them. As a servant warrior for the King, you cannot afford to fall into traps that will silence you. Warn people about His soon return. Watch for the Signs of the Times and there are more of them every week.

A Great Delusion is being prepared. When it arrives, it will be so vast, so apparently real and all-encompassing, that it will seem like insanity to stand against it. The outlines of it are all around us. When it arrives, it will be during a time of overwhelming darkness and will appear to bring salvation from Beyond. It will seem to prove with scientific certainty that Jesus is not who the Bible says He is. It will focus the world's attention onto a different god.

Purveying this lie will be a generation of wolves more empowered and dangerous than any ever seen before. Large numbers of people who call themselves Christians will fall away. Do not be one of them. Look for the Return of the King and warn those given into your care.

A last thought.

A servant warrior approaches the battlefield of ministry knowing who he is and expecting enemy attacks, both physical and spiritual. A servant warrior knows that he is not alone, he is part of a vast and ultimately powerful Army under the leadership of the greatest Warrior King.

A servant warrior lives a life worthy to be attacked. In faith, he or she takes risks for Jesus. The lives of servant warriors are not dedicated to the accumulation of comforts and protection or worldly success. In the Name of the Lord, a servant warrior is committed to doing enough damage to the enemy by fighting to set prisoners free, that the enemy's attention is drawn to him. He or she is not surprised at being attacked.

Most of all, a servant warrior obeys His Lord who has said, "Fear not, for I am with you."

To him who overcomes I will give some of the hidden manna to eat. And I will give him a white stone, and on the stone a new name written which no one knows except him who receives it. (Revelation 2:17-18)

Fight well, my friend. The King is coming. I'll see you over There.

Your brother in the Faith,
Coleman

With Deep Gratitude

This has been an extremely difficult book to write. Throughout the process it has been very important for me to be accountable to the Body of Christ. In order to do that, at various stages of manuscript completion I have asked trusted individuals of proven Christian maturity and knowledge to read and critique. I told them to be very tough on me. This was to be "no-holds-barred".

The people in this group came from a variety of leadership backgrounds including the pastorate, Christian para-church ministries, business, etc. Though all come from thoroughly conservative evangelical traditions, within the group were varying theological perspectives. No matter the background each person loves Jesus and desires to serve Him. There is not a wolf among them.

While there was agreement in many areas, also there was some disagreement. Each person expressed a different emphasis and set of concerns. All were very helpful. I deeply appreciate the time each individual took to read and formulate ideas. It was not an easy task. Due to the controversial nature of this book, I have decided that it would be in their best interests not to list their names. All have my deep gratitude. Of course, total responsibility for this work is mine alone.

As always, the support of my family has been vital. It was my daughter's experience as part of a leadership team suffering under a wolf in a Christian ministry that instigated the entire project. What she described about how he treated his employees, using the Bible to control and abuse them to the point of despair, brought back many memories and pushed me to write.

Besides designing the cover, my wife, Carel, has been a constant encouragement, reading and commenting on multiple drafts and sections. Her love and support is a mainstay of my life. My son, Cole, has read and commented on multiple drafts and edited the manuscript. The whole family has encouraged me with their words and prayer. I am very blessed.

Most of all I want to praise and thank our Savior and great King, Jesus, the Messiah, who has guided and provided every step of the way throughout my life. May this book be used to strengthen His Body, the Church, as it enters a very dark period of history.

Even so come quickly, Lord Jesus.

Coleman Luck
Fall in the Year of Our Lord, 2014
In the Sierra Nevada Mountains near Yosemite National Park

About the Author

Coleman Luck has been a Hollywood writer and executive producer known for such TV series as "The Equalizer" and "Gabriel's Fire". His Hollywood credits are available at: www.imdb.com.

His first novel, Angel Fall, was published in 2009 by Zondervan, a subsidiary of Harper/Collins. His second novel, The Mentalist Prophecies - Book One – Dagon's Illusion, was published in 2013 as was his third novel, The Singing Place.

Coleman is also the author of the non-fiction books, Proof of Heaven? A Mental Illusionist Examines the Afterlife Experience of Eben Alexander M.D. from a Biblical Viewpoint and The Curse of Conservatism.

He studied at the Moody Bible Institute of Chicago, received his undergraduate degree from Northern Illinois University (magna cum laude) and did graduate study at NIU, the University of Southern California and Simon Greenleaf School of Law where he studied under famed Christian apologist, the late Dr. Walter Martin.

As a U. S. Army infantry officer, Coleman was awarded the following decorations for combat service in Vietnam: the Bronze Star for valor, the Bronze Star for meritorious service, three Army Commendation medals for valor, the Air Medal for combat assaults by helicopter and the Combat Infantryman's Badge.

Coleman and his wife of 48 years, Carel Gage Luck, a fine artist, live in the mountains of central California. They have three adult children and four grandchildren.

All of Coleman's personal papers relating to his Hollywood career are available for examination in the Special Collections section of the Wheaton College Library, Wheaton, Illinois under the title, The Coleman Luck Collection.

Visit his website: www.colemanluck.com.

Made in the USA
Monee, IL
25 April 2021

66040879R00225